T0247561

A fascinating recounting of how we got to where we are now, what challenges our healthcare system faces as a country, as well as the paths that will propel us forward and upwards. Essential reading for anyone who wants to understand healthcare today, the necessity of transforming the world's largest industry, and the ideas, companies and people that will lead us back to the top. As a medical practitioner, federal policymaker, and health services entrepreneur, I applaud this brave book.

—William H. Frist, MD,
former U.S. Senate Majority Leader; Co-Founder and
Managing Partner, Frist Cressey Ventures

An important and provocative book on the current state of healthcare in the U.S., a plea for needed changes that have been delayed for decades, and a roadmap of innovative initiatives that could get us to a better place.

—Nancy–Ann DeParle,
former White House Deputy Chief of Staff; former Administrator,
Center for Medicare and Medicaid Services (CMS);
Managing Partner and Co-Founder, Consonance Capital

A critical warning bell for our current healthcare system and a call to arms to drive the necessary changes that will allow the United States to lead, not follow.

—Jeb Bush,
former governor of Florida; Chairman and
Founding Partner, Finback Investment Partners

Johnson and Kusserow capture the shock and awe accompanying the digital and biological advances propelling clinical care into uncharted territory. They persuaded me that widespread adoption of pre-emptive diagnostics, personalized therapies and integrated, whole-person health is not only possible, but probable within the next 10 years.

—David Feinberg, MD,
Chairman, Oracle Health

I think the healthcare system in the United States is the best in the world in many respects, but the industry, like the education industry, is terribly fragmented. This fragmentation creates inefficiencies for the system, variation in outcomes for patients, and barriers to adoption of innovative new models of care that are proven to be better. The book provides a deep analysis about the current challenges in the healthcare industry and some possible pathways forward to improve it.

—Sam Hazen, CEO,
HCA Corporation

Johnson and Kusserow have finally discovered healthcare's Holy Grail: creating one place for all your health and care needs in a seamless, easy-to-use platform will empower consumers to live better and healthier lives. Unifying benefits navigation, clinical guidance, and care delivery, within one quality experience will change everything, much as Amazon did in the rest of our world.

—Glen Tullman, CEO,
Transcarent

An insightful perspective into the current threats and emerging opportunities in the U.S. healthcare system. Change in our current system is inevitable and necessary, and this book shows us the path that got us here and a way to move forward.

—Kim Keck, President and CEO,
Blue Cross Blue Shield Association

Healthcare is the largest industry in the world and the only industry that every one of us interacts with: what choice do we have? In this essential book, healthcare executives and experts Johnson and Kusserow demystify the healthcare system and make the case for the revolutionary change that needs to happen. They eloquently reveal the coming transformation of our healthcare system and give us a glimpse as to what new and better world can evolve.

—Trevor Fetter,
Senior Lecturer and Henry B. Arthur Fellow,
Harvard Business School; former Chairman
and CEO, Tenet Health

Using surgical deftness and delightful literary references, authors Johnson and Kusserow open the reader's eyes to five societal forces that will put massive pressure on our current healthcare system. With that as a foundation, they detail five solutions capable of obviating the crisis and restoring health to our nation. *The Coming Healthcare Revolution* is a must-read for both the providers and recipients of medical care.

—Robert Pearl, MD,
Stanford University; former Executive Director and CEO,
The Permanente Medical Group

The Coming Healthcare Revolution portrays the constellation of irresistible macro-economic and market forces that are disrupting and rewiring the U.S.'s largest industry in real time. Johnson and Kusserow predict more change in the next 10 years than in the last 100. Buckle up!

—Wyatt Ritchie,
President, Cain Brothers

At Amazon One Medical, we believe deeply in working backwards, as described by Johnson and Kusserow, from customers' health and healthcare "jobs to be done." Our experience in doing so suggests that there are many ways, many of which are highlighted in the book, to reduce friction and eliminate waste, that all too often we admire rather than address in healthcare.

—Trent Green, CEO,
Amazon One Medical

The Coming Healthcare Revolution concretely describes the 10 forces rewiring America's health care industry in real time. It is a must-read for leaders navigating through a changing health care marketplace, as well as for employers who want to become better buyers of high-value healthcare to help their employees live healthier, happier and more productive lives.

—Dan Mendelson, CEO,
Morgan Health

The combined impact of the forces articulated in this insightful book will drive dramatic change and shape our healthcare ecosystem for years to come. Johnson and Kusserow provide a front-row seat to the coming revolution. You don't want to miss it.

—Jonathan Kolstad,
Henry J. Kaiser Chair at the Haas School of Business and Economics Department, Director of the Center for Healthcare Marketplace Innovation at UC Berkeley

This book eloquently highlights how we got here, what the consequences of doing the same things we've been doing have been, and what we do next.

—Richard Ashworth,
President and CEO, Amedisys

The two "B's" in the authors' clever acronym CB2E2 (Cheaper, Better, Balanced, Easier, Empowering) really resonates. Balancing health promotion and population health with better and more equitable access to treatment is exactly what will enable all Americans to thrive.

—Michelle Williams,
former Dean, Harvard T.H. Chan School of Public Health

Healthier futures for all Americans depend on aligning payment and performance metrics with desired outcomes. As Johnson and Kusserow's compelling narrative depicts, market-driven restructuring of healthcare services is now occurring through value-creation, health promotion and consumerism. It's time for all industry stakeholders to convene and legitimately address opportunities for better health outcomes for all.

—Ann Jordan, JD, CEO,
HFMA

A clarion call for change and transformation from two of the most strategic minds in healthcare.

—Lucinda Baier, President and CEO,
Brookdale Senior Living; Chair, Nashville Health Care Council; author of Heroes Work Here

THE COMING HEALTHCARE REVOLUTION

10 FORCES THAT WILL CURE AMERICA'S HEALTH CRISIS

DAVID W. JOHNSON | PAUL KUSSEROW

WILEY

For general information on our other products and services or for technical support, please contact
our Customer Care Department within the United States at (800) 762-2974, outside the United
States at (317) 572-3993 or fax (317) 572-4002.

Wiley also publishes its books in a variety of electronic formats. Some content that appears in print
may not be available in electronic formats. For more information about Wiley products, visit our
web site at www.wiley.com.

Library of Congress Cataloging-in-Publication Data is Available:

ISBN 9781394286454 (cloth)
ISBN 9781394286461 (ePub)
ISBN 9781394286478 (ePDF)

COVER ART & DESIGN: PAUL MCCARTHY
BACKGROUND PATTERN: © GETTY IMAGES | FOTOATA

SKY10085987_092624

To my younger siblings Doug, Sue and Liz.
We have suffered, survived and thrived during our long lives together.
—*Dave*

For my Mom, Suzanne Kusserow, whose pioneering and
fearless work in nursing, public health, and women's health inspired
a grateful son. With gratitude and love to my wife and partner,
Serena. And to my daughters — Maude, Marina, and Francesca,
for their enduring love and patience.
—*Paul*

Contents

Foreword

Dave Johnson and Paul Kusserow are optimists. They can foresee a time in the not-too-distant future when American health care costs will be lower, access to services will be more convenient, care will be more personalized and more focused on prevention and wellness, quality will be uniformly high, and everyone—patients and clinicians—will be more satisfied.

The authors term this future of medicine "3D-WPH"—**D**emocratized and **D**ecentralized **D**istribution of **W**hole-**P**erson **H**ealth. Maybe 3D-WHP is not something yelled at the ramparts of a revolution—even a health care revolution—but it accurately describes what they think the future will bring. What makes them optimists is that they believe this future is not just a utopian vision, but is both inevitable and imminent, **arriving** by 2034.

There was optimism and excitement after the passage of the Affordable Care Act (ACA), but that was 15 years ago. Despite concrete gains in access and costs since then, optimism about American healthcare is distinctly out of fashion. Today, pessimism about and dissatisfaction with the US health-care system are the norm. In this sense, Johnson and Kusserow are out of step with the times. But that does not mean they are wrong. . .it means they see things most Americans cannot discern.

On access, the passage of the ACA, and more recently, COVID-driven increased subsidies and prohibitions on Medicaid recertifications and rede-terminations, drove the uninsured rate down to as low as 7.7%.[1] This con-stitutes a huge achievement. However, today, those temporary COVID policies have ended, and the country is about 26 million people – and growing – short of universal coverage. There is no plausible path to that goal, certainly none in the next 10 years.

On costs, the 15 years since passage of the ACA have seen an unprecedented plateau in healthcare costs as a fraction of GDP. In 2022, the US spent about 17.3%[2] of GDP on healthcare – about the same as it was in 2010 and much lower than predicted for 2022 at the passage of the ACA in 2010. This cost plateau generated almost $4 trillion in savings for Medicare alone.[3] Simultaneously, however, premiums for family insurance coverage increased from $13,871 in 2010[4] to an average of just under $24,000 in 2023[5], which constitutes a whopping 32% of median household income. Furthermore, out of pocket costs, separate from premium costs, are nearly $1500 per person per year. And over 60% of Americans say they forego healthcare services because of cost.[6] Even worse, predictions are for 5% or higher annual growth in healthcare expenditures through 2032.[7] Whatever savings from reduced cost growth the ACA generated seem to be evaporating if they are not already gone. And predictions are for healthcare costs to be 19.7% of GDP by 2032.

Finally, healthcare quality remains uneven and not good, maybe even outright poor. Yes, the US is a world leader in cancer care, but for almost everything else, health outcomes are embarrassing.

Hypertension is a paradigm of bad outcomes in the United States. Nearly 120 million American adults, close to half of all adults in the US, have hypertension[8], of which, estimates say that between 10[9] and 24[10] million don't even know it. Hypertension control is dismal, at under 50% by a "loose" definition of controlled (a blood pressure under 140/90) and under 25% by a more "stringent" definition of controlled (a blood pressure under 130/80). The result and reality for our citizens is worse cardiovascular, renal, and stroke incidence and rising rates of maternal morbidity and mortality around pregnancy and delivery. Indeed, hypertension is associated with hundreds of thousands of deaths each year. And this number has increased, not decreased, since 2000.[11] Keep in mind, this poor American performance occurs for a disease that is relatively easy to diagnose and treat with cheap, automatic blood pressure cuffs, a clear consensus care algorithm to guide treatment, and plenty of low-cost generic medications.

The story for type 2 diabetes is not much better. Fully 38 million, or 14.7% of all US adults, have diabetes.[12] Of them, about half have their diabetes under control with a hemoglobin A1C under 7%. According to the

National Committee for Quality Assurance (NCQA), about two-thirds of people with diabetes do not have their blood pressure "controlled"[13] (by the more lax standard) and just under 65% had an annual eye exam[14]. With only half of people having their disease under control, it is no wonder diabetes causes over 100,000 deaths annually, making it the 8th leading cause of death in the United States.[15]

Given these data, it is no surprise the American public is far from optimistic about health care. According to various polls – Gallup, Ipsos, and Pew – 60% of Americans say the healthcare system is a hassle, and a similar proportion find it stressful.[16] Indeed, the proportion of Americans who think the system has "major problems" or is in a "state of crisis" is, for the first time, over 50%.[17]

Such data and the pervasive dissatisfaction expressed by Americans make one wonder how Johnson and Kusserow can be so optimistic about the future of the US health care system?

There is no doubt that if the US pushed prevention and wellness, the country would be healthier, happier, with lower costs. What is exciting about Johnson and Kusserow's book is not just that they can envision this new future that really is better for all Americans – lots of researchers and commentators have done that – but that they discern the larger and powerful forces driving system-wide transformation and have described the types of actual companies and policies, that can overcome the barriers – especially the financial barriers – to bring the country closer to their 3D-WPH.

In particular, they discern 10 large macro and -economic market forces that are coalescing at the same moment to propel the American healthcare system not just to the precipice but tipping it over into revolutionary change. These forces include demographic changes: the aging of the population and increase in the incidence of chronic illnesses and mental health conditions. They also include limits to the willingness of businesses and the public to pay more for healthcare, forcing a focus on efficiency. They also examine positive forces from advances in digital technologies to more care in the community and in patients' homes to creative redesign of care to a shift in focus toward prevention rather than more treatment once diseases have manifest.

These forces, to change metaphors, make Johnson and Kusserow believe the US is entering the steep upward portion of the S-shaped curve of healthcare improvement. In Johnson and Kusserow's view, the 10 forces are "irresistible" and that creative destruction will produce a better healthcare system. Ultimately, in their view, in "2034 US healthcare will bear little resemblance to our current system."

How do these forces manifest? One way is a massive shift to virtual or digital care. They cite a McKinsey study that suggests "virtual care could replace $250 billion of in-person care." This "decentralization" will enhance patient access and convenience and produce cost savings. Another element of decentralization is the outmigration of procedures – the profit drivers at hospitals – from expensive, inefficient institutions to lower-cost venues including ambulatory surgical centers and outpatient physician offices. They see this occurring through a small but powerful change in payment termed "site-neutral payment" in which the pay for a procedure is the same regardless of where it occurs. Many policy experts, including myself, have been advocating for this for years, and it seems as if it will finally occur in the near future. They also recognize the numerous ways in which patients can receive whole-person care in the comfort of their own homes. One is a palliative care model which encompasses more than just pain management, incorporating "non-clinical home-based care that enhances delivery of ADL and SDoH/health multiplier services." Models like these can both enhance the quality of care and save money by employing patients' families and friends to provide some services such as preparing meals or even just chatting with patients.

Johnson and Kusserow profile many start-ups that are transforming care because of a change in financial and quality incentives being offered by employers. One company they praise as "interesting and promising" is Apree Health, a primary care company that is backed by JP Morgan Chase (JPMC) and is managing care for JPMC's 36,000 employees and dependents in and around Columbus, Ohio. Apree combines "independent advanced primary care clinics with easy-to-use technologies, risked-based payment models and performance metrics" to focus on whole-person health. Their clinics serve as a single point of contact that provide integrated clinical care teams – including navigators, coaches, and behavioral health specialists – to work seamlessly for each patient. To ensure convenience, Apree augmented "its robust digital and virtual care platforms with five new clinics. . .on or adjacent to JPMC's Columbus offices." Apree is rewarded not based on fee for more services but based on prevention, patient satisfaction, quality, and costs and cost savings using metrics such as Net Promoter Score (NPS), responsiveness to appointment requests, SDoH screens, Healthcare Effectiveness Data and Information Set (HEDIS) scores for quality, emergency room use and hospitalizations. As Johnson and Kusserow conclude: "The key takeaway from this [Apree] case study is that whole-person health works at scale with aligned financial incentives and appropriate resource allocation." They admonish existing healthcare payers, hospitals, and other providers to be afraid. . ."very afraid."

With the various means to democratize care delivery, including through but not limited to virtual care, Johnson and Kusserow also detect a reduction in the enormous numbers of intermediaries in the systems. Intermediaries – insurers, pharmacy benefit managers (PBMs), pharmacy services companies, management service organizations (which implement the non-clinical services of physician practices) and others – are proliferating. According to one estimate, these intermediaries now account for over 40% of all healthcare revenue in the United States. Just this past July, the Federal Trade Commission (FTC) released a 73-page report hostile to PBMs, formally labeling them "the powerful middlemen inflating drug costs and squeezing main street pharmacies."[18] This kind of bullish activity from the federal government is a sign that the power of intermediaries may be ending. Decentralization and democratization should shrink this sector and bring patients and clinicians closer and improve satisfaction for both.

According to Johnson and Kusserow, new delivery models like Apree and fewer intermediaries portent the creative destruction that will transform the delivery and quality of care in the next decade. They foresee that the current, inefficient incumbents – what they call Healthcare Inc. –will disappear with substantial dislocations but real cost savings and thus improvements in the lives of most Americans.

It is impossible to argue with many of the social forces Johnson and Kusserow see as shaping the future of healthcare. The aging of the population and increase in chronic and mental health conditions are indisputable facts, as are the rise of digital technologies and greater biologic understandings of diseases with more insights about how to prevent and treat chronic illnesses. But even with strong forces pushing change, it is also a fact that old, deteriorating dysfunctional organizations and systems can teeter for a long time, decades, even centuries, without being replaced. Witness the Holy Roman Empire and the Ottoman Empire, not to mention antiquated and dangerous water and sewage systems, or almost any big city's public transit system in the US, or antiquated companies.

While they cite start-up examples like Apree and many others, both the existing infrastructure of healthcare – the facilities, contracts, relationships, usual practices, etc. – and Healthcare Inc. – the existing hospitals, insurers, pharmaceutical companies, device manufacturers, high-priced specialists, skilled nursing facilities, and all the other organizations that profit from the status quo – will use their tremendous financial, political, and PR resources to fight back against the innovators. But for Johnson and Kusserow, as forceful and well-financed as this counter by incumbents might be, the 10 macro and market-economic forces, acting through companies like Apree, as well as government and employer policies, are making it financially possible to bypass these giant but lumbering and antiquated parts of the healthcare delivery system. The rise of different payment models as embodied in Apree–JPMC example, and the consequent decline in fee-for-service incentives, are becoming more common and soon will reach a tipping point. And this will make it financially viable, indeed even highly remunerative, to deliver whole-person health, especially prevention and wellness. And then – to adopt yet another metaphor – the change will trigger a chain reaction that will completely refashion the system.

If you read this book with its numerous illuminating examples, you may start to believe revolutionary change in US healthcare is possible. As Johnson and Kusserow say, be afraid, very afraid, you too might shed your dissatisfaction and become an optimist about the future of US healthcare.

Ezekiel J. Emanuel, MD, PhD, is the Vice Provost for Global Initiatives, the Co-Director of the Healthcare Transformation Institute, and the Diane V.S. Levy and Robert M. Levy University Professor at the University of Pennsylvania

References:

1. National Uninsured Rate Remains at 7.7 Percent in the Fourth Quarter of 2023. (Issue Brief No. HP-2024-10). Office of the Assistant Secretary for Planning and Evaluation, U.S. Department of Health and Human Services. May 2024. https://aspe.hhs.gov/sites/default/files/documents/8fc1b15be1d96a55592c62aa35f3a4d0/nhis-q4-2023-data-point.pdf

2. Hartman, M., Martin, A. B., Whittle, L., Catlin, A., & National Health Expenditure Accounts Team (2024). National Health Care Spending In 2022: Growth Similar To Prepandemic Rates. *Health affairs (Project Hope), 43*(1), 6–17. https://doi.org/10.1377/hlthaff.2023.01360

3. Sanger-katz, M., Parlapiano, A., & Katz, J. (2023, September 5). *A huge threat to the U.S. budget has receded. and no one is sure why.* The New York Times. https://www.nytimes.com/interactive/2023/09/05/upshot/medicare-budget-threat-receded.html

4. Sep 02, 2010. (2010, September 2). *Family Health premiums rise 3 percent to $13,770 in 2010, but workers' share jumps 14 percent as firms shift cost burden.* KFF. https://www.kff.org/health-costs/press-release/family-health-premiums-rise-3-percent-to-13770-in-2010-but-workers-share-jumps-14-percent-as-firms-shift-cost-burden/#:~:text=The%20reason%20for%20the%20large,up%20from%20$779%20in%202009.

5. Published: Oct 18, 2023. (2023, December 8). *Section 1: Cost of health insurance – 10240.* KFF. https://www.kff.org/report-section/ehbs-2023-section-1-cost-of-health-insurance/#:~:text=PREMIUMS%20FOR%20SINGLE%20AND%20FAMILY,per%20year%20%5BFig ure%201.1%5D.

6. Lopes, L., Montero, A., Presiado, M., & Hamel, L. (2024, May 7). *Americans' challenges with health care costs.* KFF. https://www.kff.org/health-costs/issue-brief/americans-challenges-with-health-care-costs/#:~:text=One%20in%20four%20adults%20say,care%20because%20of%20the%20cost.v

7. Fiore, J. A., Madison, A. J., Poisal, J. A., Cuckler, G. A., Smith, S. D., Sisko, A. M., Keehan, S. P., Rennie, K. E., & Gross, A. C. (2024). National Health Expenditure Projections, 2023–32: Payer Trends Diverge As Pandemic-Related Policies Fade. *Health affairs (Project Hope), 43*(7), 910–921. https://doi.org/10.1377/hlthaff.2024.00469

8. Centers for Disease Control and Prevention. (n.d.). *High blood pressure facts.* Centers for Disease Control and Prevention. https://www.cdc.gov/high-blood-pressure/data-research/facts-stats/index.html.

9. CDC. (2023, April 27). *Million hearts® undiagnosed hypertension.* Million Hearts. https://millionhearts.hhs.gov/about-million-hearts/optimizing-care/undiagnosed-hypertension.html

10. Farley, T. A., Dalal, M. A., Mostashari, F., & Frieden, T. R. (2010). Deaths preventable in the U.S. by improvements in use of clinical preventive services. *American Journal of Preventive Medicine, 38*(6), 600–609. https://doi.org/10.1016/j.amepre.2010.02.016

11. Vaughan, A. S., Coronado, F., Casper, M., Loustalot, F., & Wright, J. S. (2022). County-Level Trends in Hypertension-Related Cardiovascular Disease Mortality-United States, 2000 to 2019. *Journal of the American Heart Association, 11*(7), e024785. https://doi.org/10.1161/JAHA.121.024785

12. Centers for Disease Control and Prevention. (n.d.-b). *National Diabetes Statistics Report.* Centers for Disease Control and Prevention. https://www.cdc.gov/diabetes/php/data-research/index.html#:~:text=Among%20the%20U.S.%20population%20overall,Table%201a%3B%20Table%201b).

13. *Blood pressure control for patients with diabetes.* NCQA. (n.d.). https://www.ncqa.org/hedis/measures/blood-pressure-control-for-patients-with-diabetes/

14. *Increase the proportion of adults with diabetes who have a yearly eye exam – D-04.* Increase the proportion of adults with diabetes who have a yearly eye exam – D-04 - Healthy People 2030. (n.d.). https://health.gov/healthypeople/objectives-and-data/browse-objectives/diabetes/increase-proportion-adults-diabetes-who-have-yearly-eye-exam-d-04

15. Centers for Disease Control and Prevention. (2024, May 2). *FAST-STATS – leading causes of death.* Centers for Disease Control and Prevention. https://www.cdc.gov/nchs/fastats/leading-causes-of-death.htm

16. Lohr, A. A. (n.d.). *MDVIP/Ipsos poll shows Americans are struggling with the …* Ipsos. https://www.ipsos.com/en-us/mdvipipsos-poll-shows-americans-are-struggling-healthcare-system

17. Saad, L. (2024, February 7). *Americans sour on U.S. Healthcare Quality.* Gallup.com. https://news.gallup.com/poll/468176/americans-sour-healthcare-quality.aspx#:~:text=The%20latest%20excellent%2Fgood%20rating,annual%20Health%20and%20Healthcare%20survey.

18. *Pharmacy benefit managers: The powerful middlemen inflating drug costs and squeezing Main Street pharmacies.* Federal Trade Commission. (2024, July 9). https://www.ftc.gov/reports/pharmacy-benefit-managers-report

Introduction: Healthcare's Roaring 2020s

This book's working title was "Gradually, Then Suddenly." The phrase comes from Ernest Hemingway's *The Sun Also Rises*, perhaps Hemingway's greatest literary achievement. In the novel, Hemingway fictionalizes his own post–World War I life in Paris and Spain as a member of what author Gertrude Stein termed the "Lost Generation." Two of the book's central characters, Bill Gorton and Mike Campbell, are hard-drinking war veterans. One evening, the two men fall into a conversation about Mike's financial problems. Bill asks Mike how he went bankrupt. Mike responds, "Two ways. Gradually, then suddenly."

Like the sigmoid function (commonly known as the "S" curve) in mathematics, Hemmingway's quote captures the underlying pattern (emergence, acceleration, climax) of transformative change. Disruptive innovations build their capabilities "gradually" before "suddenly" unleashing themselves on unsuspecting and ill-prepared incumbents.

By their very nature, markets adjust, adapt, and advance. Disruption of healthcare's status-quo business practices has been quietly underway for more than a decade. Institutional resistance and a lax regulatory environment have enabled Healthcare Inc. (our shorthand for the massive U.S.

healthcare industrial complex) to avoid the market-driven transformation forced upon other industries. Until now.

As a result, revolutionary transformation of the U.S. healthcare system is much closer to the "suddenly" stage than most incumbents can imagine. Complacency has lulled them into a false sense of security that their massive and interdependent business practices are impervious to transformational change. It's hard to fault this conclusion.

A GARGANTUAN "GAS GUZZLER"

U.S. healthcare is the largest industry ever created by human beings. "The National Health Expenditure Projections (2022–31)" published in June 2023 by the Centers for Medicare and Medicaid Services (CMS) estimates that 2024 healthcare expenditures in the U.S. will equal $4.9 trillion or 17.8% of the nation's $26.5 trillion economy.[1]

That number – $4.9 trillion – is massive. World Bank data for 2022 identifies Japan as the world's third-largest economy at $4.2 trillion. It's almost impossible to believe, but U.S. healthcare expenditure now exceeds Japan's aggregate economic activity. By itself, U.S. healthcare is the world's third-largest economic engine. If it were a car, healthcare would be a gas guzzler. Despite being the largest segment of the U.S. economy (or perhaps because of it), the healthcare industry over-consumes resources without delivering commensurate value.

An October 2022 meta-analysis in *Health Affairs* pegged healthcare's administrative costs at between 15% and 30% of total expenditures with at least half of that amount attributable to waste.[2] The high end of that percentage range for 2024 equals $1.47 trillion. Unbelievably, at that level healthcare's administrative expenses would be bigger in size than any other U.S. industry. Think about this for a moment. Administering healthcare services conceivably generates more economic activity than any other non-healthcare enterprise.

Gargantuan as it is, the $1.47 trillion figure excludes the "administrative sludge" imposed on American consumers to navigate through the system. Jeffrey Pfeffer of Stanford Business School found that Americans spend 12 million hours per week hassling with health insurance administrivia. Over half of this activity occurs on the job.[3]

CMS projects healthcare expenditures will grow 5.4% annually and reach $7.2 trillion by 2031, representing almost 20% of the U.S. economy.[4] For that to happen, healthcare will constitute 25% of the incremental growth ($2.5 trillion out of $10.0 trillion) in the U.S. economy between 2023 and 2031. With these projected growth rates, it's not surprising that private equity and venture funds are moving aggressively into healthcare. Private investment follows growth.

Healthcare Inc. operates within a hospital-, physician-, and disease-centric payment system that prioritizes treatment over prevention and disease management. One hundred years ago, healthcare created this operating model to apply scientific discipline to physician training and clinical care delivery. For its time, this revolutionary approach propelled the U.S. into becoming the global leader in medical research and discovery. That was then. Healthcare Inc.'s inability to adapt to changing consumer demands and market dynamics in recent decades makes its incumbents vulnerable to disruptive competition.

Due to its size, complexity, fragmentation, lack of accountability, and artificial economics, Healthcare Inc. is failing the American people. Rising maternal mortality, declining life expectancy, a massive misallocation of facilities and practitioners, uneven care access, skyrocketing costs, demoralized caregivers, fearful consumers, and poor customer service testify to the current system's shortcomings. Healthcare Inc. needs to die, so that a new, better, and more balanced healthcare ecosystem can replace it.

The U.S. healthcare system's structural flaws are not new. What is new are the numerous macro and market forces that are coalescing to upend Healthcare Inc.'s status-quo business practices. Despite incessant discussion of the need for system-wide reform, most incumbents don't appreciate the revolutionary change that is at their doorsteps. They apply an incremental analytic lens to a marketplace confronting exponential transformation. Indeed, the CMS expenditure projections through 2031 use a linear forecasting methodology that assumes tomorrow will be like yesterday. It misses the paradigm-shifting forces that are reconfiguring healthcare's supply–demand dynamics.

The changes coming to healthcare in the U.S. are revolutionary, not evolutionary. They will originate more outside-in than inside-out and will be messy. A transformed healthcare system will properly align its service delivery to consumers' actual health and healthcare needs. Costs will decrease as outcomes improve. Applying Reverend Theodore Parker's famous quote on justice to economics, "The arc of the marketplace can be long, but it bends toward value."

"FORTUNE" TELLING HEALTHCARE'S DYSFUNCTION

Healthcare Inc.'s systematic dysfunction has been evident for decades. In January 1970, *Fortune Magazine* published an investigative report with the provocative title, "Our Ailing Medical System." The magazine's cover is a play on Aesculapius, the ancient Greco-Roman god of medicine. Modern medicine has incorrectly added a second snake into the design of its iconic symbol (see Figure 0.1). This error is suggestive of American medicine's "original sin," an unbending commitment to volume and payment-driven business practices (medicine's "twin snakes") that place secondary importance on outcomes, value, and customer experience.

Getting it right, the *Fortune Magazine* cover (see Figure 0.2) has a single serpent wrapping itself around and strangling, boa constrictor-like, the American flag. The cover's designer, Walter Allner, made the wry observation that any resemblance between the snake and a dollar sign was purely coincidental. Then as now, money is at the center of American healthcare.

Figure 0.1

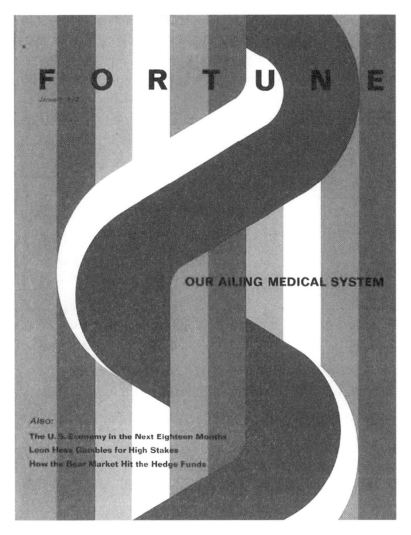

Figure 0.2 *Fortune Magazine* **cover.**

Unfortunately, the healthcare boa constrictor has gotten much larger, more predatory, and voracious since 1970. The healthcare system's fundamental organizing principle is revenue optimization. Just follow the money. Since 1970, U.S. healthcare expenditures have grown from 7% of GDP in 1970 to 18% today. In the process, Healthcare Inc. has used its economic and political leverage to enrich itself at the expense of American society. Much of Healthcare Inc.'s gains have come, in large measure, by increasing what America's beleaguered working families must pay for healthcare services.

The opportunity costs associated with this massive overpayment are incalculable. They manifest as lost wages, lower family wealth, and reduced social mobility.

Despite being written over 50 years ago, the magazine's opening commentary has a contemporary feel. Titled "It's Time to Operate,"[5] the commentary characterizes the chaos and challenges confronting the U.S. healthcare industry circa 1970 in this compelling language:

> *American medicine, the pride of the nation for many years, stands now on the brink of chaos. To be sure, our medical practitioners have their great moments of drama and triumph. But much of U.S. medical care, particularly the everyday business of preventing and treating routine illnesses, is inferior in quality, wastefully dispensed, and inequitably financed.*
>
> *Medical <u>manpower</u> and facilities are so maldistributed that large segments of the population, especially the urban poor and those in rural areas, get virtually no care at all – even though their illnesses are most numerous and, in a medical sense, often easy to cure.*
>
> *Whether poor or not, most Americans are badly served by the obsolete, overstrained medical system that has grown up around them helter-skelter. . . . The time has come for radical change.*

Remarkable! By changing the word "manpower" to "personnel," we can apply the 1970s *Fortune* language verbatim to Healthcare Inc. today. Unfortunately, the system's structural flaws have magnified since then and contribute even more to the nation's declining health status. As the *Fortune* analysis identifies, the system's inability to prevent and manage routine illnesses may be its greatest failing. That failure manifests itself in the catastrophic levels of chronic disease that now plague the American people.

The most predictive indicator of future chronic disease is the onset of obesity. Adult obesity has skyrocketed from just under 15% of Americans in 1970 to more than 40% today.[6] During the same period, childhood obesity rates have almost quadrupled.[7] Circumstances aren't improving. An analysis by the Harvard T.H. Chan School of Public Health highlights that almost 70% of American adults are currently overweight and that half will be obese by 2030.[8]

---

[1] "It's Time to Operate," *Fortune 81* (January 1970), 79.

As an industry, Healthcare Inc. has gotten much better since the 1970s at keeping sicker people alive longer. This is a logical response for an industry focused on treatment rather than prevention. The rise of chronic disease, however, is a broader societal challenge.

The explosion of highly processed foods within the American diet combined with a less-active population are causal factors of the chronic disease pandemic. This is particularly true in low-income urban and rural communities where "food deserts" make healthy eating almost impossible. Healthcare's disease- and treatment-centric orientation limits its ability to apply proven solutions to overcome these counterproductive lifestyle behaviors.

It's not that there hasn't been progress. Hepatitis C now has a cure. CRISPR technologies enabled creation of the remarkably effective COVID vaccine in under one year. The new GLP-1 drugs (e.g., Ozempic and Wegovy) appear to be quite effective at enabling and sustaining weight loss. Despite these bright spots, the long-term trends in healthcare have been ever-higher expenditures to treat an ever-sicker population. Healthcare Inc.'s strategic orientation remains reactive to disease as it manifests, not proactive to prevent disease transmission.

Under the current payment systems, however, Healthcare Inc. benefits when Americans are sicker. *It's not in Healthcare Inc.'s current financial interests to attack the root causes of chronic disease. It really is that simple.* Consequently, it is naïve to believe that this vast, intricate, and rigid healthcare system will change of its own accord.

The industry's incumbents have been strong and clever enough to maintain a stranglehold on service access, delivery, and pricing. This is why U.S. healthcare costs are higher and health outcomes worse than those found in other high-income countries. Like a volcano about to erupt, however, demographic inevitabilities and societal pressures are intensifying.

The first stanza from William Butler Yeats' 1920 poem "The Second Coming" captures the uneasiness and fatalism of an adrift American healthcare system, cut from its moorings and heading toward an uncertain future:

> *Things fall apart; the center cannot hold; …*
> *The best lack all conviction, while the worst*
> *Are full of passionate intensity.*

Overbuilt and inequitable, Healthcare Inc. is collapsing under its own weight. The forces described in this book are accelerating this collapse.

CHANGE IS THE ONLY CONSTANT

The Buddha observed, "Change is never painful. Only resistance to change is painful." As Buddha's insight implies, change and its byproducts are elemental to human experience. Consequently, it's not surprising that understanding and accommodating change are constant and recurring themes in art, literature, and theology across all cultures.

Buddhism teaches that an individual's response to change is more important than the change itself. Detachment from human experience is the ultimate objective. An individual's ability to accept and adapt to never-ending change determines their ability to find happiness and a sense of self-worth within an imperfect world.

In the blessed state of nirvana, Buddhists experience life's continuous changes with equanimity. The Sanskrit root of "nirvana" literally means to blow out flames of worry and desire, both of which increase with change. Buddhist teachings reflect a universal truth: Change is constant.

From ancient history to the current day, humankind has searched for unchanging principles to bring stability and understanding of the human condition. We rely on these truths to explain injustice, suffering, and death. Many find solace in the concept of an afterlife. Despite the human desire for stability and permanence, the tectonic plates still move. Circumstances change. Game-changing technologies emerge. Industries rise and fall.

We know that change is inevitable even though we humans often lull ourselves into complacency. We take false comfort in the permanence of institutions. Given the reality of constant change, the optimal human and organizational response is consistent, predictable adaptation. Moving from the philosophical to the economic realm, disruption within other industries (from transportation to entertainment to hospitality) reveals the vulnerability of market-leading but asset-heavy companies (e.g., Blockbuster) to more nimble digital interface companies (e.g., Netflix).

Emergent service and technology companies have lower capital needs. They rely on software more than hardware. They exhibit greater strategic flexibility within dynamic markets. Investors increasingly value "interface" companies, like Netflix and Airbnb, with seamless, easy-to-use, customer-friendly integrated service platforms that can adapt quickly to new circumstances. Market valuations reflect this. As of March 2024, Airbnb, with few tangible assets other than its digital platform, has a market capitalization significantly greater than that of Marriott and Hyatt combined.

In today's digitizing marketplace, capital-intensive industries are increasingly vulnerable to competition from disruptive asset-light companies. As a consequence, healthcare's capital-intensive sectors, notably hospitals and health systems, are highly vulnerable to the disruptive threat posed by tech-savvy, asset-light competitors. Absent external intervention (i.e., another government bailout), hospitals will decrease in size and number. As the winnowing occurs, health systems able to embrace innovation, adapt to new supply–demand dynamics, reinvent themselves, and deliver tangible value to customers will retain market relevance. Those that cannot, will not.

Purposeful deconstruction of a product's original architecture is a way for incumbent companies to internally disrupt themselves. The concept makes sense. Profitable product and service lines mature and decline. Enlightened companies anticipate this decline and incorporate strategic pivots into their assets' life cycles. In this way, the old becomes new and improved with modest reinvestment. Along with prudent diversification, purposeful deconstruction enables companies to address market evolution. Together, they provide a resilient strategy for surviving and even thriving as market environments shift, often in profound ways.

Strategists study history to divine specific patterns, improve their prognostication prowess, and avoid surprises. Mark Twain famously said, "History never repeats itself, but it does often rhyme." While companies strive for stability, they also look for ways to predict and anticipate changing market dynamics. This deductive knowledge search combined with forward preparation often differentiates successful companies from their competitors.

Going back to the 1920s can provide fresh perspectives (rhymes) on addressing the social and technological changes confronting modern-day America, particularly in healthcare.

BACK TO THE FUTURE?

Today, for the first time in history, human beings must adapt to change at a rate beyond our natural capabilities. Weaving digital technologies into the fabric of daily life to ease adaptation, reduce stress, and promote wellbeing is the challenge of our times. Big challenges require big solutions.

In a March 1944 speech to the Royal College of Physicians, Winston Churchill observed, "The longer you can look back [into history], the farther you can look forward [into the future]." With these Churchillian connections to health, history, and our collective future, let's "look back" a hundred years to the rollicking 1920s. As we do, let's search for insights into how life and healthcare will unfold throughout an equally rollicking 2020s.

America in the 1920s was a place of big ideas, boundless energy, big personalities, and big dreams. There were huge winners and losers. By the decade's end, so much had changed that it was hard to recognize or even remember the decade's humble origins. 1920s America has much to teach today's Americans about adapting to fast-paced and sometimes chaotic change.

Then and Now

The 1920s began in the immediate aftermath of World War I and a crippling global pandemic. The 1918–1919 Great Influenza killed 625,000 Americans and as many as 50 million people worldwide. Weary of global war and disease, America entered the 1920s with a profound sense of loss and deep uncertainty regarding its future.

Long roiling beneath a sunny facade, America's contradictions, conflicts, and restlessness burst forth and found expression during this turbulent decade. Efforts to resolve these tensions triggered a titanic wave of creativity, innovation, social conflict, dazzling technological advances, and status-quo-busting dynamism.

The 1920s also became the decade when American medical education, research, and clinical care were standardized, professionalized, and modernized. Breakthrough discoveries expanded medicine's healing powers.

Not surprisingly, this exuberant, freewheeling, and tumultuous decade is the only one to have its own nickname. The Roaring Twenties launched America into the modern era. For better or worse, there was no turning back.

A century later, the U.S. is just emerging from the grip of another massive pandemic. Living under COVID fundamentally changed the way people in America and around the world live, work, and play. Virtual technologies have made remote connectivity easier and better. On-demand delivery gets us what we need when we need it. On-demand transportation gets us where we need to be when we need to be there. COVID accelerated the adoption of these game-changing technologies.

During and since the COVID pandemic, long-simmering tensions exploded into the public arena. High-voltage rhetoric has politicized and polarized the national discourse. Restless Americans confront an uncertain future. There is a desperate need for creative solutions.

Like the 1920s, there's no going back to our pre-pandemic existence. Nowhere is this truer than in medicine and healthcare. Reconciling the industry's inherent contractions is putting enormous pressure on incumbent business practices even as it creates opportunities for new business models that create value and promote whole-person health. Mining the post-pandemic 1920s for insights deepens our understanding of the technological, economic, and cultural forces reshaping America today. It also provides a useful context for assessing how efforts to transform healthcare's long-calcified and counterproductive status quo will proceed.

Medicine's Golden Era

By the early 1900s, the United States had only a few elite medical enterprises that incorporated rigorous training, scientific research, and clinical consistency into their operations. The most notable was the then-new Johns Hopkins School of Medicine (founded in 1893). By contrast, most medical organizations were squalid, unregulated, clinically inadequate, and staffed by quacks. With the support of the American Medical Association (AMA), the Carnegie Foundation engaged Abraham Flexner in 1908 to survey medical education in the U.S. and Canada. Flexner published his findings in 1910.

The Flexner Report revolutionized American medicine. It called for rigorous admission criteria, adherence to scientific protocols, and state regulation of medical organizations. Few medical schools met Flexner's standards. He recommended closing more than 120 of the 150-plus medical schools then operating in the country.

Response to the Flexner Report was rapid and profound. Within four years, 31 states refused to license graduates from substandard medical schools. Within 10 years, almost a hundred medical schools closed or merged. Despite a fast-growing population, the number of U.S. medical students dropped from 28,000 in 1904 to just 14,000 in 1920.

The Flexner Report also promoted the Johns Hopkins training model of medical education: two years of science education and two years of clinical training, followed by extensive residencies at teaching hospitals. Medical schools universally adopted the Johns Hopkins model and operated within a tripartite mission (education, research, and clinical practice) that emphasized the power of science and the necessity of academic freedom.

The broad adoption of the Johns Hopkins model during the 1920s transformed American medicine and enshrined science as its core organizing principle. The decade witnessed breakthrough discoveries (penicillin, insulin, vitamins), advancing diagnostics, and the dramatic expansion of public health departments. By the close of the decade, America had become the global leader in medical research and clinical care.

While the Flexner Report did much to advance U.S. medicine, its narrowed focus within a highly segregated nation had significant negative consequences. Post-Flexner, five of the seven historically Black medical schools closed, greatly depressing the numbers of future Black physicians that continues into the current day. In 2018, only 5% of physicians were Black when Black people represented 13.4% of the total U.S. population.

The Flexner Report also led to the closure of almost all medical schools that emphasized a more expansive whole-person health approach to medical practice. These closures and the stigma assigned to "nonscientific" practices stifled development of complementary and alternative approaches to health and wellbeing. The invasive and reductionist bias embedded within American medicine today has its origins in the Flexner Report. This bias has limited the acceptance and application of functional medicine, which employs systems biology to address the root causes of chronic diseases.

Flexner's tripartite academic model promulgated during the 1920s remains largely intact today; however, it's showing its age. Despite a century's worth of medical advances, the American healthcare system was unprepared and ill-equipped to address the COVID pandemic. COVID exposed weaknesses in Healthcare Inc.'s supply chain, the inadequacy of the nation's public health infrastructure, the health risks of unchecked chronic disease, and profound disparities in access to healthcare services. The result was needless death and suffering.

Healthcare at the Crossroads

Frontline healthcare professionals battled COVID for several years. Their heroism and selflessness inspired the nation. Post-COVID, these professionals often labor with inadequate resources and suffer from high stress/burnout levels. Union organizing of healthcare employees is at record levels. Dissatisfied workers are no longer willing to accept status-quo work rules and compensation. Going forward, health companies must take better care of their workers and give them more tools to manage their own health as well as their patients' health.

The elimination of elective surgeries in March 2020 and relaxed regulatory barriers accelerated the adoption of innovative digital and virtual technologies. Almost all medical visits moved to telemedicine platforms. In the process, the healthcare industry pivoted to become more decentralized, consumer-oriented and cost-effective. Hospital-at-home care proliferated.

Concurrently, breakthroughs in vaccine development and genomic underpinnings of health suggest medicine is on the precipice of systematic improvements in diagnoses, treatments, and personalized wellness. Several virtual care, care management, and consumer health companies gained market traction. Many have become "unicorns" with valuations greater than $1 billion.

Despite these near-term advances, healthcare still largely operates in the same ways it did during the 1920s with an emphasis on hospital-centric care delivery, fee-for-service payment, and fragmented service provision. Post-COVID, most payers and providers desire a return to pre-pandemic business practices.

For example, among the AMA's top policy priorities is limiting "scope creep" by working to reinstate practice limitations in every state legislature. They're winning in many. Practicing at top of license, crossing state lines to practice without impediments, and encouraging virtual care were major improvements implemented during COVID to facilitate better and more convenient care delivery. The AMA is trying to put that "progress genie" back in its bottle.

Retrograde strategies like fighting "scope creep" are risky for healthcare incumbents. Their success relies on the belief that American society will continue to pay premium prices for sub-optimal care outcomes. That belief flies in the face of healthcare's turbulent market dynamics. Changing consumer expectations, new competitors, value-based payment models and pro-market regulatory reforms are placing enormous economic pressure on Healthcare Inc.'s status-quo business models.

Relative to other industries, healthcare has been slower to adapt disruptive and consumer-empowering digital technologies. Consequently, healthcare incumbents will experience disruptive change at an accelerated pace during the coming decade. This technological imperative represents a massive challenge for industry incumbents. Big challenges require big solutions. Successful healthcare companies must adapt to post-COVID work and market environments that empower both employees and consumers. Not easy.

Healthcare's Roaring 2020s

The conclusion is clear. The way healthcare's presently working isn't working. It's too expensive, fragmented, and ineffective. Americans want better care options, more transparency, greater convenience, and lower costs. Moreover, Healthcare Inc. isn't addressing the nation's most compelling public health challenges: the exploding levels of obesity and related chronic diseases along with major spikes in mental health conditions.

New business models are emerging to challenge status-quo practices and give consumers what they need, want, and desire. 1920s-like turbulence will eliminate many legacy businesses. Companies that promote whole-person health through high-value service provision will become market leaders. Here's the punchline: Healthcare will change more in the next 10 years than it has in the last hundred.

This is an exciting and perilous time for healthcare professionals. Properly inspired, healthcare's people can lead transformation through the industry's Roaring 2020s.

FORCE MULTIPLIERS

This book identifies five macro forces and five market forces that are rewiring the healthcare industry's supply-demand dynamics. The macro forces are broad societal megatrends that are pressing down on the healthcare ecosystem, demanding change. Healthcare Inc.'s foundation is crumbling. Its end is near.

By contrast, the five market forces capture the positioning strategies that value-creating health and healthcare companies are employing to demonstrate "market fitness." They are moving into the light created by the cracks in Healthcare Inc.'s armor. Their energy is enormous. Their intent is lethal. They win by winning over consumers.

The macro forces categorize cleanly with limited overlap. The same cannot be said for the market forces. New-age healthcare companies are pursuing strategies that combine two or more of the market forces to create value for customers.

No framework is perfect, particularly for one as large and complex as healthcare. The benefit of this framework is that it captures the simultaneous and unrelenting top-down and bottom-up pressures being applied to Healthcare Inc.'s antiquated business practices.

The other important nuance is that these 10 macro and market forces do not operate in isolation. Their individual impacts compound and magnify as they intersect with one another. Revolutionary change requires revolutionary forces that are strong enough to overcome Healthcare Inc.'s market concentration and political leverage.

The combined and compounding power of these macro and market forces will be both disruptive and transformative. As the battles for customer loyalty unfold and magnify, Healthcare Inc. will cease to exist. In its place, a revolutionary new American healthcare will emerge, phoenix-like, from Healthcare Inc.'s ashes.

The dismantling of Healthcare Inc. is long overdue. Maintaining status-quo healthcare translates into ever-higher spending to treat an ever-sicker population, lower productivity, greater inequality, worsening individual and community wellbeing, and less happiness. That is a future no one wants for the United States of America.

For incumbents, clinging to status-quo business practices is a perilous strategic mistake that risks their long-term sustainability. As management guru W. Edwards Deming noted, "Survival is optional. No one has to change."

Besides, the U.S. already spends more than enough money to provide affordable health insurance with appropriate access to everyone in the country. We must spend healthcare dollars more efficiently and effectively. This requires shifting resources out of acute and specialty care into whole-person health.

The operating and economic realities of delivering healthcare services on an outdated and clunky chassis are already causing the ecosystem to devolve in fundamental ways. Its dysfunction will widen and deepen as the top-down and bottom-up pressures on status-quo business practices magnify. Healthcare Inc. will oppose and delay logical payment and regulatory reforms, but it cannot forestall them forever.

The real challenge in American healthcare is how to implement basic and yet revolutionary reforms that will benefit the American people. The following 10 macro and market forces in combination with one another are getting the job done.

MACRO FORCES

Force #1: Demographic Determinants. The aging of America and the disease burden that accompanies it is placing greater strain on current delivery models as they struggle to find and pay caregivers. Concurrently, an aging population will place even greater financial demands on a shrinking workforce (as a percentage of total population) to fund the current system's increasing costs.

Force #2: Funding Fatigue. Healthcare expenditure has reached an inflection point that makes it impossible to continue subsidizing healthcare from other segments of the economy. Going forward, healthcare will need to fund its activities at current or lower percentages of the aggregate economy.

Force #3: Chronic Pandemics. U.S. healthcare has largely ignored its biggest challenge: the growing prevalence of chronic diseases and mental health conditions that are destroying the lives of countless Americans. Continued avoidance is not an option.

Force #4: Technological Imperatives. Breakthrough innovations in digital technologies and biology (genomics, epigenomics, proteomics, etc.) are improving the diagnosis and treatment of disease in fundamental ways as well as providing the tools to deliver better health and healthcare outcomes more efficiently and effectively.

Force #5: Pro-Consumer/Market Reforms. Shifting from a pro-industry legislative and regulatory environment that sustains status-quo business practices to one that promotes innovation and transparency, and level-field competition will improve outcomes, enhance quality, and reduce costs.

MARKET FORCES

Force #6: Whole Health. *Health* (preventive and promotive) and *health-care* (invasive and curative) are not synonymous. Making healthcare delivery cheaper, better, and easier is not enough. There needs to be a massive resource shift away from treatment into prevention and health promotion. Making America a healthier nation requires greater balance between pro-health and treatment activities.

Force #7: Care Redesign. New ways of organizing and delivering care are emerging that connect patients with caregivers more organically by delivering whole-person health at lower costs with better outcomes and personalized service delivery. Concurrently, payment policies and aligned business models are emerging to emphasize health-promoting activities and reduce demand for acute care interventions.

Force #8: Care Migration. The healthcare ecosystem is in the midst of a great outmigration of care from high-cost centralized delivery modalities (e.g., hospitals) to more convenient and much lower-cost community, home, and virtual modalities. By advancing decentralized delivery of whole-person health, Care Redesign and Care Migration pose a disruptive threat to status-quo business practices.

Force #9: Aggregators' Advantage. The emergence of holistic and seamless, consumer-friendly, whole-person health platforms will enable consumers to better navigate the system while empowering them to manage their own care needs and personal wellbeing.

Force #10: Empowered Caregivers. At its core, healthcare is a people-centered business that succeeds when dedicated caregivers practicing at the top of their license go the extra mile for customers. Optimizing human potential builds loyalty, enriches organizational cultures, drives better results, and creates market differentiation. No other business strategy generates higher overall returns.

We dedicate a chapter to each macro and market force. The book's conclusion describes a revolutionized healthcare ecosystem that is vastly different and better than the arcane one in operation today. While grounded in daunting reality and hard data, *The Coming Healthcare Revolution* is an optimistic book.

As the U.S. rewires its teetering healthcare system, it will free up enormous resources to apply elsewhere: to pay workers more; to invest in more productive industries; and to fund vital societal needs. Think of how redirecting as much as $1 trillion of wasted healthcare expenditure annually into more productive uses could benefit families and communities. Beyond economics, American society can become more equitable, productive, healthier, and happier as productive change to U.S. healthcare occurs.

Two editorial notes merit readers' attention. First, our book has two authors. Periodically, the book's narrative incorporates an author's individual experience. In those instances, we switch to third-party voice. Readers will know this is occurring when the narrative specifically mentions either Dave or Paul. We use our individual stories to add perspective and color. Like almost all consumers, we've had our fair share of good and bad healthcare experiences. Our long careers in healthcare strategy, operations, innovation, investing, and finance give us the ability to put those experiences into context.

Second, we highlight three time periods in the history of modern American medicine. The first is the 1920s, when the practice of medicine revolutionized to create a science-based framework for medical education, medical research, and clinical delivery. The second is the 1970s, when that system's fundamental flaws became apparent. The third is the 2020s, where medicine and healthcare are undergoing a second revolution. There is symmetry in this approach. Like the halfway point in a marathon, the 1970s was an unrealized opportunity to make meaningful course corrections. The industry's failure to do so has compounded its dysfunction and magnified the need for revolutionary reform.

Change is never easy, but the history of human evolution suggests that societies improve by creating ever-more complex win–win scenarios that extend benefits broadly. For too long, U.S. healthcare has been a zero-sum exchange where the industry's incumbents have disproportionately absorbed resources from an unsuspecting public that is now demanding improvement and performance accountability.

It's time to revolutionize U.S. healthcare by creating a system that serves the American people better. It's going to be a bumpy ride, but improved health and wellbeing for all Americans is just over the horizon. In the process, Healthcare Inc. will fade away. A vastly improved whole-person health system will emerge to replace it.

PART

I

Macro Forces

Introduction: Look Out Below

According to the National Weather Service there are five warning signs for a snow avalanche (see Figure 0.3). They are evident if skiers or hikers choose to look for them. We feel the same way about the macro forces pressing down on the U.S. healthcare industry. They are apparent for all industry analysts who are courageous enough to acknowledge them.

AVALANCHE
Warning Signs

- Evidence of previous slides
- Cracks forming in the snow around you
- Strong winds and/or blowing snow
- Heavy snowfall or rain in the last 24 hours
- Significant warming, or rapidly increasing temperatures

*If you see warning signs, **leave or avoid** potential avalanche terrain!*

AVALANCHE.ORG
weather.gov

Figure 0.3

Individually, each macro force is powerful. Collectively, they are irresistible. They demand attention and will require adjustment in business practices for companies that wish to achieve and/or retain market relevance.

Like the National Weather Service's list of five avalanche signs, we have identified five macro forces that will stimulate transformative change of the U.S. healthcare system. That change is imminent and existential for many industry incumbents. Like the difference between an "avalanche watch" and an "avalanche warning" (see Figure 0.4), being prepared isn't enough. It is time to take action.

As healthcare companies act, it is important for them to understand and accommodate the following five macro forces that are reshaping the industry's competitive landscape:

> *Force #1: Demographic Determinants* are increasing the demand for healthcare services even as they limit the supply of future caregivers.
>
> *Force #2: Funding Fatigue* reflects the inability of American society to continue funding healthcare expenditures at expansive rates of growth.
>
> *Force #3: Chronic Pandemics* are rapidly turning the United States into the land of the sick and home of the frail.
>
> *Force #4: Technological Imperatives* encompassing big data and biological breakthroughs are a galvanizing force that is redefining healthcare diagnosis and delivery in real time.

Figure 0.4

Force #5: Pro-Consumer/Market Reforms are taking aim at Healthcare Inc.'s anti-competitive business practices to stimulate innovation and facilitate level-field competition.

Healthcare companies ignore these macro forces at their own peril. Their combined impact creates the conditions necessary to trigger disruptive innovation, real consumerism, and market transformation.

It's adapt-or-die time for healthcare incumbents. They shouldn't be square dancing below the mountain while the avalanche is falling, and nimble competitors are changing the music.

1

Demographic Determinants

Demographics have the power of gravity. It is a quiet constant that shapes the futures of communities and nations. Like gravity, demographic trends are inevitable. It is why futurists can say with confidence that the populations of countries with low birth rates and disproportionate numbers of seniors (e.g., Japan and Italy) will shrink during the coming decades.

It is also why healthcare futurists can say with confidence that the U.S. healthcare system as currently configured is incapable of handling projected levels of patient volume without significant risk of collapse. The COVID pandemic proved these futurists right as the U.S. healthcare system buckled in response to intensified service demands.

The U.S. Census Bureau makes detailed projections to profile the evolving composition and characteristics of the nation's population. The Bureau supplements these projections with periodic reports that analyze statistical trends within the census data. These reports also incorporate interviews with polling participants to gain greater insights into the underlying reasons for their opinions.

The Bureau's most recent demographic projection and analysis of U.S. population trends occurred in 2017 (with an update in 2020) based on 2010 census data.[1] Their projections reveal that the United States is becoming more populous, older, and longer-living (see Figure 1.1). The Bureau's

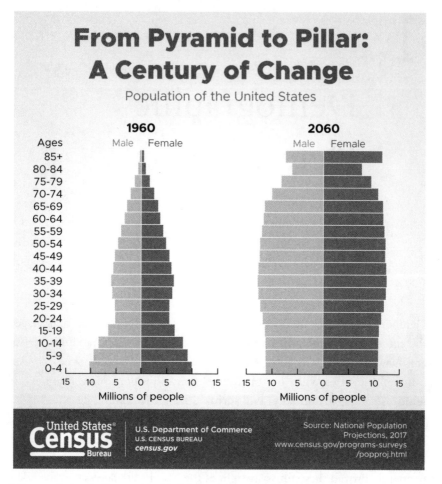

Figure 1.1   A larger and older projected U.S. population (1960 vs. 2060).

Source: Census/U.S. Department of Commerce/Public domain.

projections and analysis also reveal that America is becoming more racially and ethnically diverse.

These projected demographic changes within the U.S. will profoundly impact the nation's healthcare system. An aging society will need/demand more care services even as the supply of potential caregivers available to provide these services shrinks.

Demographics also informs how these population characteristics and trends will manifest. For example, the "age ratio" measures the mathematical relationship between workers and retirees. The shrinking age ratio within the U.S. informs assessments of the healthcare system's decreasing capacity to care for its aging citizens.

Overall, demographics is a formidable top-down force that places unrelenting pressure on the current U.S. healthcare system.

DEMOGRAPHICS, PSYCHOGRAPHICS, AND THE SEARCH FOR MEANING

In 1855, the Belgian statistician Achille Guillard first used the word "demography" in describing the mathematical characteristics of European populations during the nineteenth century. History credits Great Britain's John Graunt for conducting the first demographics study in 1662. Graunt detailed the characteristics of London's population, including its people's ages, sex, employment, and mortality rates.

Demographics literally takes its name from the Greek word "demos" for people. It is a subfield within sociology that studies populations. Demographers collect and assess statistical information on populations to understand historical and future trends. They evaluate how a population's evolving physical attributes (births, deaths, genders, ethnicity, employment patterns, income, age profiles, etc.) will shape a society's economic and communal future.

In 1838, French philosopher and mathematician Auguste Comte coined the term "sociology" from Latin and Greek root words to describe the study of human societies. Thought by many to be the "father of sociology," Comte famously observed, "Demographics is destiny." He believed that statistically measuring the hard facts of demographics was essential to understanding how people within societies evolve, function, and interact with one another.

Demographics don't lie but they do change. Understanding and anticipating those changes requires the examination of past and present population characteristics and trends. As such, demographics provide essential information for government planners. Demographic data also provide essential information for business leaders making product and service-line investments within an ever-evolving marketplace.

Used less frequently than demographics but equally important is psychographics. Psychographics measure a population's attitudes and beliefs. Knowledge of a population's opinions, choices, interests, values, and goals can provide key policy and product insights. Marketing relies on psycho-graphics to shape advertising campaigns, to literally win consumers' hearts and minds.

Psychographics complement demographics. Demographics detail a population's statistical profile. Psychographics explore that population's motivations. They try to figure out what's in their heads. Demographics and psychographics interconnect in an almost organic fashion, so we toggle back and forth between them to examine and explain the evolving healthcare ecosystem. As the U.S. population ages, it is crucial to understand both the statistical character of the nation's aging profile (the demographics) as well as our collective attitudes and opinions about aging (the psychographics).

Legendary baseball pitcher Satchel Paige defied expectations by pitching professionally into his late 40s. At age 59 in September 1965, the Kansas City Athletics signed Paige to pitch in a single game against the Boston Red Sox. He faced 10 batters, allowed one hit, no runs, and "relaxed" in a rocking chair between innings. Paige once asked, "How old are you when you don't know how old you are?" Echoing Mark Twain, Paige also observed, "Age is a state of mind over matter. If you don't mind, it don't matter." Demographics beg to differ.[2]

Paige's story is exceptional. It defies the law of averages. That's why it's so humorous and interesting. Demographics, however, depend on reversion to the mean (i.e., the law of averages) and other statistical measures to chronicle a society's demographic characteristics and assess their implications. Consequently, demographics emphasize that aging does matter. This is particularly true for U.S. healthcare as it prepares for the oncoming senior tsunami.

THE TWO-PRONGED DEMOGRAPHIC THREAT

The demographic profile of the U.S. population is changing rapidly. Two macro factors have driven the aging of American society during the last several decades. Those factors are longer life expectancy and a declining national birth rate.

An aging society requires more healthcare services for its senior citizens. Fewer births translate into a smaller labor pool for future caregivers and less societal capacity to generate the funding necessary through taxation to pay for seniors' social and healthcare needs.

These twin demographic trends are placing enormous pressure on America's current healthcare system: increasing demand for services; limiting worker supply; and diminishing capacity for societal funding support. Addressing this pincer movement will require creativity, innovation, and disruption to solve.

To paraphrase Plato, necessity is the mother of invention. It will have to be for the United States to bridge the demographic challenges confronting its fragmented and under-resourced elder care delivery system.

Boomer Time

Baby boomers, those born in the post–World War II "boom" years between 1946 and 1964, are driving the aging of America's population. The oldest and youngest boomers turned 78 and 60 respectively in 2024. *Due to their cohort's size, age, and social welfare needs, boomers will either break the United States' healthcare and retirement systems or force their transformation.*

The 71 million boomers still alive in 2024 represent only 21% of the total U.S. population but control 57% of the nation's wealth.[3] Boomers have disrupted American society in fundamental ways as they've aged, challenging established conventions and redefining social mores.

Demographers describe boomers as "independent, assertive, hard-working, ambitious, spoiled, and demanding." Not surprisingly given these descriptors, boomers are powerful and demanding consumers. They want what they want when they want it and will pay for it.

With close to 60% of the nation's wealth, boomers are now focusing on the last quarter of their lives. They are paying particular attention to health and wellbeing. Impossible to ignore, boomers will reinvent retirement, the concept of "golden years," and the role seniors should play in American society. More worrisome, at least 60% of boomers already suffer from at least one chronic disease.[4] Their care needs will strain an already overtaxed healthcare system.

Boomers are the tip of the spear as America confronts an epidemic of chronic disease. While Americans are living longer, they are not living healthier lives. Unfortunately for boomers, the onset of chronic illness still occurs as individuals enter their 60s.

Chronic illness for those past the age of 60 is ongoing and ever-present. Once Americans reach age 65, they live on average for another 13 years, often with increasingly debilitating chronic illnesses. Their lives dissipate into a long and slow chronic decline that becomes more complex and expensive to manage and treat.

Older and Sicker (Increasing Demand for Healthcare Services)

Let's first examine how American society has and will continue to age. Figure 1.2, from the U.S. Census Bureau, depicts aging trend lines over time for native and foreign-born U.S. residents.

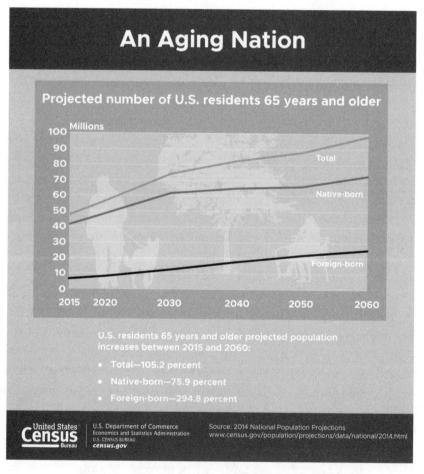

Figure 1.2   The rapidly aging U.S. population (2015–2060).

Source: Census/U.S. Department of Commerce/Public domain.

During the Roaring 1920s, the average lifespan for American men and women was 53.6 years and 54.6 years respectively. Fifty years later in the 1970s, the average lifespan for men had increased dramatically to 67.1 years and even more dramatically for women to 74.7 years. By then, women lived almost eight years longer than men.

Fast-forward to 1998. Men and women on average now lived 73.8 and 79.5 years respectively. The average lifespan for both men and women had slightly increased again by 2020, to 74.5 years for men and to 80.2 years for women.

The 2020 longevity figures were the lowest for men since 2003 and for women since 2005. In essence, the average American lifespan has plateaued. Averages can obscure powerful trends. The fastest growing demographic group in the U.S. is aged 90-plus. Their upward aging trend is offset by declining longevity in middle age, particularly in low-income communities and among ethnic populations.

On an actuarial basis, American lifespans peaked in 2019. The pandemic accelerated "expected deaths" by roughly one million people. In this way, COVID triggered a decline in American lifespans for the first time in decades. America's declining longevity has additional causes beyond COVID. They include increases in deaths due to despair (suicide, overdoses, and alcoholism), income inequality, gun violence, inequitable access to healthcare services, and unhealthy lifestyle choices.

The expectation, however, is that the average American lifespan will increase again. The U.S. Census Bureau estimates that by 2050 the average life expectancy for American men and women will be 80.9 years and 85.3 years respectively – below life expectancies of other advanced economies but longer than they are now.

Several recent reports predict that the current generation in their teens and 20s will live into their 90s. A 2009 research brief in *The Lancet* concludes that current 10-year-old children have a 50% chance of living to 100 years or beyond. Better education, advances in pharmacology, earlier diagnoses, targeted therapies, a deeper understanding of the aging process, and more effective chronic disease interventions will fuel this longevity trend.[5]

These collective advances in medical care, however, are insufficient to overcome accelerated chronic disease associated with the Standard American Diet, Lifestyle, and Environment (what we call SADLE). Medicine has become proficient at keeping sick people alive longer, often with diminished life quality, at a very high cost. It intervenes when symptoms present, often at advanced stages of disease.

As a society, the U.S. invests little in preventive care and health promotion. American consumers often prefer a pill, surgical procedure, and/or hospital visit when combatting chronic conditions instead of long-term lifestyle modification. These very American demographic and psychographic attributes compound the medical, financial, and societal ramifications of the nation's battle with chronic disease.

Obesity is the most predictive indicator of future levels of chronic disease within a population. America's obesity epidemic constitutes a clear and present danger to the nation's long-term health and wellbeing. Over two-thirds of U.S. adults are overweight or obese.

The Centers for Disease Control and Prevention (CDC) reports that "obesity prevalence" among adults increased almost 40% between 1999 and 2018, from 30.5% in 1999–2000 to 42.4% in 2017–2018 (see Figure 1.3). The average adult man and woman in America today weigh 200 and 171 pounds respectively.[6] It gets worse. A *New England Journal of Medicine* study estimates that by 2030, 67% of adult women and 75% of adult men will be either overweight or obese.[7]

Figure 1.3   Increasing obesity in the United States, 1999–2018.

Source: CDC/U.S. Department of Health & Human Services/Public domain.

According to the CDC, individuals with chronic disease and mental health conditions now account for 90% of total annual U.S. health expenditures (projected by CMS to be more than $4.9 trillion during 2024).[8] Mathematically, this translates into a whopping $4.4 trillion in projected 2024 expenditures for treating chronic disease and mental health conditions.

As depicted in Figure 1.4 this expenditure level is greater than the entire gross domestic products of the world's third and fourth largest economies (Japan and Germany) according to World Bank data for 2022.[9]

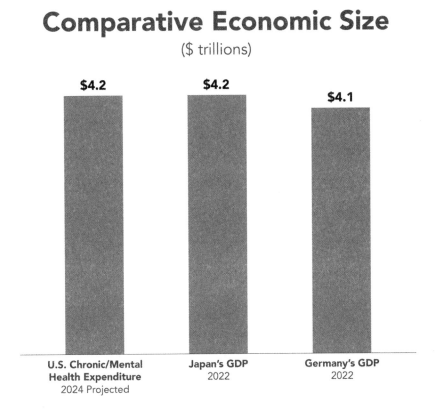

Figure 1.4   U.S. healthcare expenditures for chronic disease equivalent to the annual GDP for Japan and Germany.

Source: Adapted from CDC.

This is an astronomical and unsustainable level of expenditure to treat the rapidly increasing numbers of Americans with chronic and/or mental health conditions. The center is collapsing. Funding chronic care costs on its current trajectory is the principal reason that CMS projects the Medicare trust fund will exhaust its funding by 2036.

Absent a fundamental change in American lifestyles and a reduction in childhood and adult obesity, the levels of chronic disease, mental health conditions, and related treatment costs will skyrocket. This will increase the economic and social burden on an already beleaguered U.S. healthcare system. Policymakers will confront Hobbesian-like choices between funding healthcare and other vital services. In this inexorable way, population demographics are exerting significant top-down volume/demand pressure on the healthcare ecosystem.

Fewer Children (Decreasing Labor Supply and Reduced Funding Capacity)

While children being born today can expect to live longer, the U.S. Census Bureau projects there will be fewer American children born in the coming decades. The Great Recession of 2008–2009 initiated an absolute decline in the number of children being born each year in the U.S. (see Figure 1.5). Most forecasters believed the birth rate would return to pre-recession levels, but it has continued its slow, methodical decline.

Several factors contribute to the nation's falling birth rate. The chief ones being economic uncertainty, maternal and child health concerns, and climate change. There also are fewer "coupled households," which correlates with lower birth rates. Fewer couples mean fewer babies (see Figure 1.5).

These lower birth rates correspond with psychographic research data. A study by University of North Carolina and Ohio State researchers found that women now want fewer children than a generation ago. Their research found that women born between 1965 and 1969 at age 20–24 wanted 2.2 children. The same-aged women born between 1995 and 1999 wanted 2.1 children.

This later generation of potential mothers still want children but question whether they will have the financial means and support to raise their children without undue hardship. These concerns lead many to postpone or decide against having children.

Exploring Age Groups in the 2020 Census
Learn About Age, Sex, and Racial and Ethnic Diversity for States, Counties, and Census Tracts

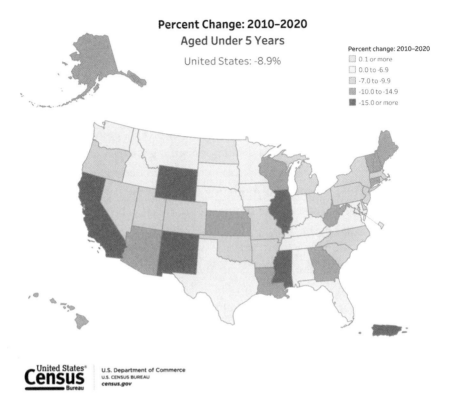

Percent Change: 2010–2020
Aged Under 5 Years

United States: -8.9%

Percent change: 2010–2020
- 0.1 or more
- 0.0 to -6.9
- -7.0 to -9.9
- -10.0 to -14.9
- -15.0 or more

United States® Census Bureau
U.S. Department of Commerce
U.S. CENSUS BUREAU
census.gov

Figure 1.5 Falling U.S. birth rate (2010–2020).

Source: Census/U.S. Department of Commerce/Public domain.

Consistent with these findings, more adult couples are opting out of parenting altogether. According to a 2021 Pew Foundation study, 85% of non-parents over 40 say they do not intend to have children. Perhaps more startling, 37% of non-parents under 40 say they also do not intend to have children.

When asked why they are less interested in having children, survey respondents most frequently answer "personal independence."[10] This answer encompasses a range of environmental and economic factors, including housing prices, climate change, safety, economic uncertainty, and the increasingly hostile political and social climates.

In essence, fewer younger American adults want children. Those who do are having fewer of them and having them later in life when they are more economically secure.

Unintended and/or unplanned births also have declined precipitously. Consistent with this decrease, teen pregnancies in the U.S. have declined an astounding 78% since their 1991 peak.[11] Corresponding with this decrease in teenage pregnancies the median age for women giving birth has increased from 27 years old in 1990 to 30 in 2015.

Absent immigration, the decline in U.S. births would be even more dramatic. Immigrants accounted for two-thirds of U.S. population growth in 2022.[12] This shift to immigrant-led population growth is occurring even as the nation's largest ethnic population, Hispanics, have experienced significant declines in their population growth during the last 15 years.

The conclusion from these demographic and psychographic studies is clear. There is less enthusiasm in the United States for having children and fewer children are being born. When combined with the overall aging of the U.S. population, the nation is on the cusp of a monumental demographic paradigm shift. By 2030, for the first time in its history, the U.S. will have more seniors than children (see Figure 1.6).

By 2030, 20% of Americans will be over the age of 65. By that time, all baby boomers will be eligible for government-sponsored retirement and health benefits. As projected by the Bureau, the seniors–children ratio widens over time. In 2060, there will be 95 million American adults aged 65 and older representing 23.4% of the population with 80 million children representing 19.8% of the population.

Fewer children today translate into a smaller labor pool tomorrow from which to draw future caregivers. It also means there will be fewer workers paying the Social Security and Medicare taxes that fund health and social care services for America's elderly population.

The corollary to the seniors–children ratio is the worker–retiree ratio that measures a society's capacity to fund safety-net services for its elderly citizens. The higher the ratio of workers to retirees, the greater the funding capacity. A high ratio also translates into less financial burden for individual workers.

Unfortunately, but not surprisingly, the worker–retiree ratio in the U.S. has declined precipitously in recent decades (see Figure 1.7). According to University of Vermont research, there were 42 workers per retiree in

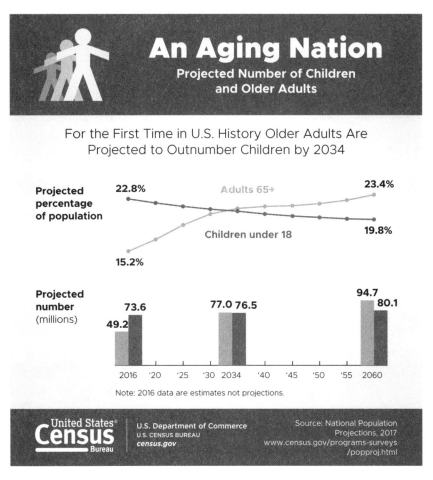

Figure 1.6 Crossover point in 2035: More seniors (65–plus) than children under 18.

Source: Census/U.S. Department of Commerce/Public domain.

1940 when the federal government began monthly payment of Social Se-curity benefits.[13] According to research by the Peterson Foundation, that number had declined to 5.1 and 2.9 workers per retiree by 1960 and 2020 respectively (see Figure 1.7).

Combined with higher spending, the declining worker–retiree ratio is the other principal reason why both the Medicare and Social Security trust funds are under enormous financial pressure. Each will eventually go bank-rupt without additional funding and/or spending cuts. Population imbalances

The ratio of workers to Social Security beneficiaries has been declining for decades

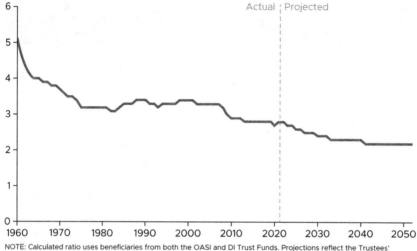

NOTE: Calculated ratio uses beneficiaries from both the OASI and DI Trust Funds. Projections reflect the Trustees' intermediate assumptions.

Figure 1.7   Declining ratio of workers to Social Security beneficiaries.

Source: ©Peter G. Peterson Foundation.

driven by the nation's aging demographics is a massive top-down force pressing against America's current safety-net programming for its elderly population. Ignoring it will accelerate and deepen the financial reckoning required to balance payment inflows and outflows.

CONCLUSION: DEMOGRAPHICS ARE NOT DESTINY

Thomas Robert Malthus (1766–1834) was a prominent English economist, cleric, and scholar who made significant academic contributions in political economy and demographics. In 1798, Malthus published *An Essay on the Principle of Population*, which explored relationships between food production, population growth, and standard of living.

Malthus opined that increased food production led temporarily to both improved living standards and population growth with the caveat that this parallel growth was not sustainable. Eventually, a larger population would consume all available foods and push the lower classes into hardship as food stores diminished.

Malthus believed that population would grow exponentially while agricultural production would grow arithmetically. This mathematical approach to the relationship between population growth and food production led Malthus to the conclusion that society would cycle between periods of surplus and scarcity to force equilibrium between food production and consumption.

The following quote captures the essence of Malthus' argument: "The power of population is infinitely greater than the power in the earth to produce subsistence for man."[14]

Malthus' description of the conflict between population growth and subsistence has become known as the "Malthusian Trap." It maintains relevance today when applied to current and unsustainable consumption patterns.

Of course, Malthus was spectacularly wrong. Advances in food production have enabled the earth's population to grow from 1 billion people in 1800 to over 8 billion people and counting today (see Figure 1.8).

Technological advances often delay and thwart dire demographic projections. The invention of the automobile overcame the "Great Horse Manure Crisis of 1894." In that year, overwhelmed by the growth of horse-drawn carriages, *The Times of London* predicted, "In 50 years, every street in London will be buried under nine feet of manure."[15]

U.S. healthcare confronts its own unique version of the "Malthusian Trap" that demographic trends are exposing to be unsustainable. The nation operates a high-cost, centralized, and fragmented delivery system ill-suited to efficiently address the expansive chronic disease that plagues the American populace.

This chronic disease "trap" is particularly alarming for baby boomers. As they approach and surpass age 65, their risk of contracting a debilitating chronic condition increases significantly.

Concurrently, the supply of caregivers available to treat this growing demand to care for these aging boomers is shrinking along with the nation's wherewithal to fund the exploding treatment costs for their chronic conditions. As *The Wall Street Journal* reports, the absolute number of American workers will decline by 4 million between 2022 and 2040.

Failure to address demographics' two-pronged attack on status-quo healthcare practices will trigger a massive funding crisis with profound moral implications for allocating societal resources. Like the war vet in

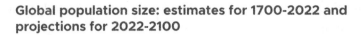

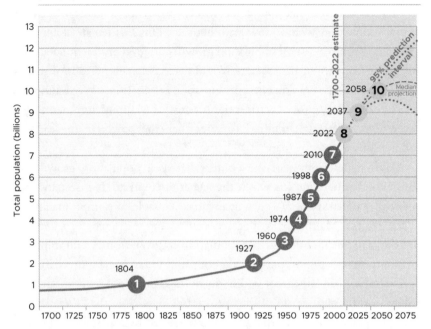

Global population size: estimates for 1700-2022 and projections for 2022-2100

Note: The solid blue line is the estimates from 1700 to today, the dotted red line the projection for the future up to 2100, and the dashed red line the upper and lower bounds of the 95% prediction interval for the projections.

Figure 1.8   Malthus' mistake: Global population estimates for 1700–2022 and projections for 2022–2100.

Source: United Nation, DESA, Population Division (2022). World Population Prospects 2022.

Hemingway's *The Sun Also Rises* who experienced bankruptcy "gradually, then suddenly," the conditions contributing to the systematic failure in U.S. healthcare have been building for decades and are about to explode. Either the healthcare system will transform itself to deliver more appropriate services at lower costs or it will break in fundamental ways.

Demographics constitute a powerful macro force zeroing in on U.S. healthcare. Demographic math paints an irrefutable and grim picture for the future of the current U.S. healthcare system. Like Thelma and Louise, U.S. healthcare is speeding toward a cliff. The industry needs to slam on the brakes and change direction. Failure to do so will be catastrophic.

Rahm Emanuel famously made the following observation when he was White House Chief of Staff in the Obama administration:

You never want a serious crisis to go to waste. And what I mean by that is an opportunity to do things that you think you could not do before.

Demographics amplify the coming crisis confronting U.S. healthcare. Contrary to Auguste Comte's assertion, demographics is not destiny. It simply cannot be. The U.S. has the knowledge and wherewithal to reinvent its dysfunctional and dystopian healthcare system. The question is whether we have the collective will to transform healthcare payment and delivery to provide appropriate healthcare services for the American people now and for the foreseeable future.

Healthcare's current existential crisis could enable revolutionary reformers to pursue fundamental system redesign to deliver better healthcare services at lower costs for all Americans. Time will tell, sooner rather than later, whether America can avoid the demographic avalanche tumbling toward its social welfare system.

KEY INSIGHTS ON DEMOGRAPHIC DETERMINANTS

- U.S. demographics will exert a powerful influence on healthcare's evolving future, which manifests through an aging population, increasing levels of chronic disease, decreasing workforce capacity to provide care services, and increasing demand for healthcare workers.
- Trends that cannot continue, won't. The current system is breaking in fundamental ways under the weight of increasing demands, ineffective operations, and rising costs.
- An inescapable conclusion is that healthcare must transform to accommodate anticipated demographic changes by creating more effective and distributed care delivery models.
- Reducing the demand for high-cost services where possible through better prevention, less waste, and more appropriate end-of-life care could liberate sufficient resources and personnel to offer enhanced elder care service provision.

2 | Funding Fatigue

In their 1973 Academy award-winning performances for the film *Cabaret*, actors Liza Minelli and Joel Grey perform "Money Money" on the cabaret stage in 1930s Berlin. Their heart-pumping rendition captures how the frenzied pursuit of cash can overwhelm all other human motivation. The song's final refrain makes this point explicitly:

> *Money money money money*
> *Money money money money.*
> *Get a little, get a little*
> *Money money money money*
> *Mark, a yen, a buck or a pound*
> *That clinking, clanking, clunking sound*
> *Is all that makes the world go 'round*
> *It makes the world go 'round!*

Money certainly makes the healthcare world go around. Healthcare's appetite for consuming resources is gargantuan. By disproportionately absorbing resources from other economic sectors (i.e., public education), Healthcare Inc. has grown its share of the U.S. economy from 7% in 1970 to almost 18% today. U.S. healthcare's defining characteristic is its unbridled pursuit of revenues across all its sectors within a historically pro-business regulatory environment.

If analysts want to understand healthcare economics, they need to follow the money. Money explains Healthcare Inc.'s unique and often counterintuitive operating realities: why hospitals become ghost towns on weekends; why preventive care is underfunded; why technology advances increase rather than decrease costs; why providers and payers both fight transparency regulations. The list of value-depleting behaviors within healthcare (like those listed above) is a very long one.

Healthcare Inc.'s artificial "supply-driven" economic model and the perverse financial incentives that fuel it are well-documented and understood. Revenue cycle management (RCM) is the practice of optimizing revenue collection. It is a massive business in healthcare, perhaps rivaling the U.S. banking industry in size.[1] Within healthcare, RCM constitutes the vast majority of Healthcare Inc.'s administrative costs, estimated to be as high as $1.47 trillion in 2024.

Less understood are the macroeconomic forces that have begun to restrain the healthcare industry's monstrous growth. Our contention is that the money trail that has funded Healthcare Inc.'s bulging coffers for decades is coming to an end, "Not with a bang but a whimper," as T.S. Eliot observed in his epic poem "The Wasteland." In essence, American society is no longer willing and/or able to fund Healthcare Inc.'s profligacy.

Healthcare Inc.'s gluttonous appetite for revenues has bled federal and state governments, self-insured employers, and individual consumers dry. They have reached a point where they have no more to give. Their cupboards are bare. These purchasers' collective resolve to become better buyers of healthcare services is ushering in an unprecedented era of austerity for a healthcare industry that has never learned how to tighten its belt.

The macroeconomic character of American society's funding fatigue for healthcare becomes evident when we detail the industry's plateauing share of the national economy (as measured by gross domestic product or GDP). Subsequent analyses of per-capita Medicare spending and commercial funding for healthcare services reveal the same pattern.

The commercial segment is vitally important to incumbent Healthcare Inc. Private health plans pay substantially higher prices/reimbursement rates than Medicare and Medicaid for identical services across the care continuum.

In each of healthcare's individual funding segments (governments, employers, and consumers), an unmistakable pattern of funding resistance to increased healthcare expenditures has emerged. Collectively, these buyers are sending a clear message through their purchasing behaviors that they expect the healthcare industry to begin living within its means.

Properly absorbed, this "scarcity" message can become a forcing function for the U.S. healthcare industry to shift its managerial orientations away from revenue optimization and toward value creation. Long-term, value creation within the healthcare sector will benefit the American people by delivering better health outcomes at lower costs with improved customer service. It also will increase the market relevance of value-creating healthcare companies.

We end the chapter by shifting from macroeconomics to family economics. GoFundMe campaigns are a uniquely American funding model for buying healthcare services. The ubiquity of these campaigns and the lengths to which desperate Americans go to pay for vital medical care (e.g., forgoing food, pill-splitting, unpaid caregiving, delaying necessary care) speak to the bankruptcy of U.S. healthcare's payment and delivery mechanics.

Overall, Healthcare Inc. has pushed large segments of American society to the brink of insolvency without delivering value in the form of improved health status. In response, echoing the famous line from the 1976 movie *Network*, American society is "mad as hell and not going to take it anymore."

MACROECONOMICS: THE END OF HEALTHCARE'S GRAVY TRAIN

The best of all monopoly profits is a quiet life.
— Sir John Hicks, Nobel Laureate in Economics

"Gravy train" is a railroad term that originated in the early 1900s. It described well-paid train runs that didn't require much effort. In modern parlance, speakers use it to describe a task that is easy to accomplish or a cushy situation. Healthcare Inc.'s gravy train has created "a quiet life" for the industry's entrenched incumbents.[2] Their monopoly and monopsony pricing power within healthcare's sub-markets limits Healthcare Inc.'s exposure to value-based competitors. Life is good.

The problem with gravy trains is that riding them too long engenders lazy, sloppy, and wasteful behaviors. New York City discovered this the hard way. Decades of overspending, overborrowing, and lax financial oversight in combination with a stagnant national economy triggered a major fiscal crisis in 1975. The city had a substantial operating deficit, could not borrow in the debt markets, and begged the Ford administration for assistance.

On October 29, 1975, President Gerald Ford stepped to the podium at the National Press Club in Washington, D.C. The president declared that he would veto any bill providing federal bailout assistance to New York City. The next day's *New York Daily News* distilled the president's pronouncement into an iconic and infamous headline: "Ford to City: Drop Dead."

Although nowhere near as obvious but just as serious, buyers of healthcare services are demanding more value for their healthcare purchases. As a result, a more parsimonious funding paradigm has emerged. After decades of consuming ever-larger percentages of the American economy, healthcare's share of the economic pie is diminishing. Healthcare Inc.'s gravy train has run out of steam. Macroeconomic realities are driving this paradigm shift. Numbers don't lie.

Inflection Point in Aggregate Healthcare Spending

The term "inflection point" ranked No. 2 on Lake Superior State University's 2023 list of banished words. Each year, the school selects and ranks "banished words" based on their overuse, misuse, and/or uselessness. Here's commentary on why *inflection point* made that year's list:

> *"Inflection point" is a mathematical term that entered everyday parlance and lost its original meaning. This year's version of "pivot," banished in 2021.*
>
> *Inflection point has reached its saturation point and point of departure. . . a pretentious way to say turning point.*

Thank you to Lake Superior State for clarifying the true definition of *inflection point*, the spot on a mathematical curve where its slope changes direction. This happens before data-infused curves reach their peaks. Inflection points occur when a curve's rate of increase (its slope) shifts upward or downward (see Figure 2.1).

The right way to measure the funding curve for healthcare expenditures is to plot its relationship as a percentage of U.S. gross domestic product. GDP measures the size of the overall U.S. economy. As the chart in Figure 2.2 depicts, healthcare's share of the U.S. economy increased dramatically from 5% in 1960 to 17.4% in 2010 as healthcare expenditures grew faster than the overall economy.

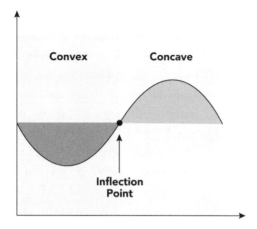

Figure 2.1 Graphic illustration of an inflection point: The point at which a signification change occurs.

Healthcare Expenditure as a Percentage of U.S. GDP

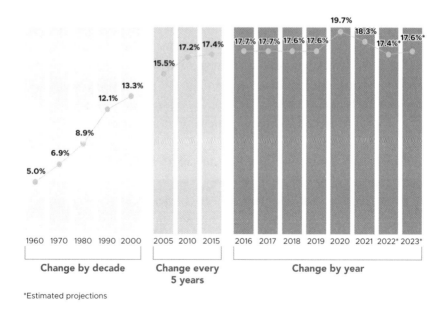

Figure 2.2 Flattening relationship: Healthcare expenditure as a percentage of U.S. GDP.

Source: Adapted from CMS Data.

By 2010, healthcare's annual growth in expenditures had begun to mirror that of the overall U.S. economy. This is the curve's inflection point. Absent COVID, the peak and eventual decline of healthcare expenditures as a percentage of the national economy would have been much more gradual.

The pandemic forced a lockdown of the global economy. In response, the federal government pumped hundreds of billions of dollars into the healthcare economy. This included $185 billion in direct financial support to hospitals and other healthcare providers.[3]

In response, U.S. healthcare expenditure grew by an astonishing 10.3% in 2020 to $4.12 trillion, representing a record 19.7% of total U.S. GDP. Overall, healthcare's share of the total U.S. economy increased by an unprecedented 2.1% that year.

There was bound to be some correction to 2020 healthcare expenditure levels. As detailed in its March 2022 forecast, the Centers for Medicare and Medicaid Services (CMS) expected the rate of increase in national health expenditures during 2021 to drop to 4.2%, accelerate to 4.6% in 2022, and remain above 5% annually through the end of the decade.[4]

In 2030, CMS projects national healthcare expenditure to be almost $7 trillion and consume almost 20% of the overall U.S. economy. Don't take that forecast to the bank. It misses the inflection point.

Traditional expenditure analyses, like the one from CMS, miss the dynamism that is changing healthcare's underlying supply–demand relationships. This dynamism explains, for example, the push by big retailers like Amazon into healthcare.

In a bottom-up, organic manner, the healthcare marketplace is reorganizing to offer higher-value, customer-friendly products and services. This is the real threat to status-quo provider and payer business models built on fee-for-service (FFS) and administrative-services-only (ASO) contracting.

Here's what actually happened in 2021. Healthcare expenditures did not increase 4.2% as predicted by CMS in March 2022. Instead, healthcare spending rose just 2.7%.[5] Healthcare's percentage of the national economy declined a staggering 1.6% from 19.7% to 18.3%. In mathematical terms, this means the overall economy grew at a faster rate than the healthcare industry for the first time in decades.

The federal government funded almost all its emergency COVID expenditures with debt. As a result, the ratio between federal debt and U.S. GDP grew from 107% in 2019 to 128% in 2020.[6] Real economic growth declined to 2.1% in 2022 and slowed even more during the first half of 2023 as the Federal Reserve raised short-term interest rates.[7]

The U.S. government's debt levels are staggeringly high and growing. Commentator John Gabriel periodically publishes the most informative chart regarding the relationship between the federal government's revenues, deficits, and debt. He published Figure 2.3 in *AZ Central* on December 2, 2023. We present it below with his permission.

As illustrated in Figure 2.3, the U.S. governmental debt has grown exponentially since the Reagan administration. Expansive borrowing under both Republican and Democratic administrations has added to the cumulative total.

The current national debt now exceeds $33 trillion.[8] It represented 123% of the nation's GDP as of September 30, 2023. This figure is just below the record percentage achieved during the Trump administration in 2020 of 127%. With rising interest rates, net interest payments on the national debt are approaching a staggering $500 billion annually.[9]

Even if it wanted to do so, the federal government doesn't have the fiscal capacity to provide more emergency funding to healthcare providers. Its cupboard is bare.

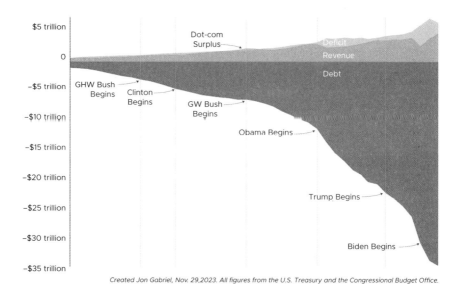

Figure 2.3   U.S. Government's astronomical debt levels.

Source: U.S. Treasury and the Congressional Budget Office/Public Domain.

Beggars and Choosers

Healthcare's new funding paradigm has been particularly difficult for hospitals. According to Kaufman Hall's January 2023 *National Hospital Flash Report*, 2022,[10] half of U.S. hospitals lost money as expenses grew faster than revenues.

To add salt to the wounds, CMS' final payment rule for FY24 increased payment rates for hospitals by only 3.1%, well below the 4.6% annualized increase in compensation reported by the U.S. Bureau of Labor Statistics (BLS). The American Hospital Association (AHA) fought for higher rate increases and was notably irate in its public comments:

> *The AHA is deeply concerned with CMS' woefully inadequate inpatient and long-term care hospital payment updates. The agency continues to finalize rate increases that are not commensurate with the near-decades-high inflation and increased costs for labor, equipment, drugs and supplies that hospitals across the country are experiencing.*[11]

These macroeconomic trends involving GDP growth, debt, productivity, and inflation explain why society writ large is unwilling and incapable of shifting resources disproportionately into healthcare despite the industry's urgent pleas. No external funding sources are riding to healthcare's rescue. Expect economic pressure on the healthcare industry to intensify.

Healthcare Inc.'s funding quagmire would be bad enough if the industry were working to transform itself, but it's not. In his keynote address at Intermountain Health's 2023 Mindshare Conference, CEO Rob Allen observed that 52% of current healthcare expenditure is unnecessary. Preventable acute conditions account for 27%[12] and waste accounts for the remaining 25%.[13]

Allen believes this expenditure pattern is both unacceptable and unsustainable. These poor-quality measures are among the many reasons that private and governmental buyers of healthcare services are demanding reform.

Bad macroeconomics and its historic lack of value creation have triggered this funding inflection point for the healthcare industry. It's leading to a "Robin Hood" moment. After stealing resources from the rest of American society for 60-plus years, Healthcare Inc. is starting to experience a significant backlash. American society is now repatriating some of its lost wealth.

Consequently, expect healthcare's share of the national economy to flat-line or decline through the balance of the decade. It's not going to be easy for healthcare incumbents to adjust to this "new normal" (another word banished by Lake Superior State in 2022). Remaining competitive within a shrinking and dynamic marketplace takes skill and resilience.

With the benefit of hindsight, many now believe that President Ford's tough-love message to New York City was critical to its financial turna-round and subsequent recovery.[14] Henry J. Stern, a former parks commissioner and city councilman, observed that "Ford was good for New York because he made us clean up our act."

Entwined within Healthcare Inc.'s new funding reality is a similar tough-love message. Both the public and private sectors, as well as Republicans and Democrats, are demanding that the healthcare industry clean up its act. Financial sustainability for healthcare companies must come from overhauling their bloated business models and by delivering more value to customers. In value there is the potential for both salvation and growth.

PLATEAUING MEDICARE AND COMMERCIAL FUNDING

Consistent with the plateauing of healthcare expenditure as a percentage of U.S. GDP since 2010, per-capita Medicare and commercial spending have exhibited the same pattern. Medicare spending exhibited exceptionally high annual growth from its origins in 1965 until 2011 (see Figure 2.4). Commenting on this Medicare funding pattern in 2011, President Barack Obama observed, "If you look at the numbers, then Medicare in particular will run out of money and we will not be able to sustain that program no matter how much taxes go up."[15]

According to a *New York Times* analysis, Medicare spent $3.9 trillion less than projected between 2011 and 2023.[16] This savings figure is astronomical, equivalent to 85% of total U.S. healthcare spending in 2023. While this time period encompasses the rollout of the Affordable Care Act, analysts cannot pinpoint the exact reasons for the moderated spending. Most highlight reduced demand for acute healthcare services, such as the elderly having fewer heart attacks and strokes. While that may be true in part, less system-wide funding capacity and the scarcity mindset it engenders are driving lower payment growth.

In this instance, Medicare may be benefiting from the commercial sector's more parsimonious funding patterns for healthcare services. The

Annual Medicare Spending Per Beneficiary

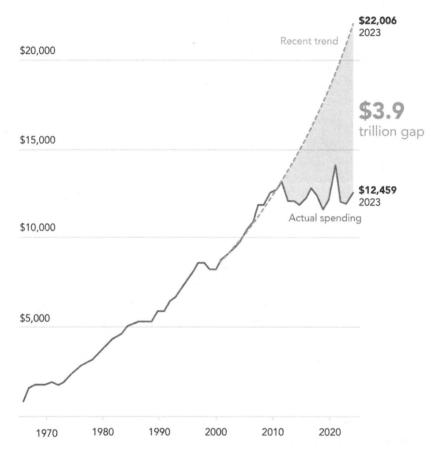

Figure 2.4   Per-capita Medicare spending.

Source: https://www.nytimes.com/interactive/2023/09/05/upshot/medicare-budget-threat-receded.html. / With permission of *New York Times*.

Healthcare Affordability Index (the Index, see Figure 2.5) is a simple and powerful metric for assessing commercial funding patterns. The Index measures the relationship between the total cost (employer and employee portions) of a commercial family health insurance policy relative to the median household income (MHI).

$$\frac{\text{Family Health Insurance Cost}}{\text{Median Household Income}} = \begin{array}{c} \textbf{HEALTHCARE} \\ \textbf{AFFORDABILITY} \\ \textbf{INDEX} \end{array}$$

Figure 2.5   Healthcare affordability index calculation.

Importantly, the Index reveals this obvious but hidden truth: The very high cost of private health insurance contributes significantly to middle-class wage stagnation. Although the percentage of Americans in Medicare is increasing with the aging of the baby boom generation, more than half of Americans still depend on employer-sponsored health insurance to cover the lion's share of the healthcare services they consume.

As healthcare costs rise, health insurance premiums also rise. As a consequence, both employers and employees pay more for healthcare coverage. The undeniable conclusion is that the cost of commercial health insurance has become an increasingly unbearable burden for American workers. Between 1999 and 2011, the Index more than doubled from 14.2% to 30.1% (see Figure 2.6).

Like healthcare's percentage of national GDP and Medicare per-capita spending, however, the Index began plateauing in 2011. Unlike healthcare's percentage of GDP and Medicare per-capita spending, the Index did not spike during COVID because incremental pandemic funding came entirely from governmental, mostly federal, sources.

This pattern of a plateauing relationship between commercial health insurance costs and household incomes confirms this chapter's core observation that healthcare funding has entered a new period of fiscal austerity. Both are increasing at roughly the rate of inflation.

Origins of the Healthcare Affordability Index

In November 2017, Zeke Emanuel, Aaron Glickman, and co-author Dave published an article in the *Journal of the American Medical Association* (JAMA) that introduced the Healthcare Affordability Index.[17] JAMA included editorial critiques from respected economists Uwe Reinhardt from Princeton and Joseph Antos from the American Enterprise Institute. The article was widely read and heavily commented upon. As a result, the Healthcare Affordability Index entered the industry's lexicon.

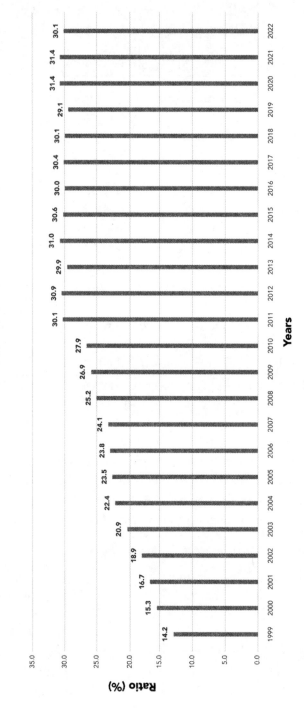

Figure 2.6 The Healthcare Affordability Index, 1999–2022.

Source: Adapted from https://jamanetwork.com/journals/jama/fullarticle/2661699 / American Medical Association.

The authors' intention was to create a comprehensible measure of health insurance affordability using readily available and highly trusted data elements. The Kaiser Family Foundation's (KFF) annual Employer Health Benefits Survey documents employer and employee contribution levels for commercial health insurance plans. The U.S. Census Bureau annually publishes the U.S. median household income (MHI), the most widely used measure of family income. These two bedrock measures became the Index's respective numerator and denominator.

The Index's most compelling feature is its depiction of the increasing financial burden placed on working American families by Healthcare Inc. All other things being equal, a constant 14.2% Healthcare Affordability Index would translate into a 2022 median household income of $86,430. That hypothetical figure is almost $12,000 more than the actual 2022 MHI figure of $74,580. Any way analysts slice that figure, it's a significant amount of incremental income for average American families.

The academic reaction to the Index largely focused on defining affordability and income. Some suggested the Index's formula was misleading because it did not include employer health insurance contributions as a component of family income. Adding employer-paid health insurance premiums to income lowers the Index but does not change its upward trajectory.

While debating the economic definition of affordability has merit, that debate misses the far more important relationship over time between commercial health insurance costs and middle-class family incomes. Debating definitions of affordability and income distracts from the unassailable conclusion that health insurance has consumed an ever-greater percentage of family resources and contributed significantly to stagnant income growth for working families.

In 2022, however, the Index's ever-upward pattern reversed. The Index was 30.1% in 2022, the same as it was in 2011. This decline in the Index from 31.4% in 2021 to 30.1% in 2022 was the result of wages, as measured by MHI, rising at a much higher rate (5.4%) than commercial health insurance premiums (1.1%).

The good news here is that the overall plateauing of healthcare costs means that the absolute burden of healthcare costs on American workers, while still very high, is not increasing. To the extent that future healthcare costs grow at a rate below natural inflation, as they did in 2022, the financial burden as measured by the Healthcare Affordability Index will decrease.

PIZZA, PRODUCTIVITY, AND HEALTHCARE

Co-author Dave's favorite pizza joint at Colgate University in Hamilton, New York, was Ye Olde Pizza Pub. Students like Dave from the late 1970s referred to it as Pepe's (its former name). It's still there. Customers use napkins to soak up the excess grease that pools on the pizza before gobbling it down. In 1978, a slice of cheese pizza at Pepe's cost 50 cents. Rounding up, that same slice of greasy cheese pizza cost $2 in 2022, four times as much. This time-based pricing relationship creates a perfect metric for calculating real (inflation-adjusted) costs.

Rounding up, a full year at Colgate University in 1978 – including tuition, room, board, and expenses – cost $5,000. That seemed like a gargantuan sum to student Dave. Minimum wage was $2.30 an hour. With student loans but no scholarships, Dave worked year-round and paid for 70% of his college education.

In 2022, Colgate's full annual cost, including health insurance, was $86,000 (17.2 times greater in nominal dollars than 1978). Dividing today's annual cost of a Colgate education by the pizza-inflation metric of 4, Colgate's inflation-adjusted cost in 2022 becomes $21,500. That is over four times greater in real dollars than the comparable 1978 cost of $5,000!

Despite the beautiful campus, the many new buildings, and its reputation for educational excellence, there's no way a Colgate education is *worth* four times what it was in 1978. There's also no way a non-scholarship student with ample student loans and great part-time jobs (like Dave in the 1970s) could come close to funding the total current $350,000 four-year cost of that Colgate education.

The key word in the paragraph above is *worth*, which links productivity with value. In economic terms, increasing productivity creates value by stimulating wealth creation, wage growth, and improved living standards. Value decline creates *negative worth* when prices increase without a corresponding increase in productivity. Healthcare leaders should take note. There's correlation with higher education's skyrocketing costs and diminishing relative value.

Productivity and Healthcare's Relative Value

Before examining healthcare's relative value, let's first consider the fundamental relationship between productivity and value creation. The website for the U.S. Bureau of Labor Statistics has a short video that explains the basic concepts underlying labor productivity. The video uses a fictitious birdhouse builder named Beth to illustrate how productivity statistics measure the relationship over time between inputs (materials and labor) and outputs (in this case, birdhouses).

At first, Beth makes one birdhouse per hour. By becoming more efficient, she increases her per-hour birdhouse production to two, doubling her labor productivity. Higher productivity enables Beth to earn more money for the same effort or earn the same amount of money by working less. Either way, Beth's economic wellbeing (i.e., standard of living) improves. The video ends by correlating Beth's experience to the broader economy:

> *Similarly, the standard of living for the country as a whole depends on improvement in overall productivity. Historically, productivity growth has led to higher wages for workers and higher profits for businesses.*

A college education has worth because it imparts knowledge, teaches new skills, and expands an individual's network of contacts. These attributes not only enrich individuals' lives, but also increase their productivity, market value, and income potential.

The skyrocketing cost of a college education, however, has diminished its relative value. Paying more (remember the pizza productivity metric) for a college education requires young people today to work longer and harder to match their parents' standard of living. In this sense, the rising cost of a college education has become a drag on the overall U.S. economy and diminishes its aggregate human potential.

The same logic applies to healthcare. In 1978, the Health Care Financing Administration (the precursor to CMS) reported that the national, per-capita healthcare expenditure was $863.[18] CMS estimates that the per-capita 2022 healthcare expenditure was $13,591 (15.8 times greater in nominal dollars than in 1978).[19] Using the pizza-inflation metric of 4, healthcare's inflation-adjusted, per-capita cost was $3,398 in 2022. Like higher education, inflation-adjusted healthcare costs today are approximately four times greater than their 1978 cost.

Despite whizbang medical technologies, palatial care centers, and breakthrough drugs, America is not four times healthier today than it was in 1978. By some health measures, including incidence of chronic disease and maternal mortality, we're far less healthy. The healthcare industry has gotten very good at enabling sick people to live longer. It has not improved our ability to live longer, healthier, more productive lives.

Waste Not. Want Not.

The U.S. is currently in a prolonged productivity slump. After adjusting for an anomalous one-time COVID productivity bump of 5% in 2020, labor productivity has averaged less than 1% in annual growth since 2011.[20] This compares to the long-term annual growth rate of 2.1%. As demonstrated in the birdhouse example, less labor productivity growth translates into less national wealth creation.

The sub-1% growth rate since 2011 includes a dismal negative 1.7% drop in productivity during 2022. That drop reflects a new economic reality. Americans are working fewer hours but receiving higher pay. Given the lack of current productivity improvement, it is unlikely that the U.S. can grow its way back to higher living standards anytime soon. Spiking inflation reflects this unhappy economic reality.

Historically, increases in median household income (MHI) paralleled improvements in labor productivity. Beginning around the millennium, however, MHI stagnated as productivity continued its upward march (see Figure 2.7). Life has gotten harder.

This productivity–income divergence fuels political anger on the left and right. Despite the recent supply-driven uptick in wages, Americans today are working harder than ever but have less to show for their efforts. Inflationary pressures add to their financial strain.

Healthcare's Increasing Burden for Working Americans

The U.S. boasts the world's most productive workforce. High worker productivity creates wealth and sustains high living standards. The U.S. outspends all countries on healthcare services, generally by two to three times. Logic suggests that generous health spending enhances national

U.S. Productivity and Median Household Incomes
1992 to 2022

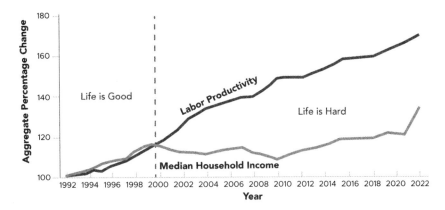

Figure 2.7   Americans are working harder but earning less, 1992–2022.

Source: Adapted from information obtained from the Bureau of Labor Statistics (Productivity); U.S. Census Bureau (Household Income).

productivity, competitiveness, and wealth creation. In the U.S., however, the opposite is true.

On almost all relevant measures (life expectancy, maternal mortality, infant mortality, etc.), America's health status is lower than that found in other developed economies. While all Americans bear the cost of increasing health insurance premiums, the financial burden of paying for health insurance falls disproportionately on lower-income households whose stagnant wages have risen more slowly than their health insurance costs.

Lower-income individuals and families also suffer disproportionately from health disparities and chronic disease as well as increasing out-of-pocket expenditures to pay for healthcare services. This is why so many Americans with low incomes forgo vital healthcare services, which makes them sicker.

In both indirect and direct ways, paying for commercial health insurance contributes to the nation's widening health disparities and income inequality.

Healthcare expenditures have contributed significantly to this widening gap between labor productivity and MHI. As mentioned above, if the cost of a family health insurance policy had remained 14.2% of MHI in 2022, all other things being equal, the average family's income would have increased from $74,580 to $86,430. This almost-$12,000 jump would have closed 60% of the productivity–income gap. American pocketbooks would be fuller and American spirits would be brighter.

Consequently, Healthcare Inc.'s rising costs are an underappreciated component of the wage stagnation afflicting U.S. workers. Increasing health insurance premiums reduce monies available for wage increases. In this way, rising health insurance premiums act as tax on worker incomes. Unfortunately, the U.S. healthcare system has become more dependent on this "tax" to fund its high expenditure levels.

Consumers Disconnected from Rising Healthcare Costs

Americans understand that healthcare is expensive but generally do not recognize the direct connection between health insurance premiums, healthcare costs, and incomes, particularly in employer-sponsored plans. This disconnection compromises consumers' ability to be good purchasers of healthcare services. The following factors contribute to these perception failures and blunt optimal consumer-purchasing behaviors:

- **Employers cover the lion's share of health insurance costs:** This subsidy of health insurance premiums insulates consumers from bearing the actual costs of healthcare services. Although changing, Americans, on average, typically worry more about access to healthcare services than their cost. This compromises their ability to become better purchasers of healthcare services.
- **Consumers experience the healthcare marketplace through the purchase and use of health insurance products:** The relevant economic measures for Americans with health insurance are not healthcare costs, but their contributions to paying for healthcare services (employee health insurance premiums, deductibles, and copays). Consequently, healthcare seems much less expensive than it really is.
- **Healthcare principals negotiate prices without customers:** Patients see doctors who prescribe treatments for which a third party

(e.g., a health insurance company) pays predetermined and/or negotiated prices. This transaction process severs the traditional buyer–seller relationships that govern product and service purchases between informed parties in efficient markets.

- **Employees focus on income, while employers focus on total compensation:** Consequently, most workers underappreciate the negative impact rising healthcare and health insurance costs exert on their take-home pay. They also have little say in deciding which health insurance plans their employers offer.

Given these embedded mechanics and perceptions, the rising costs of employer-sponsored health insurance costs exert a double whammy on employee wages. Workers pay more for health insurance through increases in premiums and out-of-pocket costs. This decreases discretionary spending.

Meanwhile, escalating health insurance costs limit employers' ability to increase wages. Even as they funnel more resources into their employees' healthcare, employers rarely see any incremental improvement in health outcomes or productivity. The net result of these unusual market dynamics is that workers pay more for health insurance *and* receive lower pay. As a consequence, healthcare costs are strangling middle-class incomes.

Funding America's highly expensive, inefficient and often ineffective healthcare delivery system through high-cost private health insurance plans that discourage consumerism has consequences. It weakens the American economy. It reduces the global competitiveness of U.S. companies. It robs workers of higher wages and lowers living standards. It also siphons investment from more productive industries.

Declining Healthcare Inflation

Employer-sponsored health insurance subsidizes America's inefficient and exceptionally high-cost healthcare delivery system. Between 1999 and 2022, commercial health insurance premiums rose almost 2.5 times the rate of inflation and 1.75 times the rate of medical inflation (see Figure 2.8).

High-cost healthcare could not exist in America without very high-cost private health insurance. Importantly, Healthcare Inc. has become increasingly dependent upon high-cost commercial premiums to fund their operations. In chasing higher payment rates for commercially

Inflation Statistics
1990-2022

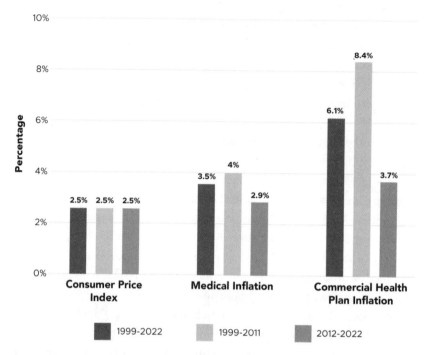

Figure 2.8   Commercial health plans subsidizing the rising costs of U.S. healthcare, 1999–2022.

Source: Adapted from information obtained from the U.S. Bureau of Labor Statistics, Kaiser Family Foundation.

insured patients, healthcare providers disproportionately invest resources in more affluent communities.

This investment pattern has resulted over time in a profound maldistribution of medical facilities and practitioners. Higher-income communities get more, and lower-income communities get less. Unequal deployment of healthcare resources contributes significantly to healthcare disparities, including reduced access to care and declining life expectancy in low-income communities.

Digging deeper, the medical inflation figures break into two distinct time periods. Between 1999 and 2011, the cost of a commercial health insurance policy for a family increased annually by 8.4%. Between 2012 and 2022, that annual rate of increase dropped by more than half, to 3.7%.

Annualized medical inflation, which incorporates both commercial and governmental rates, decreased more modestly between the two periods, from 4.0% to 2.9%. Since general inflation remained constant at 2.5% during the two periods, healthcare's differential inflation figures reflect a tightening marketplace for healthcare service providers.

Albert Einstein wryly observed that "compound interest is the eighth wonder of the world. He who understands it, earns it . . . he who doesn't . . . pays it." Even as Healthcare Inc.'s desire for commercial health insurance business has increased, its ability to realize above-market rate increases has decreased dramatically. Providers are running harder for incrementally smaller benefits. At-risk health plans and self-insured employers clearly have learned the benefits of limiting providers' ability to "compound" their price increases.

More broadly, these declining medical inflation figures support our Funding-Fatigue thesis. Those paying for healthcare services have less capacity to do so. As a result, they are actually paying less. The obvious conclusion is that a healthcare spending trend that could not continue, hasn't continued.

GoFundMe Healthcare

During the chaotic runup to the 2020 elections, President Trump nominated Judge Amy Coney Barrett to fill Ruth Bader Ginsberg's vacated seat. On September 26, 2020, Trump held a White House Rose Garden ceremony to celebrate Coney Barrett's nomination. It became a COVID superspreader event.

At least 11 of the attendees contracted COVID. They included President Donald Trump and First Lady Melania Trump, Senators Mike Lee and Thom Tillis, advisor Kelly Ann Conway, lawyer Rudy Giuliani, former New Jersey Governor Chris Christie, and press secretary Kayleigh McEnany. It's possible that President Trump was contagious when he debated Democratic presidential nominee Joe Biden three days later.

COVID had struck the White House even before the September 26 event. The most serious case involved Crede Bailey, the director of the White House security office. Bailey required three months in an intensive care unit to recover from COVID. The disease cost him the lower part of his right leg and his left big toe. Upon discharge, Bailey required substantial rehabilitation that included a prosthetic leg. Even with good healthcare insurance, Bailey's medical bills were staggering.

Without his permission, Bailey's friend Dawn McCrobie launched a GoFundMe campaign on November 13, 2020, to help him and his family cover his medical care and rehabilitation costs.[21] With a $50,000 goal, the campaign ultimately raised over $85,000 from 1,200 donors.

A December 14, 2020, article in *Bloomberg News* turbocharged campaign donations.[22] A post that same day on the GoFundMe website reported that the Crede family were "blown away by your generosity and very appreciative of all your positive thoughts, prayers and belief in his recovery!"

Bailey is hardly alone in receiving support for medical care from GoFundMe campaigns. According to the GoFundMe website, 250,000 medical campaigns annually raise a whopping $650 million to fund vital treatments. This represents a third of total money raised from all GoFundMe campaigns.

Recipients of GoFundMe medical campaigns almost always pay full commercial prices for their treatments. It has become routine at some hospitals to suggest that patients, families, and/or friends launch GoFundMe campaigns to pay for expensive procedures, such as transplants.

Many, perhaps most, Americans are one medical tragedy away from financial ruin. Access and affordability go hand-in-hand. Unaffordable healthcare is unavailable healthcare. Paying commercial healthcare rates places an enormous financial burden on working Americans, as well as increasing stress and compromising health status. So, it comes as no surprise that medical bills are the leading cause of personal bankruptcies, particularly among seniors.[23]

A 2020 pricing analysis by the RAND Corporation found that hospitals charge commercial health insurers 2.5 times more than Medicare for the same treatments.[24] Despite arguments to the contrary, these markups constitute profiteering. They make healthcare unaffordable. Healthcare needs and costs collide in GoFundMe medical campaigns. They provide a remarkable window into the American psyche as ordinary people confront extraordinary medical bills.

Americans' compassion and generosity in supporting medical campaigns, often for individuals they don't know personally, is awe-inspiring. The annual need for hundreds of thousands of GoFundMe medical campaigns, however, reflects the sad truth that many Americans cannot afford healthcare when they need it most.

This financial tragedy has its roots in the frantic pursuit of individuals seeking to access and pay for vital care services within a system of fragmented health insurance provision and inflated healthcare prices. Entrenched providers rarely worry about being undersold.

Most healthcare services are routine, yet there is enormous price variation. This occurs because of arcane pricing formularies, cross-subsidization, and limited pricing transparency. Cutting through the complexity, the underlying reason that providers charge excessive and varied prices for healthcare services is because they can. They exercise monopoly pricing power within regional healthcare markets. Even large employers with thousands of employees cannot realize the benefits of competitive markets with transparent prices.

How significant is the price variation? A UnitedHealth Group report found that their commercial insurance clients experienced between 3-fold and 20-fold pricing disparities for seven routine diagnostic tests in 2017.[25] Their clients overpaid for these tests by $18.5 billion.

The Health Care Cost Institute (HCCI) tracks the cost of healthcare services nationally through their "Healthy Marketplace Index" funded by the Robert Wood Johnson Foundation. In a 2019 study, HCCI found that price variation for routine visits in 2016 "between" markets varied by as much as 25-fold:

- The median price for C-sections in San Francisco/Oakland/Hayward, California ($20,721) was nearly 4.5 times that in Knoxville, Tennessee ($4,556).
- A common blood test in Beaumont, Texas ($443) costs nearly 25 times more than the same test in Toledo, Ohio ($18).
- Patient office visits had median prices three times larger in Anchorage, Alaska ($165) than in Miami/Fort Lauderdale/West Palm Beach, Florida ($60).[26]

The HCCI study found even greater variation "within" markets, as high as a "39-fold price difference for the exact same service, even after removing the top and bottom 10% of prices to exclude outlier effects."

How is that possible? Some examples of extreme pricing/payment differentials include the following:

- The median price of a normal vaginal delivery without complications in Boston/Cambridge, Massachusetts, and Newton, New Hampshire was $8,074, but actual prices ranged from $4,701 at the 10th percentile to $15,973 at the 90th percentile, a difference of $11,272.
- The price of a screening mammogram varied by more than fourfold in Allentown/Bethlehem/Easton, Pennsylvania, where the median price is $177.
- Some new patient office visits cost over three times more than other new patient office visits in Minneapolis/St. Paul/Bloomington, Minnesota, where the median price was $229.

At the receiving end of the current system are ordinary Americans overpaying for health insurance that often isn't sufficient to cover their costs during a medical crisis. They turn to GoFundMe campaigns out of desperation. It is unrealistic to expect private philanthropy to overcome the systematic funding gap that exists between patients' medical needs and their ability to pay sky-high medical bills. While there are numerous successful GoFundMe medical campaigns, 90% of them fail to reach their funding goals. On average, medical campaigns raise just 40% of their funding goals.[27]

During a 2019 interview with Kaiser Health News, GoFundMe CEO Rob Solomon said they didn't expect to fund medical expenses when they launched the company in 2010.[28] "We didn't build the platform to focus on medical expenses . . . It saddens me that this is a reality. Every single day on GoFundMe, we see the huge challenges people face. Their stories are heartbreaking."

Solomon emphasizes that he'd "love nothing more than for *medical* not to be a category on GoFundMe." He notes, "We [at GoFundMe] feel good that our platform is there when people need it," but also asserts that Americans die when they can't pay for healthcare services they need. Solomon saves his most stinging criticism for the U.S. health system itself:

The system is terrible. It needs to be rethought and retooled. Politicians are failing us. Healthcare companies are failing us. Those are realities. I don't want to mince words here. We are facing a huge potential tragedy. We provide relief for a lot of people. But there are people who are not getting relief from us or from the institutions that are supposed to be there.

We shouldn't be the solution to a complex set of systemic problems. They should be solved by the government working properly, and by healthcare companies working with their constituents. We firmly believe that access to comprehensive healthcare is a right and things have to be fixed at the local, state and federal levels of government to make this a reality.

As Solomon makes clear, U.S. healthcare violates a principal rule of bioethics, "First, do no harm." In its pursuit of revenues over outcomes, the U.S. healthcare system overtreats, undertreats, overcharges, and neglects far too many patients who come under its care. Patients suffer physical, emotional, and financial harm as a result. Anyone with a heart wishes for Go-FundMe medical campaigns to be successful. Anyone with a heart and a brain recognizes that these campaigns shouldn't be necessary.

Perhaps GoFundMe healthcare is the most powerful evidence that American society is at the end of its rope when it comes to paying for the nation's massive healthcare expenditures.

CONCLUSION: SWIMMING NAKED

Warren Buffett has a knack for using common vernacular and concepts to make penetrating observations about the marketplace. He has repeatedly observed, "It's only when the tide goes out that you learn who has been swimming naked."

The tide is going out on American society's willingness to fund its current healthcare system. Funding Fatigue for Healthcare Inc. is real. There is abundant evidence that business-as-usual in healthcare is struggling mightily to maintain its legacy practices.

Funding Fatigue is reshaping the healthcare operating environment. Whether through value-driven purchasing, blunt-force funding cuts, or both, buyers of healthcare services are making their intentions known. Through this grinding restructuring process, Healthcare Inc. will learn which of its members are swimming naked.

KEY INSIGHTS ON FUNDING FATIGUE

- Historic funding patterns for healthcare service provision reached an inflection point in and around 2010 as measured by healthcare's percentage of GDP and the trajectory of the Healthcare Affordability Index.

- Contrary to CMS forecasts, healthcare expenditures and the funding required to pay for them will grow at or below the levels of national economic growth and general inflation. This longer-term expenditure trend will manifest unevenly but relentlessly.

- As an industry, healthcare detracts from national productivity and is a drag on economic growth.

- The existence of a massive crowdfunding ecosystem to pay for vital medical care is a powerful indicator that healthcare's current delivery and payment mechanics are unsustainable. Desperate people seek desperate solutions at great emotional cost and usually fail. It's cruel and inhuman that the U.S. healthcare system creates this almost-impossible-to-meet funding requirement for so many Americans.

3

Chronic Pandemics

Exploding chronic disease is the most potent top-down force pressuring Healthcare Inc.'s "sick-care" operating model. The four faces of chronic diseases' death and human devastation are heart disease, cancer, diabetes, and dementia (HCDD). Despite the enormous resources U.S. healthcare spends to treat chronic conditions, America is getting sicker.

Without system-wide transformation, America's aging demographics translate into ever-higher levels of debilitating chronic disease and premature deaths. As mentioned previously, the U.S. spends the equivalent of Japan's entire economy ($4.2 trillion) each year to treat individuals with chronic disease and mental health conditions.

Equally disturbing, this expenditure level excludes the monumental unpaid care costs, borne mostly by women. Like the albatross around the Ancient Mariner's neck, expansive chronic disease is imposing an increasingly heavy burden on the American people. It is robbing us of our collective vitality.

Moreover, the United States confronts a moral imperative to reverse the spread of chronic disease. Chronic HCDD diseases ravage every American community, but they are particularly virulent among low-income and ethnic populations. The rise of chronic disease to epidemic levels makes American society less equitable and less free.

Under severe duress, the nation's healthcare ecosystem must reorganize to confront the Chronic Pandemic's massive threat to the American way of life. It can no longer ignore or avoid its responsibilities to reverse disease spread. The Chronic Pandemic is already on our shores and attacking our most vulnerable citizens in record numbers.

Understanding comes before action. What are the contours of this pandemic and how dangerous is it to national wellbeing? Here are two patient stories, one rural and one urban, that illustrate the depth and magnitude of the chronic disease onslaught confronting America.

CHRONIC DILEMMAS: STORIES FROM THE FRONT LINES

Keith: Byron, Ohio

Brian Alexander's book *The Hospital: Life, Death, and Dollars in a Small American Town* chronicles the ups and downs of Byron Hospital, a community hospital in rural northwest Ohio fighting for its economic survival. Alexander describes how this rural hospital fights against regional competitors in Toledo and Fort Wayne to deliver higher-paying specialty care services in its local community. To gather material for his book, Alexander embedded himself within the hospital's management team and lived in the community for two years ending in August 2020.

The book also chronicles the daily travails of residents seeking vital primary and mental healthcare services they desperately need and often cannot access. Among them is Keith, an affable, mechanically gifted, heavy-set man who enjoys playing with remote-controlled cars and trucks. When we first meet Keith, he has a well-paying factory job that requires him to make a round trip each day taking two or more hours. He also has type 2 diabetes, a dying wife, and a special-needs son.

During the book's narrative, Keith's wife dies and leaves him with over $40,000 in unpaid medical bills. He quits his factory job to have more time to care for his son. Working long shifts at the local Menards for $12 per hour, Keith struggles to make ends meet. Insulin is expensive, he's drained his 401(k) accounts, and is constantly warding off medical bill collectors.

Shortly after starting at Menards, he goes to the emergency room with a swollen big toe on his right foot. To stop the infection from spreading, a surgeon amputates the toe. During the next year, diabetes costs Keith more of his right foot and much of his eyesight. Only 39, Keith hobbles to endless medical appointments and has numerous eye surgeries at the University of Michigan.

After diabetes had ravaged Keith's body, fee-for-service (FFS) medicine kicked in to pay for his acute treatments. In U.S. healthcare, there's abundant funding for amputation but little to none for diabetes prevention and management. The nation "rescues" people when they're drowning but doesn't teach them to swim.

An effective diabetes management program could have kept Keith active and productive. Instead, as he spirals downhill, American society funds Keith's enormous treatment and disability costs after the fact – an entirely preventable tragedy.

Maria: Houston, Texas

The People's Hospital: Hope and Peril in American Medicine by Ricardo Nuila provides a first-hand account of caring for uninsured patients within the sprawling confines of Houston's Ben Taub Hospital. Ben Taub is among the nation's largest and best public hospitals.

Nuila, an internal medicine physician and hospitalist, is a second-generation immigrant from El Salvador. Nuila and his father, a pediatrician in private practice, share a passion for medicine but have different and strong opinions regarding doctor and patient responsibilities. Their conflicts provide context for the larger healthcare policy debates regarding healthcare access, costs, payment, and resource allocation.

When he first started seeing patients at Ben Taub as a medical student, a senior resident ordered Nuila to update the medical history for a female ER patient being admitted to the hospital for a urinary tract infection. Let's name her Maria.

Admitting patients with UTIs to the hospital is unusual. Armed with a rudimentary "Pocket Medicine" guidebook and a one-page script for collecting patient stories, Nuila set about his task. He arrived to find a fit Hispanic man in his thirties holding the hand of an older woman – the patient with the UTI.

Reviewing the medical record and talking to the young man, Nuila discovered the woman was this man's wife and that they were the same age. Maria was urinating so frequently that she had to wear diapers. She didn't have a fever and was otherwise stable.

Nothing in "Pocket Medicine" corresponded with her symptoms. Maria's eyes drifted as Nuila asked her questions. She was largely unresponsive. Nuila began to wonder if Maria had some type of early onset dementia. He tested this hypothesis with one of Ben Taub's senior internal medicine professors named Dr. Robert Graham.

Graham and Nuila sat down at the computer together and scrolled through the young woman's medical records. Her latest CT scan revealed no signs of dementia. Graham concluded that untreated diabetes had triggered thousands of small strokes which obliterated Maria's cognitive function.

Seeking to learn from the experience, Nuila scoured "Pocket Medicine" but found no listing of symptoms for "untreated diabetes." The book's working assumption is that patients would receive care to manage their diabetes so it wouldn't spiral out of control so explosively. Lacking insurance that could have quelled Maria's diabetes, her disease spread like wildfire. It robbed Maria of her youth, livelihood, and independence.

The direct and indirect costs of treating type 2 diabetes are massive, exceeding \$300 billion each year.[1] More than 1 in 10 Americans have diabetes. The average annual per-capita cost for diabetes care is roughly \$10,000. This figure doesn't account for lost productivity and non-compensated care that diabetes causes and requires.

In Maria's case, her husband cared for her since their family lacked resources necessary to arrange for external assistance. After Ben Taub discharged Maria into her husband's care, Nuila never saw her again. He often wonders what happened to her.

HEALTHCARE'S PROFOUND SERVICES– NEEDS MISMATCH

Keith is white and lives in rural Ohio. Maria is Hispanic and lives in urban Houston. They are both poor and uninsured. As a result, each lacks access to basic and vital healthcare services. Chronic HCDD diseases are indiscriminate. They attack all vulnerable people. For Keith and Maria, their lack of affordable health insurance created an early death sentence.

There are millions of people like Keith and Maria living today in America, especially in low-income urban and rural communities. They suffer disproportionately from chronic diseases, like diabetes. U.S. healthcare is not providing them with the basic care services they need to lead longer, healthier, happier, and more productive lives.

THE FOUR FACES OF CHRONIC DISEASE (HCDD)

There are many chronic diseases but the four most virulent are heart disease, cancer, diabetes, and dementia. Heart disease and cancer are the two leading killers of Americans. Diabetes and dementia, including Alzheimer's disease, are relentless, long, slow-building chronic diseases that wreck countless lives. The collective impact of chronic HCDD diseases on the American pocketbook, psyche, and sense of wellbeing is monumental.

There are various definitions of what diseases fit into the chronic category. In addition to the HCDD diseases, other chronic diseases include kidney disease, COPD, depression, and, surprisingly, tooth decay. For our purposes, we will focus on the big four.

Heart Disease

The CDC's National Center for Chronic Disease Prevention and Health Promotion (NCCDPHP) is the most authoritative source for data on chronic diseases. NCCDPHP bunches heart disease and stroke together as a chronic disease category. Their March 2023 report details the deadly impact of heart disease, including stroke, on the American people.[2] Heart disease accounts for a third of all deaths in the U.S. – 877,500 Americans. The annual cost of these two diseases is $216 billion. Lost productivity adds another estimated $147 billion in cost.

By itself, heart disease causes one in five American deaths each year. It kills approximately 695,000 Americans annually. Almost 50% of those who suffer from heart disease or stroke have high blood pressure, high cholesterol levels, and/or use tobacco. These are controllable through medication and behavior modification. According to CDC data, 58% of American seniors (65-plus) have high blood pressure, followed by 47% with high cholesterol, and 29% with heart disease. According to a 2020 USC Health report, heart disease and stroke are the two most expensive chronic conditions to treat and cure.

Cancer

According to the Commonwealth Fund, there are approximately 1.8 million cases of cancer diagnosed each year in the United States. Cancer is the nation's second leading cause of death; it kills almost 600,000 Americans each year, and its mortality rate is 183 per 100,000 people. The CDC predicts that cancer will overtake heart disease as the leading cause of death in the U.S. by 2030. On the plus side, there are approximately 16.9 million cancer survivors living in the U.S.

According to the CDC's United States Cancer Statistics (USCS), the rate of increase for new cancers (1999–2000) is modestly declining even though the absolute numbers of new cancer cases are increasing with the aging of the U.S. population.[3] Overall, the USCS statistics demonstrate that cancer care in the U.S., as measured by outcomes, is improving.

The USCS's map (see Figure 3.1) of new cancer diagnoses indicates that the Northeast and Midwest are seeing greater growth in cancer diagnoses along with some Southern states. This might have to do with average age in these regions. The South has disproportionately high levels of all types of cancers driven by its high numbers of poor and rural communities that lack adequate access to regular cancer screenings and timely follow-up care. Access to preventive care, screenings, and aligned treatments are essential to beating cancer.

The USCS data from 2013–2019 underscores the importance of early cancer detection. Survival rates were 87.8% for localized cancer diagnoses (stage 1 in the cancer severity index), 71.3% for regional diagnoses (stage 2), and 15.8% for cancers that have spread beyond the site of origin (stage 3 and stage 4).

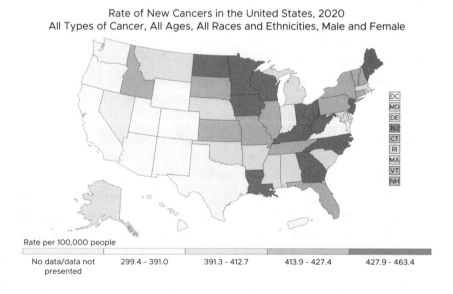

Figure 3.1   **Cancer rates differ significantly by state.**

Source: U.S. Cancer Statistics Working Group. U.S. Cancer Statistics Data Visualizations Tool, based on 2022 submission data (1999–2020): U.S. Department of Health and Human Services, Centers for Disease Control and Prevention and National Cancer Institute; https://www.cdc.gove/cancer.dataviz, released in November 2023 /Public Domain.

Cancer survivability also depends on the type of cancer. Some are less deadly. According to Mayo Clinic research, for example, the five-year survivability for bladder cancer is a high 77% when it is detected in stages 1 or 2. Early detection of lung cancer also increases survivability to 60%. With late detection, only 5% survive. By contrast, pancreatic cancer's five-year survival rate is a very low 7.2%

The COVID pandemic wreaked havoc with early cancer diagnosis. During COVID, at-risk individuals delayed screening exams. The result was a spike in late-stage cancer diagnoses, particularly for lower-income individuals and those without health insurance. Beyond COVID, cancer prevalence varies by region due to a host of behavioral, cultural, and environmental factors, including access to care services.

The CDC's National Center for Health Statistics (NCHS) tracks the prevalence of disease throughout the country. It's NCHS data that enables researchers to identify cancer "hotspot" regions.

The highest cancer death rates per 100,000 of population run right through the middle of the country, along the Ohio and Mississippi rivers. These are largely rural, high-poverty areas with poor diets, widespread obesity, sedentary lifestyles, and limited access to vital primary care services, including early cancer detection. These are the perfect Petri dishes for cancerous cells to spawn and multiply.[4]

In this way, most cancers (like all chronic diseases) are the product of multiple genetic and environmental factors. Chronic diseases defy reductionist medical diagnostic reasoning – there are rarely single causes.

Given the complexity of chronic cancers and the need to have a comprehensive and holistic approach to diagnostics and treatment, Healthcare Inc. rarely gives those living on the margins of society a fighting chance to stop the cancers that attack them. They lack access to early detection and timely interventions. Instead, the poor and disadvantaged often receive their diagnoses late (stages 3 and 4) and die in disproportionate numbers relative to those with adequate care access.

Historically, medicine has identified cancers by the organ (e.g., breast, liver, lung) where the cancer originates (see Figure 3.3). This is both helpful and problematic. Organ cancers do display similarities as the cancer cells metastasize and spread. However, all cancer tumors have genetic fingerprints. Understanding the tumor's genetics can be more important than the cancer's location for achieving curative therapies.

Needless to say, cancer is complicated. It seems the more we learn about the various types of cancers, the more there is to learn. At the same time, there are now diagnostic tests that can pinpoint a cancer diagnosis as well as an individual's genetic propensity for certain types of cancer.

Unfortunately, health insurance often doesn't cover these types of tests, so their availability depends on individuals' ability to pay. This is another example of medical advances being less available to lower-income people and therefore another factor contributing to the nation's inequitable care access (see Figure 3.2).

What we do know for certain is that behavior modification to reduce environmental risk factors can prevent cancer from taking hold. A World Health Organization (WHO) report concludes that 30–50% of all cancers are preventable.[5] The American Cancer Society (ACS) agrees. Their report

Mortality | All Races | All Malignant Cancers | Both Sexes | State | 2016 to 2020

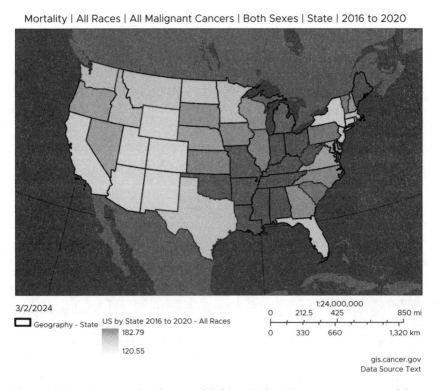

3/2/2024

☐ Geography - State   US by State 2016 to 2020 - All Races

▓ 182.79

120.55

1:24,000,000

0   212.5   425   850 mi

0   330   660   1,320 km

gis.cancer.gov
Data Source Text

Figure 3.2   Cancer death rates highest in low-income communities.

Source: U.S. Department of Health & Human Services/Public domain.

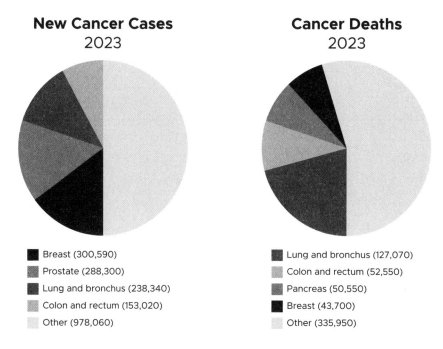

New Cancer Cases
2023

Breast (300,590)
Prostate (288,300)
Lung and bronchus (238,340)
Colon and rectum (153,020)
Other (978,060)

Cancer Deaths
2023

Lung and bronchus (127,070)
Colon and rectum (52,550)
Pancreas (50,550)
Breast (43,700)
Other (335,950)

Figure 3.3 Categorization of cancer types and deaths by organ, 2023.

Source: U.S. Department of Health & Human Services/Public domain.

indicates that 42% of cancer cases and 45% of cancer deaths are preventable.[6] Never has Ben Franklin's observation that "an ounce of prevention is worth a pound of cure" had more applicability.

Diabetes

Diabetes is the country's most rapidly growing chronic disease. According to research cited by the CDC, more than 37 million Americans (11% of the population) have diabetes. A third of the population will develop diabetes sometime in their life.

Moreover, diabetes and pre-diabetes are spreading at plague-like levels, particularly among young people of Black and Hispanic origin (see Figure 3.4). The growth of diabetes among children and young adults is the disease's fastest-growing subsection of the population. Type 2 diabetes

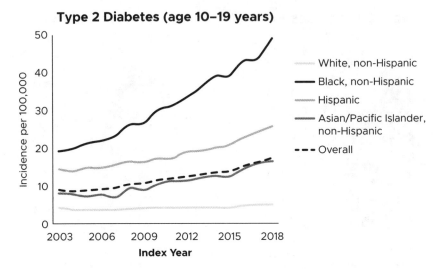

Figure 3.4   Skyrocketing incidence of Type 2 diabetes in the 10–19-year age group, 2003 to 2018.

Source: CDC/U.S. Department of Health & Human Services/Public domain.

follows obesity rates, and obesity is exploding within the nation's youth population.[7]

Not only does rampaging diabetes shorten and diminish countless American lives (remember Keith and Maria), but it also drains the nation's coffers. According to the CDC, diabetes has become America's most expensive chronic condition.[8]

Treatments for patients with diabetes consume a quarter of all U.S. healthcare expenditure. This includes $237 billion spent annually on direct diabetes care and an additional $90 billion in lost productivity. The average cost to treat a person with diabetes is 2.6 times higher than treating those without diabetes.[9] Absent interventions to slow Type 2 diabetes' spread, the nation's aggregate treatment costs for the disease will increase markedly.

The scope of America's diabetes challenge is daunting. A University of Southern California (USC) study reports that the healthcare system diagnosed 28.7 million Americans in 2020 with diabetes.[10] Another 8.5 million people were undiagnosed diabetics. It gets worse. The CDC estimates that 96 million Americans are pre-diabetic. They are ticking healthcare time bombs waiting to explode.

Here's the dilemma. Type 2 diabetes is 100% preventable. Given the devastation diabetes causes and the enormous resources required to treat it, the United States needs to declare war not only on this disease, but also on its primary cause (rising obesity).

Dementia and Alzheimer's Disease

Like diabetes, dementia and Alzheimer's disease (a sizable subset of the broader disease category of dementia) are fast-growing chronic diseases that are becoming a clear and present danger to America's wellbeing.

According to CDC data, almost 6 million Americans currently live with Alzheimer's.[11] It is the nation's fifth leading cause of death. The CDC expects this number of Americans afflicted with Alzheimer's to reach 14 million by 2060.

The prevalence of dementia and Alzheimer's disease is doubling every five years among Americans aged 65 and older. The CDC estimates that these cognitive diseases cost the current healthcare system $321 billion in 2022.[12] By 2050, dementia and Alzheimer's disease will afflict 12.7 million Americans and its annual cost will exceed a trillion dollars.

According to Lancet research, the average onset age for Alzheimer's is 68.8. The average age of diagnosis is 74.2. The average life expectancy after diagnosis according to Lifeline research is 5.8 years. Putting these numbers together, Alzheimer's is a neurological disease accompanied by a long, slow mental deterioration and physical decline.

Families bear 70% of Alzheimer's caring costs through out-of-pocket expenses and/or unpaid care. Forty-one percent of families with Alzheimer's patients have incomes at or below $50,000. Tragically, like other chronic diseases, the incidence of Alzheimer's falls disproportionately on low-income and/or ethnic individuals (see Figure 3.5), which contributes significantly to broader societal inequities.

Due to their long durations and care intensity, both the CDC and the USC studies referenced earlier identify Alzheimer's and diabetes as the nation's most expensive diseases to treat. Most dementia and Alzheimer's patients receive home-based care, at least during the initial stages, according to the *Journal of Gerontology*. The Alzheimer's Association says that two-thirds of Alzheimer's caregivers are women, one-third of whom are daughters of the afflicted.

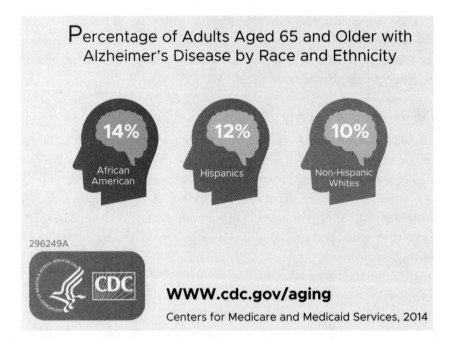

Figure 3.5   Higher percentages of U.S. Black and Hispanic adults aged 65 and older experience Alzheimer's disease, 2014.

Source: CDC/U.S. Department of Health & Human Services/Public domain.

These caregivers, often poor and stretched beyond capacity, have a high incidence of depression- and stress-related diseases. The burden of caring for dementia/Alzheimer's patients is so heavy that caregivers often die before the loved ones for whom they're caring. Even families that can afford institutionalized care carry a very heavy care and cost burden.

Individuals with Alzheimer's require an estimated 47 hours per week of caregiving. According to Alzheimer's Association data, annual unpaid caregiving represents a $340 billion cost borne by families and friends of the afflicted.

Estimates for the direct and indirect costs for Alzheimer's patients range widely between $17,000 and $77,000. That level of variation suggests there isn't a precise understanding of appropriate care protocols nor how to appropriately identify and fund treatment regimens. We do know, however, that dementia and Alzheimer's costs are already high and climbing higher.

As referenced earlier, the prevalence of dementia and Alzheimer's increases with age. According to the Alzheimer's Association, 73% of those currently diagnosed with dementia/Alzheimer's are 75 years old and older.[13] It is a devastating disease that lasts for years, even more than a decade.

Co-author Dave's mother-in-law, Mary Brady, suffered with Alzheimer's for 13 years before finally succumbing to the disease. At the time of her death, Mary was physically compromised, mute, and uncomprehending. The smart, vibrant, witty, caring, and fun-living Mary had long-since disappeared. Alzheimer's carries the nickname "the long goodbye" for a reason. It is a devastating disease that afflicts its victims and their caregivers with equal venom.

Like other chronic diseases, there appears to be no single causal factor for dementia or Alzheimer's. Big pharma has invested billions seeking to demonstrate that reducing amyloid plaques in the brain would lessen or eliminate the disease. Despite a massive effort, no drug has yet proven efficacious.

Like most cancers, it seems likely that a multiplicity of environmental and genetic factors combines to cause dementia and Alzheimer's. This would explain why a cure has been so elusive. There is some promising evidence that behavior modification (diet, exercise, sleep, keeping the brain active, etc.) can mitigate or even reverse early-onset Alzheimer's.

Today, heart disease and cancer cost American society more to treat than diabetes and dementia. They also cause more deaths. Diabetes and dementia, however, are faster-growing chronic diseases and the most expensive to treat as individual cases. Collectively, these four HCDD diseases pose a grave and increasing threat to America's health, safety, and productivity.

These chronic HCDD diseases share a long gestation period, become more virulent over time, and arise as a byproduct of multiple genetic and environmental factors, many of which relate to lifestyle behaviors. The origins of chronic HCDD are complex and likely require multifactorial prevention and treatment protocols to reverse their growing presence. A whole-person health "systems biology" approach to understanding and treating chronic diseases has the greatest potential to moderate the spread of chronic HCDD diseases.

THE ORIGINS OF CHRONIC DISEASE

As an adjective, *chronic* is a dreary word. It describes persistent, endlessly reoccurring, and troublesome phenomena. Those experiencing chronic conditions develop a sense of hopelessness in response to ongoing misery and pain.

Chronic gamblers, alcoholics, and liars are not well-adjusted, joyful people. They dread their harmful proclivities yet give into them. It takes strength, persistence, and the development of new habits to overcome addictive behaviors. That is why most individuals fail to change behaviors they know are bad for them.

The term *chronic* has specific application in healthcare. Medicine often divides diseases into two broad categories: acute and chronic. As defined by the CDC's NCHS, acute diseases occur suddenly and require immediate treatment. The National Council on Aging includes injuries caused by accidents as well as viral and bacterial infections among its list of afflictions requiring acute interventions.

By comparison, chronic conditions are sneaky. They emerge slowly and increase in virulence over time. The NCHS describes chronic diseases as those that "last three months or more, can't be prevented by vaccines and/ or cured by medication, nor do their symptoms just disappear."

The National Council on Aging observes that chronic diseases and conditions are slower to develop and progress over time. They may have many potential warning signs or none at all, but generally persist throughout an individual's lifetime. Based on these characteristics, the National Council on Aging draws this compelling conclusion: "Unlike acute conditions, chronic conditions cannot be cured – only controlled."

The working title for our book, "Gradually and Then Suddenly," describes the slow onset and development of chronic diseases and their virulent expression once they achieve a critical threshold (remember Keith and Maria).

We chose this title initially because the onset and progression of the dysfunction afflicting U.S. healthcare mirrors the progression of chronic conditions that afflict the human body. In other words, chronic dysfunction afflicts U.S. healthcare in the same way that chronic diseases afflict the U.S. populace.

Unlike acute conditions triggered by external pathogens or accidents, individual lifestyle choices and behaviors, sometimes in combination with genetic predisposition, can cause and amplify chronic diseases. These individual "choices" occur often within uniquely American cultures that encourage and reward unhealthy lifestyles. Phrases like "couch potato," "party hardy," "fat and happy," "horizontally challenged," "food coma," "cheesy good," and "betcha can't eat just one" have entered the American lexicon to give meaning and justification to unhealthy behaviors.

The ironic acronym SAD describes the "standard American diet." We have expanded this acronym to SADLE – standard American diets, lifestyles, and environments – to encompass the totality of forces "weighing" Americans down. SADLE is literally killing us.

The spread of chronic disease has become so ubiquitous that the Centers for Disease Control (CDC) added the word "Prevention" to its title in 1992 and launched its own *Preventing Chronic Disease* journal in 2004. The CDC identifies the following four lifestyle behaviors as causal factors contributing to the turbocharged growth of chronic HCDD diseases: poor nutrition, a lack of physical activity, tobacco consumption, and alcohol use. Let's explore them individually.

Poor Nutrition

Americans consume too much harmful food. Instead of food becoming health inducing, it becomes poison. As previously stated, over 75% of Americans are overweight or obese, a percentage that continues to grow consistently, particularly among children and young adults. Fewer than 1 in 10 adults eat recommended amounts of fruit and vegetables. Six out of 10 children and 5 of 10 adults have one or more sugary drinks per day. Nine out of 10 Americans consume too much sodium.

The standard American diet is a source of significant malnutrition as well as a trigger for excessive weight gain. The food industrial complex mass-produces inexpensive, convenient, addictive, pre-packaged, long-lasting, and high-calorie processed foods (with high levels of sugar, fat, and salt) that can overwhelm the body's natural defenses against overeating.

Portion sizes have increased with American waistlines. Sugar and manufactured high-fructose corn syrup are particularly dangerous. Some researchers even characterize sugar as the "new tobacco" and "a toxin in its own right" because of its easy access and addictive qualities.[14]

Diets filled with high amounts of sugar, salt, fats, and carbohydrates make people chronically ill. No one refutes this. Consequently, avoiding these dangerous, highly processed foods is essential to better health.

Getting the mass of Americans to change their eating habits is a monumental challenge. Junk foods' enticing marketing, prevalence in food deserts, low prices, and the poisonous political sloganeering (e.g., "food nannies" or "food Nazis") against efforts to restrict their consumption is formidable. Moreover, counterproductive governmental policies (e.g., subsidizing sugar and cheese production) amplify the negative nutritional impact that junk foods impose on American society.

Physical Inactivity

A surprising percentage of Americans get little or no physical activity. According to the CDC, a remarkable 25.3% of Americans do not participate in any non-job-related physical activities.[15] Physical inactivity has regional and social characteristics.

At a stunning 49.4%, Puerto Rico has the highest percentage of physical inactivity of any U.S. state or territory. In the continental U.S., the South earns that distinction at 27.5%, followed by the Midwest at 25.2%, the Northeast at 24.7%, and the West at 21%. Not surprisingly, lack of physical activity (see Figure 3.6) correlates with the incidence of chronic disease.

According to the NCCDPHP, only one out of two adults get the right amount of aerobic exercise on a regular basis. Even more startling and disturbing, 77% of high school students do not engage in the recommended amount of physical activity for their age group. This amalgamated lack of physical activity adds an estimated $117 billion dollars of incremental cost to our healthcare system.

Exercise is universally beneficial. Proper amounts of exercise reduce the probabilities of contracting heart disease, Type 2 diabetes, and many cancers. Proper exercise also mitigates the effects of high blood pressure, combats obesity, and potentially reduces the probability of contracting Alzheimer's disease.

Tobacco Consumption

Many consider the anti-smoking campaign begun in the 1960s to be the nation's most successful public health campaign. Despite

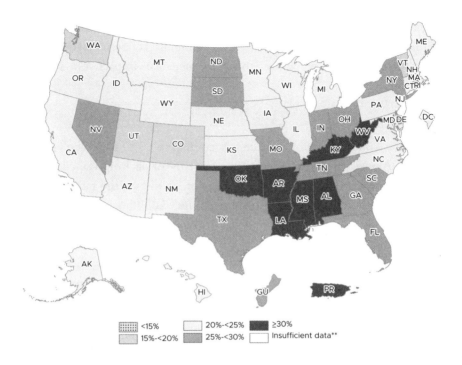

Figure 3.6 Moving less.

eliminating smoking in public places and the decline in tobacco consumption among the general population, the U.S. still has a smoking
problem. The tobacco products industry in the U.S. had $52.7 billion in
revenues during 2022. This market now includes the fast-growing e-
cigarette segment.

Despite the national decline in tobacco consumption, the CDC asserts
that tobacco usage remains America's "leading cause of preventable disease
and death." In 2019, there were 34 million American adults who smoked
cigarettes. Of these individuals, 16 million have tobacco-related diseases.
Everyday 1,600 children and young adults have their first cigarette or
e-cigarette. One in four Americans is exposed to second-hand smoke, which
can trigger chronic respiratory diseases and cancer.

The CDC assesses the annualized direct costs of smoking to be $170
billion, over three times greater than annual U.S. tobacco sales. Tobacco's
costs are even higher when incorporating tobacco's indirect costs (e.g.,
lower productivity due to higher absenteeism and greater use of sick days).

Even more worrisome, the emergence of vaping on e-cigarettes, popular with younger adults, adds to tobacco's spreading use. It doesn't take a mathematical wizard to recognize tobacco's negative impact on societal wellbeing.

Alcohol Use

Too many Americans drink to excess. According to CDC data, alcohol kills 140,000 Americans a year, accounting for 10% of all American deaths.[16] Among American adults between the ages of 20 and 49, the ratio doubles to 1 in 5 deaths. Alcohol abuse costs the country an estimated $249 billion annually, approximately $2.05 per drink. More prevalent in the U.S. than in other high-income countries, binge drinking triggers 40% of alcohol-related deaths.

There have been frequent claims that moderate alcohol consumption enhances health. A 2023 WHO report categorically refutes these claims:

> Alcohol is a toxic, psychoactive, and dependence-producing substance and has been classified as a Group 1 carcinogen by the International Agency for Research on Cancer decades ago – this is the highest risk group, which also includes asbestos, radiation, and tobacco. Alcohol causes at least seven types of cancer. . .
>
> The risk of developing cancer increases substantially the more alcohol is consumed. However, latest available data indicate that half of all alcohol-attributable cancers in the WHO European Region are caused by "light" and "moderate" alcohol consumption.[17]

The occasional drink may be fun but there's little to no evidence that alcohol has any beneficial effect on health.

Beyond counterproductive behaviors, irregular health screenings also contribute to America's excessive chronic disease levels. Chronic diseases can take years, even decades, to manifest as acute conditions. Regular health screenings can diagnose chronic diseases earlier when interventions against them are more effective. As witnessed in our accounts of Keith and Maria, a lack of access to basic screening services amplifies the mortality, morbidity, and treatment costs for chronic diseases.

In the second song of the Broadway play *Hamilton*, Alexander Hamilton meets Aaron Burr for the first time. Burr advises Hamilton to "speak less and smile more" if he wants to have greater influence in the new nation's affairs. Playing on Burr's assertion, Americans need to "eat less and move more" while avoiding tobacco and alcohol to optimize their health and forestall the onset of chronic diseases. These types of behavioral changes are hard but necessary to lessen the levels of chronic diseases that plague the American people.

Often in combination, poor eating, a sedentary lifestyle, and tobacco and alcohol consumption are the four behaviors that trigger the onset of chronic diseases. Interwoven with these behaviors are a host of economic, cultural and social factors that encourage these behaviors and amplify their negative impact.

Reversing the spread of chronic diseases will require comprehensive responses that address both the biology of specific chronic diseases as well as the social factors that make disease onset more likely and more deadly. The challenge is made even more acute because younger populations are adopting lifestyle behaviors that incubate chronic diseases at increasing levels.

CONCLUSION: TACKLING AN IRRESISTIBLE FORCE

Chronic HCDD diseases appear to have unstoppable momentum. Collectively, they have become an almost irresistible force – too strong for our natural defenses to combat. The conditions necessary for chronic HCDD diseases to continue flourishing in the U.S. are ideal.

Unhealthy lifestyle behaviors combine with a "sick-care" system that treats the symptoms of chronic HCDD diseases without addressing their root causes. Who wouldn't take the bet that chronic disease will continue its onslaught against beleaguered Americans? Yet, the U.S. must tackle these seemingly irresistible chronic diseases or risk a steady and continuous decline in national productivity, prosperity, confidence, and wellbeing.

Despite the rise of chronic disease, Americans are living longer by 10, 15, or 20 years than they did 50 and 100 years ago. This increase in longevity has occurred even though the onset of chronic diseases continues to occur on average as individuals enter their sixties.

What explains this increased longevity in the face of exploding chronic disease? Essentially, American medicine has become adept at keeping sick people alive longer, often with significantly diminished life quality. The financial and human costs of this "improvement" can be astronomical.

According to CDC data, 80% of adults 65 and older have a chronic disease; 68% have two or more. The incremental costs of caring for chronically ill adults is three to four times higher than those costs for equivalently aged adults without chronic disease, even as these chronically ill Americans live into their seventies, eighties, and nineties. Absent change, this irresistible chronic disease force will gain momentum as baby boomers age into their sixties, seventies, and beyond.

A January 2023 article by John Ansah and Chi-Tsun Chiu in the National Library of Medicine paints an alarming picture:

> *The number of people in the U.S. aged 50 years and older will increase by 61.11% from 137.25 million in 2020 to 221.13 million in 2050. Of the population 50 years and older, the number with at least one chronic disease will increase by 99.5% from 75,522 million in 2020 to 142.66 million by 2050.*[18]

More than any other high-income country, the United States cares for its chronic HCDD patients in hospitals. Designed to address acute episodes, hospitals are ill-suited to manage chronic diseases. High engagement, light-touch care delivery models that emphasize monitoring and coaching are much more effective and lower cost.

The U.S. spends more per capita on healthcare with worse health outcomes than all other advanced economies (see Figures 3.7 and 3.8). Continuing to tolerate this imbalance will lead to a significant decline in America's financial and political standing among nations.

Beyond treating chronic HCDD diseases more effectively once they've manifested, American society needs to reorder its priorities and resource allocation to prevent these diseases from taking hold in the first place. This responsibility expands beyond the healthcare system to encompass social

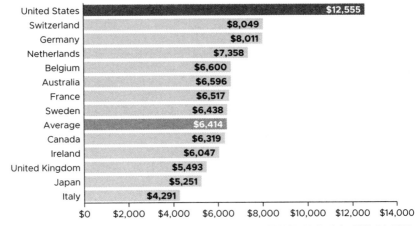

Healthcare Costs per Capita (Dollars)

SOURCE: Organisation for Economic Co-operation and Development, *OECD Health Statistics 2023,* July 2023.
NOTES: Data are from 2022 and include provisional values from some countries. Average does not include the
United States. The five countries with the largest economies and those with both an above median GDP and
GDP per capita, relative to all OECD countries, were included. Chart uses purchasing power parities to convert
data into U.S. dollars.
© 2023 Peter G. Peterson Foundation   PGPF.ORG

Figure 3.7   U.S. spending more on healthcare.

Source: ©Peter G. Peterson Foundation.

care, education, recreation, and nutrition. In this fundamental way, health differs from healthcare.

By investing in health, U.S. society will need to spend less on healthcare. This may be our book's most obvious and important conclusion.

Although the United States spends more on healthcare than other developed countries, its health outcomes are generally not any better

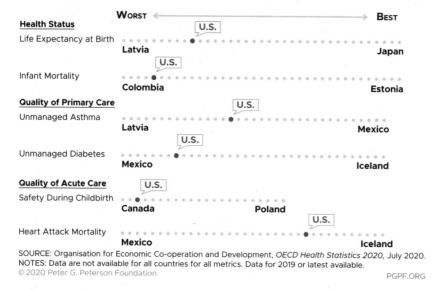

SOURCE: Organisation for Economic Co-operation and Development, *OECD Health Statistics 2020,* July 2020.
NOTES: Data are not available for all countries for all metrics. Data for 2019 or latest available.
© 2020 Peter G. Peterson Foundation   PGPF.ORG

Figure 3.8   And achieving poor or mediocre health outcomes.

Source: ©Peter G. Peterson Foundation.

KEY INSIGHTS ON CHRONIC PANDEMICS

- SADLE (the Standard American Diet, Lifestyle, Environment) supports behaviors that induce chronic diseases.
- Aging demographics and treatment regimens that extend lifespans make the onset of chronic HCDD diseases more widespread and more expensive to treat.
- Younger populations are becoming obese and sedentary at alarming rates, leading to earlier onset of chronic conditions.
- Socioeconomic conditions make low-income and ethnic populations less able to prevent and more likely to contract debilitating chronic HCDD diseases.
- A medical system riddled with perverse incentives that underinvests in preventive care in favor of providing high-cost, late-to-the-game disease care is ill-prepared to address the tsunami of chronic disease hitting America's shores.

4 | Technological Imperatives

The healthcare marketplace is ripe for disruption because Healthcare Inc.'s organization and delivery of care has changed little since 1970. Then, like now, the industry's core activity was the pursuit of treatment volume at the expense of better health outcomes.

Mentioned in the Introduction to this book, *Fortune* magazine's January 1970 investigative report[1] on America's "ailing medical system" makes this sobering conclusion painfully clear:

> *Our hospital system is being severely strained, and money — unless accompanied by rational organization and careful controls — is not going to bring much relief. The strain comes from the fact that Medicare, Medicaid and most insurance schemes are designed in such a way as to encourage more frequent and longer stays in the hospital. Instead, they should hold out incentives for the use of less expensive facilities.*

Fortune's investigative report, however, saw hope amid the darkness. With faith in America's managerial prowess, the report makes a compelling argument that bringing "modern methods" to managing healthcare operations could deliver "good care to every American with little increase in cost." Their report observes with obvious relish that "the management of

91

medical care has become too important to leave to doctors, who are, after all, not managers to begin with."

Professional administrators and managers have come to healthcare in a big way. Since 1970, the number of healthcare administrators has risen by 3,800%.[2] In contrast, the number of doctors in the U.S. has risen by only 200%. In U.S. healthcare today, there are now 10 administrators for every doctor.[3] These numbers are particularly staggering in contrast to other industries as outlined in a 2021 *JAMA* article by Nikhil Sahni, David Cutler, and Brandon Carrus citing research by McKinsey:

> *To run any organization, a base of administration is necessary. A typical U.S. services industry (for example, legal services, education and securities and commodities) has approximately 0.85 administrative workers for each person in a specialized role (lawyers, teachers and financial agents).*
>
> *In U.S. health care, however, there are twice as many administrative staff as physicians and nurses, with an estimated 5.4 million administrative employees in 2017, including more than 1 million who have been added since 2001.*[4]

Despite the expansive increases in healthcare administration or perhaps because of them, Healthcare Inc.'s costs have continued to spike upward even as Americans' collective health status has sputtered and by many measures declined.

How can it be true that healthcare has failed to demonstrate incremental cost and health status improvement for over 50 years? Why hasn't American ingenuity and technology transformed healthcare's antiquated 1970s–era operations? There is a deeper economic truth underlying the answers to these fundamental questions. *The U.S. healthcare system, as currently designed and operating, functions to optimize its performance within an activity-based payment system.*

The late Charlie Munger, Warren Buffett's long-time investment partner, observed, "Show me an incentive and I'll show you an outcome." Munger further noted, "Show me a dumb incentive structure and I'll show you dumb outcomes." Unfortunately, U.S. healthcare proves Munger's thesis. "Modern" healthcare management focuses the majority of its energy on exploiting perverse economic incentives.

Healthcare's "dumb" incentive structure enriches self-interested industry incumbents without delivering value to consumers. A lack of market accountability combined with a lax regulatory environment create the underlying conditions that enable incumbents to prosper by optimizing their own enrichment. There's little punishment and often lucrative incentives for inefficient and ineffective care delivery. Conversely, there's little reward and often negative financial consequences for pursuing health promotion and value-based care delivery.

Healthcare's perverse economic incentives explain why technological advances, unlike in other industries, have increased rather than lowered costs. They also explain the profound maldistribution of facilities and practitioners, which in turn limits access and the system's ability to provide the highly integrated and coordinated service delivery necessary to limit chronic disease spread.

Perverse financial incentives also explain why Healthcare Inc. spends exponentially more than any other industry on lobbying to sustain a favorable legislative and regulatory framework. It's in their interest and nature to do so.

Healthcare Inc., however, cannot fight gravity forever. Digital and biological technological advances are so powerful and coming so fast that Healthcare Inc. can no longer forestall their ascendance.

This is good news. Unlike the previous three macro forces (Demographic Determinants, Funding Fatigue, and Chronic Pandemics), Technological Imperatives are a galvanizing as well as a disruptive force. They provide new tools and capabilities that innovative companies can apply to revolutionize healthcare service provision.

Properly harnessed, the Technology Imperatives described in this chapter incorporate the data, tools, and bandwidth necessary for U.S. healthcare to finally achieve the goal (as articulated by *Fortune* magazine in January 1970) of delivering "good care to every American with little increase in cost."

To understand how this will happen, this chapter first explores the dynamics of living in an age of accelerating innovation. From there, we explore the rise of human–machine collaboration and its potential to reconfigure care services delivery in fundamental ways.

Technological Imperatives' largest benefit will be disrupting the unbelievably massive army of healthcare intermediaries that add unnecessary layers of cost and deplete value. As these powerful Technological Imperatives take hold and rewire healthcare delivery, they will transition America's failing sick-care system into a whole-person health system that generates better outcomes at lower costs.

ACCELERATING DIGITAL AND VIRTUAL
TECHNOLOGIES

Paradigm shifts occur when there is a fundamental change within economic systems that creates new perceptions and opportunities for innovation. "When he was budget director in the George H. W. Bush administration, Richard Darman often quipped, "Brother, can you paradigm," which plays on the popular Depression-era Broadway song, "Brother, can you spare a dime."

Despite Darman's skepticism, there have clearly been times in human history where discovery and innovation have spurred dramatic paradigm shifts in humanity's economic and cultural evolution. They occur haphazardly followed by long periods of adaptation. The term "punctuated equilibrium" describes this phenomenon.

Seven thousand years ago, *Homo sapiens* first learned to use and control fire for cooking, clearing land, and making tools. The wheel emerged 5,500 years ago to make transport and farming easier. Two thousand years ago, the Romans invented concrete and nails and revolutionized humanity's building capabilities. Around the same time, the Chinese invented the compass for navigation. Johannes Gutenberg's invention of the printing press in 1450 enabled Western civilization to emerge from the Dark Ages, share knowledge expansively, and set the stage for the Renaissance.

In the mid-1700s, the widespread application of steam power led to the first industrial revolution. The second industrial revolution emerged in the late 1800s with electrification, the internal combustion engine, and widespread use of assembly lines in manufacturing. The dawn of computing in the mid-1900s triggered the emergence of a third industrial revolution as production shifted from analog to digital capabilities.

The first mention of the fourth industrial revolution occurred in Germany during 2011 with the amplification of autonomous systems powering production. A fifth industrial revolution stressing the collaborative interconnection between autonomous systems, robots, and humans emerged just six years later in Japan.

This abbreviated tour of human economic history illustrates the quickening pace at which paradigm-busting technological advances are occurring. In reciprocal fashion, the time between periods of punctuated equilibrium where society adapts to emergent technologies has shortened dramatically.

Newton's Second Law of Motion holds that *Force* equals the product of *Mass* times *Acceleration*. Both the mass of increasing digital and biological capabilities as well as their accelerating rate of emergence into real-world applications amplify the immense force of Technological Imperatives pressing down on Healthcare Inc.

Contemplating and keeping up with this brave new technological world is both exhilarating and exhausting. This is what author Tom Friedman proclaims in his 2016 book *Thank You for Being Late: An Optimist's Guide to Thriving in the Age of Accelerations.*[5] Friedman envisions a new age of relentless, accelerating change where everyone and everything is connected, and no one is in charge.

In Friedman's Chapter 2, titled "What the Hell Happened in 2007," he describes a confluence of emergent companies and innovations emerging that "reshaped how people and machines communicate, create, collaborate and think." A quick scan of Figure 4.1 reveals how 2007 became a period of punctuated equilibrium to which humanity has been adapting ever since.

Friedman positively gushes as he summarizes the collective impact of these technological advances:

> . . . the platform birthed around the year 2007 surely constituted one of the greatest leaps forward in history. It suffused a new set of capabilities to connect, collaborate and create throughout every aspect of life, commerce and government.
>
> Suddenly there were so many more things that could be digitized, so much more storage to hold all the digital data, so many faster computers and so much more innovative software to process the data, and so many more organizations and people. . .who could access those insights or contribute to them, anywhere in the world through their handheld computers – their smartphones.

Astro Teller's Truth

Extreme interoperability and associated technological innovations are increasing human capabilities at an accelerating rate, but they also are increasing the levels of individual and societal discontent. The current pace of change can feel overwhelming.

In healthcare, unlike other industries, technology has increased rather than decreased the time and energy required to make the system function.

What the Hell Happened in 2007?

Apple introduced the iPhone

Facebook moved from college campuses to the whole world

Google acquired YouTube and launched Android

AT&T dramatically expanded its capacity to handle cellular traffic

Amazon released Kindle

AirBnB launched

The internet crossed one billion users

Intel introduced non-silicon chips, turbocharging micro-processing speeds

IBM began building Watson

The "clean power" revolution began

Twitter spun off on to its own platform

Cost of DNA sequencing plummeted

Figure 4.1   Major technological advances in 2007.
Source: Adapted from Tom Friedman, *Thank You for Being Late: An Optimist's Guide to Thriving in the Age of Accelerations.*

Workarounds abound. Indeed, the term "workaround" has become ingrained into healthcare vernacular as described by this widely cited meta-study from BMC Medical Research:

> *Workarounds circumvent or temporarily "fix" perceived workflow hindrances to meet a goal or to achieve it more readily. Behaviors fitting the definition of workarounds often include violations, deviations, problem solving, improvisations, procedural failures and shortcuts. Clinicians implement workarounds in response to the complexity of delivering patient care.*[6]

Much of the research literature on workarounds focuses on how electronic health records (EHR) paradoxically increase rather than decrease caregiver burden. For example, a 2021 BMC research report found that healthcare professionals frequently create workarounds to overcome "mismatches between their working practices and what the EHR allows or directs them to do."[7] Doctors and nurses often refer to the increased administrative requirements imposed on them by EHRs as a pivotal cause of burnout.

The challenge of accelerating technologies extends well beyond healthcare. Trying to make sense of the magnitude of technological change and seeking strategies for helping organizations and individuals adapt constructively, Friedman chronicles an interview in his book with Eric "Astro" Teller from Google. Astro is the grandson of Edward Teller, the creator of the hydrogen bomb. Astro's official job title at Google is "Captain of Moonshots."

For the first time in human history, Teller asserts that the rate of technological change is occurring faster than the natural ability of human beings to adapt to change. It's why we all feel so tired. Consequently, individuals and society as a whole must develop new and faster ways to accommodate change. Teller offers two strategies for speeding up this aspect of human evolution:

1. Individuals have to learn faster and longer (i.e., continuous lifelong learning is prerequisite for being productive).
2. Public, private, and governmental organizations must govern smarter by cutting red tape and pursuing continuous performance improvement.

Each of these strategies is an essential component of enhancing society's overall ability to adapt to technological advances, but they are insufficient to accomplish the mission without adding undue stress to the body politic. This is where the machines ride to our rescue.

In a 2018 *Harvard Business Review* article, authors H. James Wilson and Paul R. Daugherty describe the potential of "collaborative intelligence" as follows:

Never before have digital tools been so responsive to us, nor we to our tools. While AI will radically alter how work gets done and who does it, the technology's larger impact will be in complementing and augmenting human capabilities, not replacing them.[8]

In the digital economy, aggregating, analyzing, and applying knowledge from large diverse data sets is a prerequisite for maintaining organizational competitiveness. In healthcare, companies will differentiate and gain market share by fully engaging and supporting their employees in solving consumers' "jobs to be done." These companies will succeed by harnessing the power of human–machine collaboration.

For better or worse, the advent of generative AI and human–machine collaboration marks the beginning of another period of punctuated equilibrium. Friedman's self-described age of accelerations is accelerating. This is particularly true in healthcare, which has lagged other industries in its adoption of new technologies and business models. While other industries are racing to stay abreast of breathtaking advances in technology, healthcare is playing catch-up.

In the fifth industrial revolution, which is now underway, human–machine collaboration has established an early foothold. Writing in 2024, the machines are coming or, in many cases, are already here.

If that wasn't clear before, the launch of ChatGPT by OpenAI on November 30, 2022, confirms that machines are now learning to think and create like humans. There's no turning back. Human evolution now requires interdependent collaboration with machines to advance to higher levels of civilization. This dawning reality has profound implications for healthcare.

We have augmented Astro's original graph to incorporate this scary, awesome, and powerful tool of human–machine collaboration to humanity's

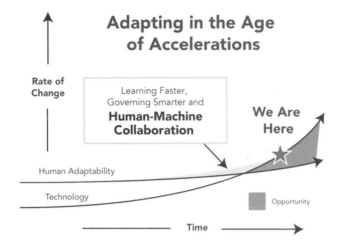

Figure 4.2 Humans cannot out-compute machines: Adapting to accelerating rate of technological change.

arsenal for adapting to an even faster-paced age of acceleration (see Figure 4.2). This is our collective future. It's not hard to imagine that some-day soon we'll all have personalized bots helping us navigate a more complex and fast-paced world with relative ease. We will use the tools of human–machine collaboration with the same ease that we now conduct Zoom meetings.

Multidimensional Machine Intelligence

Like telebanking for banking, AI is becoming an archaic descriptor for ma-chine intelligence. Originally meaning artificial intelligence, users of the term have modified the "A" to give it more precision. Ironically, their mul-tiple efforts to clarify AI (see Figure 4.3) make its definition more fluid and opaque.

Ultimately, there are just two types of intelligence, human and ma-chine. Like human intelligence, machine intelligence is multidimension-al. The multiple "A" adjectives used to describe machine intelligence speak to its expansive capacity to support almost all elements of human endeavor.

Indeed, advances in human–machine collaboration should become this decade's hallmark achievement. As referenced above, OpenAI launched a

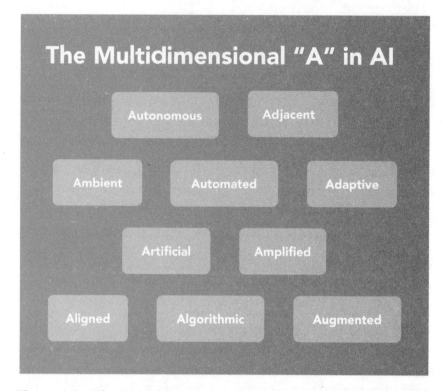

Figure 4.3　The "A's" have it: Machine versus human intelligence.

user-friendly chatbot named ChatGPT (model 3.5) in late 2022. ChatGPT-4 followed shortly thereafter on March 14, 2023. OpenAI's generative models and others like them strive to answer open-ended questions in an intelligent way by analyzing massive data with natural language processing (NPL) and machine-learning (ML) algorithms. Here's how OpenAI describes ChatGPT:

> *We've trained a model called ChatGPT, which interacts in a conversational way. The dialogue format makes it possible for ChatGPT to answer follow-up questions, admit its mistakes, challenge incorrect premises, and reject inappropriate requests.*

Within days of its launch, ChatGPT had over a million users. The platform's responses are so convincing that the *New York Times* reports that universities across the country are revamping their teaching methods to prevent students from using the app to write essays and term papers.[9] According to a *Wall Street Journal* article, OpenAI is in discussions with investors to sell existing shares at a valuation of $29 billion.[10]

By early 2023, commentators, researchers, and academics had gone absolutely crazy for ChatGPT. They announced each new application with breathless awe. ChatGPT passed all three medical licensing exams without any specialized training. It also passed a final exam for a core MBA class at Wharton.

ChatGPT is short for Chat Generative Pre-Trained Transformer. It is a form of conversational artificial intelligence (AI or Generative AI, GenAI). The concept is not new. IBM's Watson that launched in 2007 claimed to have many of the same capabilities as ChatGPT, but it never achieved critical mass. What underlies ChatGPT's remarkable success is its broad accessibility, ease of use (everyone knows how to conduct internet searches), and ability to create novel, understandable output.

Given the media hype, 4sight Health's January 27, 2023, Roundup podcast, which includes co-author Dave Johnson, debated AI's potential impact in healthcare.[11] The conversation included an overview of a new National Bureau of Economic Research (NBER) paper written by McKinsey and Harvard economist David Cutler.

The NBER paper claimed that AI could reduce healthcare spending by $200 billion to $360 billion within the next five years without sacrificing quality or access. The biggest potential savings came from reducing administrative burden, harnessing medical knowledge to enhance the accuracy and timeliness of diagnoses, and improving clinical operations.

To test ChatGPT's prowess, Dave initiated an exchange for the podcast that addressed the same questions studied in the NBER paper. Here's that exchange:

> **How will ChatGPT disrupt U.S. healthcare in the next five years, specifically, how much money will it save?**
>
> . . .it is likely that ChatGPT could have a significant impact on the healthcare system by streamlining processes and improving efficiency.
>
> One potential application of ChatGPT in healthcare is in automating administrative tasks, such as scheduling appointments and filling out medical forms. By using natural language processing, ChatGPT could understand and respond to patient inquiries, reducing the need for human staff to handle these tasks. This could lead to cost savings for healthcare providers by reducing labor costs.
>
> Another potential application of ChatGPT in healthcare is in triage and diagnosis. By using machine learning and natural language processing, ChatGPT could assist healthcare professionals in quickly and accurately identifying potential health concerns. This could lead to cost savings by reducing the need for unnecessary tests and procedures and by allowing patients to receive prompt and effective treatment.
>
> . . .it is worth noting that according to a recent study by Accenture, the potential savings for the US healthcare industry from the use of AI technologies, including natural language processing, could reach up to $150 billion per year by 2026.

Not bad! That exercise took less than two minutes, a minuscule fraction of the time it took the NBER authors to complete their 35-page paper.

The NBER paper employs a logical analytic approach, and its conclusions seem reasonable. From a pragmatic perspective, however, it is almost impossible to predict any transformative technology's compounding impact on innovation and business practices. Moments of punctuated equilibrium are, by definition, surprising.

Consequently, no one really has any idea how and to what magnitude ChatGPT and related AI technologies will alter healthcare delivery. What we can say with confidence is that AI will be far more disruptive to current business practices than any predictions being made today.

The pace of AI integration into human affairs has reached an inflection point. With seemingly unlimited data access and computing power, machines will soon be helping humans solve problems that once seemed beyond our capabilities.

The Vast AI Opportunity in Healthcare

As the NBER paper referenced above does, it is essential to imagine how AI might transform healthcare delivery. The most effective method for engaging in this form of prognostication is to establish a baseline and apply "what-if" thinking to it.

The key to market competitiveness in the digital economy is the ability to aggregate, analyze, and apply knowledge from large and diverse data sets. To differentiate their service offerings and gain market share, healthcare companies must engage and support their employees in solving consumers' "jobs to be done." They can best accomplish this by harnessing the power of human–machine collaboration.

Human–machine collaboration has the power to transform healthcare delivery by removing soul-crushing burdens from caregivers and consumers alike, freeing both to pursue higher-value activities related to individualized therapies and wellbeing. Rather than being in competition with the machines, human–machine collaboration should optimize human potential in unexpected, new, and profound ways.

HEALTHCARE'S VAST INTERMEDIARY PROBLEM

Bing Crosby and the Andrews Sisters sang a jazzy tune in the 1940s with a misspelled title. Originally written by Harold Arlen and Johnny Mercer, "Ac-Cent-Tchu-Ate the Positive" climbed to No. 2 on the Billboard Charts and earned an Academy Award nomination for best original song. Its catchy refrain was the source of its initial and continued popularity:

> *You've got to accentuate the positive*
> *Eliminate the negative*
> *Latch on to the affirmative*
> *Don't mess with Mister In-Between*

Messing with "Mister In-Between" is exactly what many of healthcare's innovative companies are intent upon doing. Up to this point, our GenAI discussion has focused on the ways in which human–machine collaboration will reduce caregivers' administrative burden, enhance customer engagement, and improve diagnostic and therapeutic decision-making as well as streamline care navigation. This is as it should be. GenAI has enormous potential to drive better care outcomes with much better customer experience at significantly lower costs.

Significant cost savings will emanate from machines' ability to guide better human decision-making at the point of care. Far more savings, however, will result from machines' ability to eliminate intermediary functions altogether. As the process unfolds, integrated platforms optimizing human–machine collaboration will "eliminate the negative" economic drag by reducing transaction friction. They will "latch on to the affirmative" improvement in health outcomes and customer experience.

Healthcare has a gargantuan number of intermediaries who broker transactions between parties. Armies of actuaries, accountants, administrators, advisors, agents, bankers, billers, brokers, care navigators, coders, compliance personnel, collectors, distributors, expediters, lawyers, lobbyists, regulators, retailers, and schedulers clog healthcare arteries at enormous cost to American society. They consume enormous amounts of societal resources without adding incremental value. Far too often, they create unnecessary transaction friction that frustrates consumers and caregivers alike.

As referenced in the McKinsey analysis presented earlier in this chapter, most industries have fewer than one administrator for everyone employed in service delivery. In U.S. healthcare, there are over five administrators for every doctor and nurse. Much of healthcare's excessively high administrative cost burden, perhaps as much as 80%, relates to complex pricing formularies and the titanic battles that occur between payers and providers to secure revenues.

Healthcare providers characterize the coding, billing, and collection for healthcare treatments as revenue cycle management (RCM). On the flipside, healthcare payers use the term "revenue integrity" to describe their efforts to document accurate and appropriate payment for treatments. For our purposes, we'll refer to both as RCM.

Whatever they're called, activities related to healthcare billing and payment constitute a massive industry employing hundreds of thousands of healthcare professionals. According to a report issued by Grand View Research, the U.S. market in 2022 for outsourcing healthcare revenue cycle functions was $140.4 billion.[12] The report projects this market to grow

10.3% annually through 2030. By comparison, Ibis World estimates the 2022 market for U.S. automobile manufacturing to be $100.9 billion, growing at just 2.6% this year.

In today's America, processing medical claims by third parties is far more lucrative than manufacturing all the nation's cars and trucks. That's just outsourced RCM activities. The $140.4 billion figure excludes in-house provider and payer RCM activities. Given the RCM market's size, it's remarkable there isn't more aggregate data on the sector. The Grand View Research report is one of only a handful on the RCM marketplace.

Given healthcare's payment dynamics and complexity, it's difficult to pinpoint the exact level of healthcare's RCM and other administrative expenses. As referenced in this book's Introduction, Healthcare Inc's 2024 administrative costs could be as high as $1.47 trillion, representing 30% of $4.9 trillion in projected healthcare expenditure. The most conservative estimate we've seen is 15%. Most estimates center around 25%.

The variation in estimates is exceptionally wide and leaves abundant room for error. It speaks to the alarming lack of clarity regarding healthcare's administrative costs. What is clear is that the vast majority, perhaps 80% or more, of healthcare's administrative expenditure encompasses claims coding, billing, and collections. These activities are the guts of RCM. Providers and payers account for much of their RCM activities within ongoing operations in ways that are difficult to isolate. Opaque accounting makes an insightful analysis difficult to undertake.

Our best guess is that the economic cost associated with healthcare RCM is $1 trillion. This is an unimaginably big number, almost beyond human understanding. Most people, for example, have no concept of how many years it would take to record a trillion seconds. The answer is an astounding 32,000 years. A trillion dollars spent each year to process medical claims is incomprehensible, but let's put it into perspective.

As Figure 4.4 shows from Ibis World documents, healthcare's core industries (hospitals, pharmacies, drug wholesaling, and health insurance) were the four largest U.S. industries as measured by revenues in May 2023. At their highest levels, Healthcare Inc.'s administrative expenditures are larger by a wide margin than the biggest non-healthcare industry, commercial banking (No. 5 at $1.21 trillion).

The 10 Biggest Industries by Revenue

U.S. Industry Revenue (May 2023)

1.	Hospitals in the U.S.	$1.42T
2.	Drug, Cosmetic & Toiletry Wholesaling in the U.S.	$1.36T
3.	Pharmaceuticals Wholesaling in the U.S.	$1.29T
4.	Health & Medical Insurance in the U.S.	$1.24T
5.	Commercial Banking in the U.S.	$1.21T
6.	New Car Dealers in the U.S.	$1.12T
7.	Life Insurance & Annuities in the U.S.	$1.12T
8.	Public Schools in the U.S.	$.99T
9.	Retirement & Pension Plans in the U.S.	$.93T
10.	Gasoline & Petroleum Wholesaling in the U.S.	$.92T

Figure 4.4   Healthcare dominates U.S. industry.

Source: Adapted from Ibis World.

Reducing Administrative Drag

Unlike other technological revolutions, GenAI's ability to conduct non-routine cognitive tasks threatens the livelihoods of knowledge workers far more than manual laborers. A Goldman Sachs report suggests GenAI technologies could affect two-thirds of all occupational tasks and fully substitute for a quarter of them.[13]

That percentage will be much higher in healthcare because Healthcare Inc. employs so many administrators and intermediaries. GenAI will devour healthcare's middle. Great software with the ability to replicate non-routine human cognition will eliminate the need for most of healthcare's intermediaries.

Machines will do the routine tasks like scheduling appointments, adjudicating claims, and managing payments, but they also will take increasing responsibility for diagnosing medical conditions and suggesting treatment regimens based on individual patient characteristics.

The transition to AI-supported work will generate enormous productivity improvement and wealth creation. A McKinsey analysis suggests that AI can boost annual productivity worldwide by as much as $4.4 trillion.[14] That's the equivalent of adding "a Japan" with the world's third-largest GDP to the global economy each year. Again, the opportunity for productivity improvement employing AI technologies is far greater in healthcare than in other industries because of the industry's historic lag in adapting to technological innovation.

Broadly speaking, productivity improvement occurs when an industry uses the same or fewer resources to produce more products and better services. U.S. healthcare spending tends to go in the opposite direction, using more resources to produce the same amount or less service provision. A 2019 McKinsey analysis highlights healthcare's significant and negative correlation between economic growth and job creation within the overall U.S. economy:

Between 2001 and 2016, healthcare delivery contributed 9% of the $8.1 trillion ($4.2 trillion in real terms) growth in the US economy – but 29% of the 14.4 million net new jobs.

As illustrated by the McKinsey figures, incremental hiring without productivity improvement creates a drag on the overall economy. Remember that the number of healthcare administrators has increased 3,800% since the 1970s. *The key to improving healthcare's productivity is dramatically reducing its exceptionally high administrative costs.*

Despite their prolific and constant increases, reining in Healthcare Inc.'s administrative costs has proven exceptionally difficult to do. There are just too many industry incumbents with a vested interest in maintaining inefficient business practices. For the first time in decades, however, buyers of healthcare services with the help of GenAI can demand more value for their healthcare purchases. In the process, the numbers of healthcare intermediaries will wither.

GenAI also will help improve the effectiveness and efficiency of care delivery. Together with GenAI-driven reductions in administrative activities, enhanced healthcare productivity has the potential to turbocharge the entire U.S. economy. Instead of being a drag on the economy as it has been, healthcare could become an accelerant. This is the inherent power and potential of the "Technological Imperatives" described in this chapter.

BYTES AND BITS

Here's an awe-inspiring concept. Science's understanding of biological systems and the ability to manipulate them to advance treatments and strengthen immunity (i.e., the genetic revolution) appears to be progressing as quickly as the digital revolution. It is now almost as easy to edit genetic code as it is computer code.

Indeed, advances in machine intelligence and analytics are turbocharging medical innovation. Digital bytes are enabling scientists to better understand genetic bits in a symbiotic dance where breakthrough digital and genetic discoveries build upon one another. Perhaps the best illustration of the Technological Imperatives' potential is the development and application of CRISPR technologies.

Forgive the short science lesson. CRISPR is an acronym for Clustered Regularly Interspaced Short Palindromic Repeats. CRISPRs are repeated bits of genetic code that ward off attacking viruses. RNA and DNA work together to replicate genetic information into cells to make the proteins that enable all living things to function. CRISPR alters "messenger" RNA to eliminate genetic mutations that cause disease.

CRISPRs can identify attacking viruses, latch on to the viruses' destructive DNA sequences, and eliminate them. This is why the Swedish Royal Academy for Sciences described CRISPR as a "genetic scissors" when it awarded the 2020 Nobel Prize in Chemistry to Emmanuelle Charpentier and Jennifer Doudna. Cas9 is an RNA-guided enzyme that cleaves to and eliminates targeted DNA strands:

Emmanuelle Charpentier and Jennifer Doudna are awarded the Nobel Prize in Chemistry 2020 for discovering one of gene technology's sharpest tools: the CRISPR/Cas9 genetic scissors.

Researchers can use these to change the DNA of animals, plants and microorganisms with extremely high precision. This technology has revolutionized the molecular life sciences, brought new opportunities for plant breeding, is contributing to innovative cancer therapies and may make the dream of curing inherited diseases come true.

Bacteria evolved CRISPR over the millennia as part of the back-and-forth battle for biological dominance with viruses. In an elegant evolutionary response, some viruses have developed anti-CRISPR mechanisms to thwart CRISPR attacks on their genetic structure. They operate in much the same way as anti-missile defenses that seek and destroy incoming missile attacks. In fact, the U.S. Department of Defense is researching these anti-CRISPR mechanisms to counter biological warfare attacks.

Charpentier and Doudna along with several other researchers led a global effort to understand the basic science underlying CRISPR. Their efforts began in the early 2000s and culminated in a pathbreaking article published in *Science* on June 28, 2012. In short order, the publication of this article triggered patent applications by five newly formed companies to develop genetic engineering tools to use on human beings.[15]

The first application of CRISPR to cure an inherited genetic disease occurred on July 19, 2019, at the Sarah Cannon Research Institute in Nashville, Tennessee.[16] Sickle cell anemia is a debilitating and deadly disease caused by a mutation in genes forming hemoglobin proteins.

On that July day, a 34-year-old African American woman from Mississippi named Victoria Gray received an injection of billions of genetically modified stem cells to treat her sickle cell anemia. Researchers had employed CRISPR technology to eliminate the genetic mutation distorting her hemoglobin proteins within these injected stem cells. It took about eight months for the genetically modified stem cells to work their magic. Gray woke up one morning with no pain. It's been smooth sailing since.

After more successful trials, the FDA approved two gene therapies (Casgevy and Lyfgenia) using CRISPR/Cas9 on December 8, 2003, to treat patients 12 years and older suffering from sickle cell anemia.[17] Other potential CRISPR applications include therapies to treat lung cancer by enhancing patients' immune system responses, cure congenital blindness, and enhance genetic defenses against viral pandemics, Alzheimer's, heart disease, leukemia, high cholesterol, and even male-pattern baldness.[18] Medical science is only beginning to understand CRISPR's potential in therapeutics, immunology, botany, and animal husbandry.

Beyond CRISPR, the collaborative power of big data and breakthrough biology will enable medicine to discover very early pre-disease markers of chronic diseases and intervene effectively to treat and/or eliminate the diseases. This type of "pre-emptive diagnostics" will correlate minor changes in biological markers over time with very early and accurate predictions of disease onset.

It's almost impossible not to hyperventilate when considering the potential of Technological Imperatives to revolutionize human existence. Not normally prone to hyperbole, tech wizard Bill Gates predicts in his 2023 annual letter that "the road ahead" will soon reach a "turning point" as "AI supercharges the innovation pipeline."[19]

Gates sees multiple AI-driven health and healthcare innovations. They include new and affordable medicines for AIDS, TB, and malaria; more effective antibiotic drugs; more effective treatments for high-risk pregnancies; enhanced HIV assessments using chatbots; easier access globally to vital medical information; reduced malnutrition based on a deeper understanding of the microbiome; and improved vaccine effectiveness.

These remarkable technologies bring significant moral challenges with them. CRISPR makes it possible to edit inheritable traits (i.e., cross the germline) that would pass to succeeding generations. When and under what circumstances should society allow this to happen?

GenAI blurs the line between human and machine intelligence. When does that go too far? These complex moral questions demand resolution that will take time to manifest. As with the dropping of the first atomic bombs, it's entirely possible that the application of AI and genetic discoveries will occur before clear use guidelines have formalized.

Notwithstanding these significant moral dilemmas, innovations in AI and genetics make this a remarkable moment in human history – a time where it's possible to consider the eradication of many debilitating diseases and sufficient wealth creation to eliminate global poverty. Shakespeare found the words, albeit ironically, to describe human potential operating at its highest levels in this passage from *The Tempest*:

> *O wonder!*
> *How many goodly creatures are there here!*
> *How beauteous mankind is!*
> *O brave new world,*
> *That has such people in 't!*

Appropriating Shakespeare's language and its ironic application, Aldous Huxley titled his classic science-fiction novel *Brave New World*. Published in 1932, Huxley presents a dystopian future where an elite leisure class of

Alphas uses genetic engineering to create working classes of Gammas, Deltas, and Epsilons to service its needs.

Baby "hatcheries" divide newborns into one of five classes or castes to determine and guide their lives. In Huxley's fictional society, science enhances evil intent. An authoritarian elite uses the fruits of scientific discovery (genetic engineering, mind-altering drugs) to marginalize their fellow citizens and sustain their privilege.

We prefer the more humane and generous future that Bill Gates envisions — where technological advances expand opportunity, improve health, and increase wellbeing for all. In that brave new world, inefficient, inequitable, and ineffective healthcare practices don't stand a chance.

CONCLUSION: THE MACHINES ARE COMING! THE MACHINES ARE COMING!

Legend has it that just after midnight on April 18, 1775, Paul Revere rode his horse north through Lexington to Concord shouting, "To Arms! To Arms! The British are coming! The British are coming!" Revere's warning enabled American patriots to ambush British soldiers later that day as they marched toward a munitions depot in Concord. The American Revolution was underway. Massachusetts celebrates April 18 as Patriots Day, and the legendary Boston Marathon runs that day.

Another type of revolution is underway now. GenAI, CRISPR and other amazing Technological Imperatives are reshaping industries and economies in real time at an accelerating rate. It's hard for mere mortals to keep pace, particularly with GenAI. As mentioned earlier, ChatGPT launched on Nov. 30, 2022. It had over a million users within five days and has spread geometrically since along with other Large Language Models (LLMs) by Alphabet, Amazon, Anthropic, Meta, and X, among others.

Unlike other technological breakthroughs (e.g., personal computers and smartphones), GenAI requires no hardware. Its capabilities manifest through already well-developed consumer habits in search. With virtually no learning curve, GenAI provides an immediate boost to worker productivity.

LLMs are boldly going where humanity has never gone before. They employ machine learning and natural language processing within deep neural networks to think and create like human beings. They're solving math word problems. AI art generators like DALL E2 use prompts to fashion original works. If that's not thinking and creating, we don't know what is. ChatGPT-4's capabilities are already awe-inspiring. Imagine what ChatGPT-10 will be able to do.

Sitting directly in GenAI's sights is U.S. healthcare. It is the largest industry ever created by human beings and still largely operates the way it did in the 1970s. It is an industry riddled with intermediaries, inefficiencies, and inferior outcomes. Healthcare also generates 30% of the world's total data. Most of that data is disconnected and unstructured.[20] It's begging for effective application. We need machines to help us make sense of it all.

We're not riding a horse like Paul Revere, but we are proclaiming that the machines are on our shores and coming to revolutionize America's broken healthcare system. The Technological Imperatives described in this chapter are sufficiently strong to rewire Healthcare Inc.'s obsolete operating system into one that fully embraces human–machine collaboration.

Fans of *Star Trek* (aka Trekkies) celebrate April 5, 2063, as First Contact Day based on events that occur in the 1996 film *Star Trek: First Contact*. On that future day, Zefram Cochrane travels at warp speed (beyond the speed of light) for the first time. This catches the attention of Vulcans who initiate contact. This "first contact" between Vulcans and humans leads to the creation of the Federation, order in the universe, and broad advancement of civilizations.

Unlike *Star Trek*, GenAI and CRISPR aren't fiction. These breakthrough technologies, however, have the same potential as warp speed to trigger equivalent epoch-changing achievements.

Like Trekkies do today, it is altogether possible that the world will honor the anniversary of ChatGPT's launch date in future years. On that day, the global community witnessed the first meaningful connection between human and machine intelligence. As GenAI achieves its full potential, November 30 could become the day we collectively choose to recognize and celebrate the rise of human–machine collaboration.

Rather than go to the third decimal point predicting the impact of generative intelligence and genetic engineering tools, let's take a moment to appreciate the awe of living in a time where digital technologies are transforming human existence before our eyes. Then let's get to work to make U.S. healthcare better!

KEY INSIGHTS ON TECHNOLOGICAL IMPERATIVES

- Almost unbelievably, the healthcare industry operates largely the same way in the post-digital era as it did in the 1970s pre-digital era. In the process, it has become an enormous drag on the U.S. economy.
- The pace of paradigm-shifting technologies and innovation is accelerating rapidly and has the potential to rewire healthcare's current operating models in fundamental ways.
- Generative AI (GenAI) is powering a society-wide fifth industrial revolution by enabling machines to learn, think, and create like human beings. GenAI's ability to undertake non-routine cognitive functions will displace knowledge workers broadly and trigger exponential productivity gains.
- Healthcare is more vulnerable to the disruptive threat posed by GenAI and related AI technologies because the industry has been slower to adapt to previous technological advances and has outsized dependence on intermediaries to conduct transactions. Great software devours intermediaries.
- Entrenched in antiquated, inefficient, high-cost, and fragmented business models, healthcare incumbents cannot fight gravity forever. The advent of human–machine collaboration will fundamentally change healthcare service delivery in beneficial ways while massively disrupting and streamlining current business practices.

5

Pro-Consumer/ Market Reforms

The year 2020 was a watershed year in U.S. healthcare. COVID changed everything. Providers needed a government bailout to stay afloat. Payers had record profits. Virtual care delivery exploded. Caregivers crossed state lines in unprecedented numbers. Gaping access issues revealed vulnerabilities and weaknesses with the nation's care delivery systems. American ingenuity created and distributed a new vaccine at scale in record time. Public health became a political football. Venture funding stalled and then skyrocketed.

Post-COVID, healthcare has stumbled into an uncertain future with federal, state, and local governments taking an ever-larger role in designing, funding, and regulating care delivery. Despite incontrovertible evidence that the U.S. healthcare system has major structural flaws, Healthcare Inc. has largely returned to status quo business practices. Few incumbents are stepping up to the challenge of strategically repositioning business models to accommodate potential changes in the industry's supply–demand dynamics.

At least for a time, the pandemic disrupted Healthcare Inc.'s rigid adherence to hospital-centric medicine and stimulated innovation. Originating in China during the latter months of 2019, the COVID pandemic spread worldwide and shuttered the global economy. The U.S. began a full lockdown in March 2020 that lasted until July when the first COVID wave receded.

Subsequent COVID variants deepened the pandemic's impact. On March 27, 2020, President Trump signed the CARES Act into law. It provided $2 trillion in emergency funding for hospitals, small businesses, and governments.

As hospitals scrambled to care for the exploding numbers of COVID patients, the Centers for Medicare and Medicaid Services (CMS) prohibited elective procedures and relaxed regulations governing state licensure of healthcare practitioners. CMS also equalized payment for virtual care patient visits. Americans adapted with varying degrees of acceptance to wearing masks, taking vaccines, disease testing, and limiting social exposure.

Meanwhile, the economy sputtered as almost 10 million Americans lost their jobs. With the pandemic still raging in 2021, Congress passed the $1.9-trillion America Rescue Plan (ARP) to continue funding the pandemic response and provide additional economic stimulus. Newly elected President Biden signed the ARP into law March 11, 2021.

The COVID emergency officially ended on May 11, 2023. Its overall impact on America's wellbeing was catastrophic and tragic. Over a million Americans died from COVID. The pandemic exposed devastating disparities in health equity. COVID disproportionately debilitated and killed individuals from low-income communities, particularly those with advanced chronic diseases.

Despite the human carnage or perhaps because of it, the American system displayed remarkable agility in shifting to virtual and in-home care modalities. Telemedicine visits skyrocketed, jumping from 0.3% to 23.6% of total clinical visits between March and June 2020.[1]

While telemedicine visits have declined back to roughly 5% of all clinical visits, they have remained well above pre-pandemic levels. Telehealth interactions, a much broader measure, also skyrocketed during the pandemic and have reset at just over 20% of all current interactions.[2]

More than anything else, the COVID pandemic forced Healthcare Inc. to accept new care delivery models. The widespread adoption of virtual and home-care services demonstrated that the historic barriers to delivery innovation were more political and economic than practical and logistical.

Meanwhile, innovative companies have emerged with significant financial backing to offer more efficient, convenient, and lower-cost care delivery modalities. As occurred during the Roaring 1920s, a pandemic has set the stage for a massive technology-driven shift in healthcare delivery.

The "x" factors in the scope and pace of transformation within the U.S. healthcare system are the degrees to which governments and agencies will shape healthcare's changing supply–demand dynamics. Relative to other industries, federal and state governments exercise disproportionate influence on the design, delivery, payment, and evolution of healthcare delivery. This is due to government's expansive healthcare mandates, which encompass the following activities:

- **Regulation:** Federal and state regulators oversee regulatory compliance with regard to patient safety, licensure, capital adequacy, and data exchange.
- **Payment:** Government funds roughly half of the $4.9 trillion in annual expenditure through Medicare, Medicaid, veterans, military, and prison programs.
- **Enforcement:** Through various local, state, and federal agencies, government seeks to ensure level-field competition, lawful billing and distribution for medical products and services.
- **Public Health:** The CDC oversees the nation's efforts to promote better health and protect against the spread of infectious diseases.
- **Healthcare Delivery:** Government administers healthcare services through the Veterans Administration, branches of the U.S. military, and through government-owned hospitals and clinics.
- **Research:** The National Institutes of Health are the primary funders of basic medical research.
- **Innovation:** The Food and Drug Administration (FDA) oversees the approval and protection of novel drugs and devices.

Given healthcare's complexity and their already expansive role, federal and state governments have ceded responsibility for credentialing medical professionals and facilities to medical associations and non-profit organizations (e.g., the Joint Commission). These intermediaries exercise significant influence in shaping the industry's operating character.

For example, the American Medical Association (AMA) develops the Medicare Physician Fee Schedule using a copyrighted procedure that incorporates relative value units (RVUs) for specific procedural codes (current procedural codes, or CPTs). Likewise, the Medical Payment Advisory

Commission (MedPAC) advises Congress on policies related to Medicare payment, quality, and access issues.

It doesn't take an organizational genius to recognize that healthcare's massive scale, breadth of responsibilities, competing jurisdictions, turf battles, and numerous invested parties make the U.S. delivery system overly complex and vulnerable to manipulation. Exploiting complexity for pecuniary gain is exactly what President Dwight D. Eisenhower warned against in his January 1961 "Farewell Address" when he coined the term "military-industrial complex":

> *Now this conjunction of an immense military establishment and a large arms industry is new in the American experience. The total influence – economic, political, even spiritual – is felt in every city, every Statehouse, every office of the Federal government.*
>
> *We recognize the imperative need for this development. Yet we must not fail to comprehend its grave implications. Our toil, resources and livelihood are all involved. So is the very structure of our society.*
>
> *In the councils of government, we must guard against the acquisition of unwarranted influence, whether sought or unsought, by the military-industrial complex. The potential for the disastrous rise of misplaced power exists and will persist.*
>
> *We must never let the weight of this combination endanger our liberties or democratic processes. We should take nothing for granted.*

When Eisenhower gave this speech, military and healthcare constituted 9% and 5% of the U.S. economy, respectively. Today, the military has shrunk to 3% of the economy and healthcare has grown to 18%. Healthcare Inc. is the equivalent of the military-industrial complex on steroids. It seeks its own advantage at the expense of American society by exercising "unwarranted influence" in the design and administration of the U.S. healthcare system.

As with the other macro forces weighing down on the U.S. healthcare system, our purpose here is not to demonize Healthcare Inc.'s size (the largest industrial complex in human history) and influence (overwhelming). Rather, it is to explain how the changing dynamics of governmental involvement in healthcare are exerting pro-consumer and pro-market influence on Healthcare Inc.'s operations.

More effective governmental payment, regulation, and enforcement policies add considerable heft to the other macro forces described in the previous four chapters. Their collective and compounding impact of all five macro forces will impose revolutionary change on Healthcare Inc.'s operations.

For reasons outlined in Chapter 2, the federal and state governments do not have the fiscal wherewithal to pay for healthcare expenditures at rates greater than the overall growth of the economy. As government grapples with fiscal austerity, it has less capacity to accommodate Healthcare Inc.'s ravenous appetite for consuming societal resources. This fiscal reality combined with the desire to make U.S. healthcare more equitable and accountable are pushing the federal and state governments to design and execute more substantial payment and regulatory reforms.

Likewise, antitrust enforcement is targeting market concentration more aggressively to prevent excessive profiteering. On September 21, 2023, the Federal Trade Commission (FTC) filed suit in Texas against U.S. Anesthesia Partners and its private equity sponsor Welsh, Carson, Anderson & Stowe for anti-competitive practices. This marks the first time the FTC has implicated a private equity firm as well as its portfolio company in a fraudulent scheme to generate illicit profits.[3]

Subsequently, Congress began writing legislation to address profiteering by pharmacy benefit managers (PBMs). With similar objectives, the FTC is investigating the business practices of drug wholesalers and group purchasing organizations (GPOs), and the Justice Department is investigating the business practices of the nation's largest commercial health insurance companies. This increasing level of regulatory scrutiny suggests that government regulators are taking more aggressive actions to address Healthcare Inc.'s anti-competitive and consumer-unfriendly behaviors.

In ways big and small, governments are demanding more value and accountability from Healthcare Inc. This chapter explores the changing character of governmental approaches to regulation and payment, the two areas of the healthcare economy where governments exercise the most influence. On balance, we conclude that the federal and state governments are attempting to improve healthcare's market dynamics.

Let's first turn to regulation. Better regulation achieves appropriate balance between oversight and efficient market functioning: too tight stifles innovation and too loose encourages anti-competitive behaviors.

BETTER REGULATION

During 2020, the federal government implemented new rules governing data interoperability (i.e., access to healthcare data) and pricing transparency for healthcare procedures. These new regulations have the potential to become game changers. They seek to liberate clinical, pricing, and claims data frozen within fragmented, inaccessible silos.

Once fully enacted, the new data-sharing and transparency rules will deliver enough sunlight to melt the data silos and light the path to making all relevant health data available to inform and guide both consumers and caregivers. Absent COVID, these new interoperability and price transparency rules would have been 2020's most important healthcare stories.

The War for Data Interoperability

On March 6, 2020, the Office of the National Coordinator for Health Information Technology (ONC) and the Centers for Medicare and Medicaid released their long-awaited final rules governing healthcare data sharing and patients' access to their own health data. This moment was a victory for health data liberation and innovation.

The new data access rules require health insurers and providers to grant third-party developers access to patient health records, including screenshots, through standardized protocols. They further require providers to inform one another regarding patient admissions, discharges, and transfers. Finally, the rules enable patients to get access to their health information through third-party apps that they authorize.

Expansive and secure data interoperability has driven technological value in other vital industries (e.g., banking, telecommunications, transportation). Despite lagging 10–15 years behind other sectors, healthcare will not be an exception. As the new interoperability rules become fully functional, they will unleash America's innovation engine on the nation's most fragmented, inefficient, and consumer-unfriendly industry.

It is important to note that entrenched incumbents within the current healthcare ecosystem do not give ground without a fight. The gloves come off and the big guns come out. Epic Systems Corporation, the nation's largest supplier of electronic health records (EHRs), fought tirelessly to dilute the Department of Health and Human Services' (HHS) well-crafted data interoperability rules.

Epic's fight against the interoperability rules is a textbook case study in how Healthcare Inc. frustrates attempts to improve operating efficiency within the healthcare marketplace. This is the principal reason that healthcare operations still exhibit a 1970s-era character. Chronicling Epic's ultimately unsuccessful attempts to prevent enactment of ONC's interoperability rules illustrates both that pro-market healthcare regulation is possible and that it takes concerted effort to bring it into existence.

Under the banner of patient safety, Epic's normally taciturn CEO and founder Judy Faulkner stepped out of the shadows to persuade health systems to join Epic's cause. She contacted leading health system CEOs in January 2020 to request that they co-sign a letter to then-HHS Secretary Alex Azar requesting a delay in finalizing the proposed rules. Faulkner employed strident language in making her case:

We are concerned that healthcare costs will rise, that care will suffer, and that patients and their family members will lose control of their confidential health information.[4]

Founded in 1995, Epic remains a privately held company. Data on the company's size, impact, and financial performance can be difficult to deduce. A 2023 *Modern Healthcare* report, titled "How Epic Took Over the Hospital EHR Market," found that 47.6% of hospital beds in the U.S. employed the Epic EHR.[5] A separate analysis provided to the authors by David Butz, Ph.D., of the University of Michigan's Ross School of Business, pegs Epic's EHR market share as high as 68% based on hospital discharges.

Like many large companies, Epic pushes hard to conflate its interests with patient interests. Despite Epic's assertions to the contrary, their "walled garden" system of patient data collection, curation, and application contributes to suboptimal care outcomes. It frustrates both practitioners and patients, complicates standardization and limits innovation. Epic's long-held insistence on limiting external access to source patient data may be the single largest impediment to liberating patient data.

There are hundreds, if not thousands, of micro-economies in healthcare where healthcare companies exert monopoly or monopsony pricing power. Epic is among them. The company has monopoly pricing power within the EHR micro-economy. Healthcare monopolists, like Epic, rely upon lax regulation and enforcement to optimize their market positions and profitability. In opposing the new interoperability rules, Epic sought to maintain its control over the use and dissemination of EHR data.

In the Oxford dictionary, "audacity" has two very different definitions:

1. A willingness to take bold risks. *"Her audacity came in handy during our most recent emergency."*
2. Rude or disrespectful behavior; impudence. *"She had the audacity to pick up the receiver and ask me to hang up."*

After earning a graduate degree in computer science from the University of Wisconsin in the 1970s, Judy Faulkner exhibited the first type of audacity. She and a dozen fellow programmers pooled their money to launch Epic in Faulkner's basement. This is the bold, risk-taking type of audacity that people admire and applaud.

Today, more often than not, Epic exhibits the second form of audacity. It pursues its corporate interests with limited regard for others. This is the type of audacity that people deride and fear. More than one health system CFO has told us that Epic has monopoly pricing control over their service arrangements. There are no alternative service providers. If Epic chose to raise its prices expansively, health systems would have no alternative but to accept and pay the increased prices.

Epic restricts innovative companies from accessing source patient data to build vital apps that could improve care outcomes and delivery efficiency. For example, Epic forces companies that participate in its App Orchard to share aspects of their intellectual property while preserving Epic's rights to develop similar technologies. Epic also maintains de facto control over health systems' ability to share patient data with other vendors through licensing agreements.

Still running on 1960s-era Mumps programming language, Epic's data platform is cumbersome. It requires enormous effort to clean and normalize data. This makes even routine template changes expensive and time-consuming to implement. As it increases its share of the EHR market and standardizes its service provision, Epic expects health systems to align their data semantics to Epic, not the reverse. Atul Gawande noted this in his insightful *New Yorker* article, "Why Doctors Hate Their Computers."[6]

While receiving Epic training at his Boston-based health system, Gawande realized that standardizing data entry across hospitals, physician offices, and health systems complicates data entry. What used to take two keystrokes now takes seven. Checking boxes in pre-populated dropdown lists is a repetitive, time-consuming, mind-numbing exercise in frustration that impedes patient care. Gawande concludes the following after using Epic's EHR for three years:

> *But three years later I've come to feel that a system that promised to increase my mastery over my work has, instead, increased my work's mastery over me.*

Gawande is hardly alone among physicians in castigating EHRs. A 2019 study found 70% of physicians suffer stress related to health IT usage. Epic and other EHR vendors have become a form of *Star Trek's* "Borg," a collective organism that acquires knowledge from captured individuals and then forcibly assimilates them into its drone army. The emergence of Borg-like EHRs has increased burnout among frontline caregivers as they endlessly feed clinical data into patients' EHRs for subsequent coding and collection.[7]

In February 2019, ONC and CMS issued its proposed new rules for data interoperability, restrictions against data blocking, and denying patient access to their health records. The rules took two years to draft. They originated from a clear statutory mandate contained in the 21st Century Cures Act as outlined in a summary of the law compiled by the Health Information and Management Systems Society.[8]

> *While the bill is largely known to help fund efforts such as precision medicine, it contains some provisions to improve healthcare IT – most notably, in relation to nationwide interoperability and information blocking. Certain sections are focused on "improving quality of care for patients," with interoperability a main concern. It also places strong emphasis on providing patients access to their electronic health information that is "easy to understand, secure and updated automatically."*

The 21st Century Cures Act received broad bipartisan support. In one of his last official legislative duties, President Barack Obama signed the bill into law by December 13, 2016. Republican Senator Lamar Alexander of Tennessee, chairman of the Senate Health Committee, described the Cures Act as "the most important bill of the year."

Epic opposed the proposed rules from the moment of their release by ONC and CMS. By contrast, Cerner, the industry's second largest EHR

Figure 5.1   Campaigning against ONC's new interoperability rules: Screenshot of Epic homepage on its website from early March 2020.

vendor, was a full-throated supporter of the new interoperability regulations. In an open letter the company's then–CEO and Chairman Brent Shafer wrote that Cerner "opposes any businesses and practices that prevent health data interoperability because empowering consumers is the right thing to do."[9]

It is ironic that Epic led the charge against the new data-sharing rules when it owes so much of its corporate success to the federal government's massive investment in EHR technologies. In 2009, the Health Information Technology for Economic and Clinical Health (HITECH) Act provided $40 billion in new funding to accelerate digitization of U.S. health records.

As the new interoperability rules moved toward adoption, Epic enlisted former Wisconsin Governor and HHS Secretary Tommy Thompson to support its fight against the interoperability rules. During the George W. Bush administration, Thompson oversaw HHS's initial efforts to institute EHRs.

Thompson penned an op-ed in the *Wisconsin State Journal* singing Epic's praises and warning that the proposed new rules would damage both Epic and the Wisconsin economy. In a world where up is down and black is white, Thompson claims the new rules would force Epic to share its hard-earned intellectual property with competitors. The new rules do require Epic and other EHR vendors to share source patient data; however, the rules do not require vendors to share their intellectual property.

Immediately prior to the issuance of the final interoperability rules for public comment, Epic devoted its entire homepage (see Figure 5.1) to discuss the rule's potential negative consequences. A hypothetical "Jim and Ken" case study depicted how an unregulated app publicly revealed Ken's opioid usage through Jim's medical record. Epic compared this to the Cambridge Analytica–Facebook scandal. A second hypothetical case study illustrated how an unregulated wellness app received all the lab results for "Liz" when she thought she had only approved the release of her cholesterol levels.

In both cases, Epic positioned its actions as stepping up to protect the vulnerable public:

> *We have always, and will always, support patients' right to use their data as they see fit. However, it is the role of government to ensure that patients have the information they need to make those decisions knowledgeably, like they have for nutrition and food or labels in the clothes they buy.*
>
> *Patients must be fully informed about how apps will use their data, and apps and other companies must be held accountable to honor the promises they made to patients.*

Despite the intense political pressure, the government didn't blink. In a keynote address at the ONC's annual meeting on January 27, 2020, then–HHS Secretary Azar declared that "scare tactics" would not prevent HHS from implementing necessary reforms.[10] Azar might have had Epic in mind when he made the following observation:

> *Health records today are stored in a segmented, balkanized system. Unfortunately, some are defending the balkanized, outdated status quo and fighting our proposals fiercely. But defending the current system is a pretty unpopular place to be.*[11]

The moment of truth arrived, and HHS implemented its new rules to improve data interoperability, prevent inappropriate data blocking, and grant patients better access to their health data. Better consumer-facing apps are bound to follow.

Ironically, Epic's share of the EHR market has increased since the enactment of the interoperability rules even as it continues to operate a largely closed system. In 2023, CMS expanded the scope of its interoperability rules to incorporate prior authorization information that will become fully operational in 2026. Epic objected to these new provisions as well.

Blocking data is anti-competitive and un-American. Like all data, health data wants to be free, free-flowing, and protected. It wants to move to the places where it can have the most positive impact. Pro-market regulations like HHS's data-sharing rules level the competitive playing field, stimulate innovation, and create value. They make healthcare better.

Transparent Hospital Pricing Data

In another bold regulatory move announced on November 15, 2019, HHS issued a proposed transparency rule governing hospital treatment prices. As documented in a 2020 RAND study, payments by commercial health insurers to hospitals are 2.5-times more than Medicare's for the same treatments.[12] This remarkable payment discrepancy makes healthcare increasingly unaffordable to average Americans.

In an accompanying press release, HHS asserted that the proposed rule would require hospitals to give patients accurate out-of-pocket costs in advance of scheduled treatments.[13] It also would require hospitals to disclose negotiated commercial treatment rates as well as discounted prices for cash payment. These transparency requirements will enable consumers to exercise more control in their healthcare purchases.

Almost immediately, the American Hospital Association and other hospital groups filed suit to block the implementation of the price transparency rules. On June 23, 2020, Judge Carl Nichols of the D.C. District Court dismissed the suit, opining that hospitals' resistance to transparency measures was anti-competitive and restricted fair access to treatment prices.

The AHA appealed the ruling to a three-judge panel of the D.C. Court of Appeals. Oral arguments on October 15, 2020, did not go well. Skeptical judges questioned why patients could not know the price of

X-rays in advance of treatment, since hospitals issue bills for all treatments. The court ultimately decided in HHS's favor and the new pricing transparency rules went into effect on January 1, 2021, for hospitals and July 1, 2022, for health insurers.

The new transparency rules require that hospitals and health insurers post a comprehensive list of standard charges, have a consumer-friendly list of shoppable services, and display contact information for patients who want cost estimates. Hospitals initially slow-walked compliance with the new rules. Many have chosen to pay fines and/or complicate public retrieval of the data.

In response, the Biden administration increased the maximum annual fine on individual hospitals from $109,500 to over $2 million. In addition, CMS has stepped up its enforcement of fines, warning letters, and mandated correction action plans for hospitals. Compliance has improved but still leaves much room for improvement.

One analysis of semi-annual compliance reports that the percentage of hospitals complying with the new transparency rules has increased from 5.6% in July 2021 to 36% in July 2023.[14] It now seems just a matter of time until full and comprehensible pricing information becomes available for all routine elective procedures.

While the Affordable Care Act has increased access to affordable health insurance and established the foundation for greater data interoperability and pricing transparency, it has not yet led to better outcomes, personalized service delivery, and/or lower costs. Expanded data interoperability and pricing transparency have the compounding power to transform healthcare services for the better. Innovative, customer-friendly companies will lead the change.

More Effective Licensing, Resourcing, and Monitoring

"Liquifying" healthcare data represents the beginning, not the end, of the regulatory reforms necessary to create a high-performing healthcare marketplace, one that creates value for consumers and solves their health and healthcare "jobs to be done." These "jobs" are "fix me when I'm broken," "sustain my health," and "enhance my health."[15] The U.S. can only reach this state of market equilibrium when healthcare payment and regulation align with consumer needs and preferences within open and transparent market environments.

CMS is attempting to put its payment mechanics consistent with its care management goals. The agency has implemented several payment codes that support efforts to expand primary care service provision and whole-person health. They include specific payment codes for behavioral health integration (BHI), chronic care management (CCM), principal care management (PCM), remote patient monitoring (RPM), remote therapeutic monitoring (RTM), and transitional care management (TCM).

While noteworthy, these new payment programs are small steps on the journey to value-based care delivery and whole-person health. Other regulatory improvements could and should include the following:

- A complete overhaul of licensing requirements for medical professionals to practice at top of license (no more artificial limitations created to limit supply).
- Elimination of barriers to cross-border service provision (let practitioners, data, and services flow freely across state lines).
- Removal of third-party input in determining fee schedules for Medicare services (get the AMA fox out of CMS' henhouse and stop direct/indirect funding of antiquated academic models for medical education).
- Development of metrics to assess the overall health of distinct populations (focus on outcomes, not process fulfillment).
- Rational patent protection for medical innovation (no more regulatory manipulation to extend patent lives).
- Level-field competition for healthcare's commodity products, most notably generic drugs and vaccines.

Given Healthcare Inc.'s political power and influence, it is impossible to conceive of enacting this magnitude of regulatory reform at the federal level. The industry has captured too much of the nation's regulatory process to achieve the type of revolutionary overhaul required to drive effective market-based reforms.

The anemic federal legislative response to surprise billing (unexpected and usually high-priced bills from out-of-network providers) testifies to the industry's power to shape legislation and regulation in ways that benefit incumbents at the expense of the American people.[16] Fortunately, there are other paths to revolutionary reform.

Taking It to the States

Federal systems, like the one employed in the United States, distribute power between federal and state governments. Among the many powers granted to states by the U.S. Constitution are the ability to levy taxes and regulate commerce. By design, the Constitution grants expansive jurisdiction to the states and limits the powers of the central government. Indeed, the Constitution's 10th Amendment makes this determination explicitly clear:

> *The powers not delegated to the United States by the Constitution, nor prohibited by it to the States, are reserved to the States respectively, or to the people.*

A key attribute of a federalist system is the ability for individual states to become laboratories to test public policies. For example, Massachusetts became the first state to legalize same-sex marriage in 2003. By 2015, when the Supreme Court codified same-sex marriage into law, 70% of the total U.S. population lived in states where same-sex couples could marry legally.

Canada also has a federalist governance model. Its movement to universal healthcare coverage began in the province of Saskatchewan in 1947 with the passage of a hospitalization act that granted its citizens full access to hospital services. It took another 15 years for Saskatchewan to grant universal access to physician services. After withstanding a three-week doctors' strike, Saskatchewan became the first government in North America to offer universal insurance coverage for the equivalent of U.S. Medicare's Part A (hospital) and Part B (physician care) services.

The popularity of universal health insurance spread quickly to Canada's other provinces. By 1972, all 13 Canadian provinces had enacted equivalent coverage. The Canadian government codified its financial contribution to provincial healthcare systems in 1984 with the passage of the Canadian Health Act. On a comparative basis, Canada's life expectancy exceeds that found in the United States by more than five years (81.6 years versus 76.4 years) even though it spends roughly half as much per capita ($6,278 versus $12,318) on healthcare services.[17]

Federalism also plays an active role in U.S. healthcare. In essence, each state (and the District of Columbia) has a unique health system created and governed by applicable state law in concert with federal mandates and coverage requirements.

Among the states, Maryland's "all-payer" model is the most exceptional. It combines uniform payment for all healthcare services within global budgets that cap all hospital and non-hospital expenditure.[18] Since the global budgeting went into effect in 2015 through a CMS waiver, Maryland's per-capita costs of providing healthcare have declined significantly relative to other states. A 2020 review by the Center for Medicare and Medicaid Innovation (CMMI) of its 54 alternative payment programs found that only the Maryland program had achieved cost savings at scale without compromising care quality.[19]

Far-reaching state-based reforms will not be easy to accomplish, but they are doable. Just like Saskatchewan overcame a doctors' strike to achieve universal health insurance coverage, individual states must overcome opposition from powerful and entrenched interests that wish to preserve a broken status quo.

At the same time, first-mover advantages will be significant. A powerful commitment to whole-person health will attract healthcare professionals tired of practicing fragmented care delivery within a broken system. It also will attract investors looking to capitalize on health-oriented business models. Most importantly, it will unleash untold human potential to catapult the state's economic, cultural, and civic initiatives.

BETTER PURCHASING

As mentioned above, governments fund about half of all healthcare expenditure in the United States. That percentage will increase with the aging of the U.S. population. Medicare is the nation's largest single payer for healthcare services.

Medicare uses complex payment formularies to determine payment/reimbursement levels for specific treatments by specific providers. There are over 80,000 ICD (International Classification of Disease) and CPT (Current Procedural Terminology) codes in use today for diagnosing, treating, and receiving payment for medical conditions. These codes are the backbone of American healthcare payment models.

The complexity of healthcare's payment mechanics makes it relatively easy to manipulate claims submissions to optimize reimbursement for services provided. This is the role revenue cycle management plays within the healthcare ecosystem and why it has become such a large segment of the healthcare industry.

Unlike commercial transactions, which are subject to negotiation, Medicare payments flow explicitly from documenting diagnosis and treatment activities in accordance with CMS' payment guidelines. As a result, Medicare payments are usually lower, sometimes much lower, than commercial payments for equivalent services.

Management of Medicare healthcare payments falls to CMS with advice from MedPAC, an independent and non-partisan congressional advisory agency established in 1997. From a macro perspective, CMS tries to manage the overall flow of payments to achieve cost-effective healthcare delivery. Still, its mechanisms for adjusting payment to achieve targeted performance improvement are incremental and often trigger unintended consequences. For example, CMS has reduced payment for homecare services significantly even though home-based care done well epitomizes value-based care.

In an ideal world, Medicare payments would correspond to improvement in care outcomes through better care coordination at lower costs. This rarely occurs. Medicare payment requires significant internal compliance by providers and external oversight/enforcement by the Office of the Inspector General. Even with rigorous oversight, there are high levels of fraud and abuse associated with Medicare payment.

In addition, political influence shapes Medicare payment policies, often in counterproductive and/or value-depleting ways. Under intense political pressure from Big Pharma, CMS allocated future funding at great expense for Biogen's controversial Alzheimer's drug, Aduhelm. Lack of commercial acceptance for Aduhelm enabled CMS to rescind its funding allocation for the drug and add back a full two years to the projected life of the Medicare trust fund.

The passage of the Affordable Care Act in 2010 included the creation of the Center for Medicare and Medicaid Innovation (CMMI) to experiment with new payment models. Even as CMMI's understanding of the market dynamics of payment reform have increased, success has been elusive. The 2020 review mentioned earlier of CMMI's 54 alternative payment models found only five models that generated a positive investment return for CMS. Of these, only Maryland's global budgeting model (described earlier) achieved savings at scale.

Healthcare's Reverse Commons Tragedy

From an economics perspective, tragedies of the commons occur when individuals have financial incentives to overconsume public goods (e.g., individual ranchers overgrazing their cattle on public lands). The "tragedy" occurs when overconsumption lessens or eliminates a public good's future utility. To overcome these types of economic "tragedies," societies establish and enforce rules to govern the use of public goods to preserve their continued utility (e.g., limitations on water use to preserve reservoir capacity).

U.S. healthcare reverses the commons tragedy. It underuses vital primary care services, a very public good. Just as occurs with traditional tragedy-of-the-commons economics, healthcare's reverse commons tragedy reduces societal wellbeing.

Relative to other advanced economies, the U.S. underinvests in preventive, primary, and promotive health and social care services that would both improve overall population health and lower healthcare expenditures. This is a well-documented phenomenon.[20] Why does this occur even as the nation's overall health and average life expectancy decline?

Almost all healthcare providers and payers acknowledge that more investment in primary health and social care services would benefit their communities, yet few organizations make those investments. Providers don't make pro-health investments because they reduce patient volume (i.e., fewer hospital admissions) and revenues.

Likewise, payers don't make pro-health investments because they increase member premiums before they reduce healthcare utilization. Upset with higher premiums, their members disproportionately switch to lower-cost health plans. Asking either providers or payers to make pro-health investments that generate negative financial returns is a recipe for economic and policy failure.

Promoting Whole-Person Health

Many of CMMI's unsuccessful payment models attempted to address healthcare's reverse-commons tragedies through "accountable care" programs that incentivized pro-health service provision. Despite their progressive intent, almost all of CMMI's alternative payment programs have failed to improve the public's health at scale. The programs have been too small in scope, too short in duration, too permissive in design, and too difficult to administer to make a meaningful economic difference.

Beyond CMMI's alternative payment programs, CMS has undertaken other payment initiatives designed to stimulate more pro-health investments and better care outcomes. The most notable is the Medicare Advantage (MA) program, which shifts care management risk from the U.S. government to commercial insurers.

The MA program has had mixed success. MA beneficiaries like the lower premiums and expanded services that generally come with MA plans. Providers, however, often feel short-changed financially by the prices MA plans pay for the clinical services they provide. This perception of underpayment led the Mayo Clinic to stop providing elective services to out-of-network beneficiaries in UnitedHealthcare Group's MA plans.

UHG is the nation's largest insurer of MA beneficiaries and a notoriously tough price negotiator. After several months, Mayo and UHG settled their dispute. However, the fault lines between providers and commercial payers embedded within the private administration of government-funded healthcare programs, like MA and exchange-based plans, remain.

On the plus side, voluntary dual-eligible programs that serve individuals who qualify for both Medicare and Medicaid benefits (basically poor, old, and often very sick people) have been an unqualified success.[21] These programs "solve" healthcare's reverse-commons-tragedy problem through robust monthly payments to enhanced primary care providers.

Dozens of enhanced primary care companies, including Oak Street Health where co-author Paul served on the board, have entered the dual-eligible marketplace with the belief that they can deliver desired care outcomes profitably by providing holistic care management services. These enhanced primary care companies are delivering real value to their members and are well-positioned for growth.

Addressing healthcare's reverse tragedy of the commons requires governments to become better buyers of healthcare services. Governments must apply their purchasing power to advance better health outcomes at lower cost. The Medicare Advantage and dual-eligible programs are examples of health insurance programs that governments are employing to align payment with desired results.

AHEAD and Away

On September 5, 2023, CMMI announced the launch of a new payment model to promote broader and more effective care management. The States Advancing All-Payer Health Equity Approaches and Development (AHEAD) program seeks to replicate the successful Maryland program described previously by partnering with up to eight states on a long-term, voluntary population health payment model. Here's how CMMI described the program in its press release:[22]

The AHEAD Model will test state accountability for constraining overall growth in healthcare expenditures while increasing investment in primary care and improving population health and health equity. More specifically, the AHEAD model will:

- *Focus resources and investment on primary care services, giving primary care practices the ability to improve care management and better address chronic disease, behavioral health and other conditions.*

- *Provide hospitals with a prospective payment stream via hospital global budgets, while including incentives to improve beneficiaries' population health and equity outcomes.*

- *Address healthcare disparities through stronger coordination across healthcare providers, payers and community organizations in participating states or regions.*

- *Address the needs of individuals with Medicare and/or Medicaid by increased screening and referrals to community resources like housing and transportation.*

The AHEAD program seeks to align payment with desired health outcomes at scale. It offers the type of state-based reform that can work within a federalist governance model. Moreover, it addresses the reverse commons tragedy by granting providers guaranteed revenue streams within hospital global budgets. This frees providers to both improve their operating efficiency and make investments in primary and social care services.

Building on the design parameters embedded in its AHEAD program, CMMI announced the launch of an Innovation in Behavioral Health (IBH) model on January 18, 2024.[23] It seeks to integrate behavioral health services more organically into care delivery. Like the AHEAD program, CMMI seeks to test the IBH model in eight states. The program will run for eight years.

The best regulatory and payment reform requires tinkering. It's too early to tell, but the AHEAD and IBH programs may be exactly the type of uniquely American, pro-market payment model that could succeed where so many others have failed.

CONCLUSION: LET THERE BE LIGHT

It is impossible to transform the U.S. healthcare system without governments playing a large and crucial role in regulating and funding an evolving healthcare ecosystem. Constructive governmental regulatory and payment programs can assist in achieving better population health, greater equity, and more efficient healthcare delivery.

The components of transformation are within the reach of America's federal, state, and local governments. It's less about what to do than how to do it. Managing the transition from a vast and reactive "sick-care" system to a smaller, more agile and effective "healthcare" system is an enormous undertaking. Given the fiscal and demographic realities that confront the nation, however, governments really have no other choice but to take up that challenge, manage the transition, and let the chips fall where they may. No more kicking the can down the road.

KEY INSIGHTS ON PRO-CONSUMER/ MARKET REFORMS

- Federal, state, and local governments exercise an expansive role within the massive and highly regulated healthcare ecosystem.
- Of the numerous governmental responsibilities, regulating the healthcare economy and becoming better buyers of healthcare services are increasing in importance.
- The COVID pandemic beginning in 2020 has created a period of punctuated equilibrium that can foster revolutionary transformation of the broken American healthcare system.
- Implementation of new interoperability and pricing transparency rules are illustrative of the types of expansive pro-consumer/market regulatory reforms that can reduce transaction friction and improve supply–demand dynamics within the healthcare industry.
- Healthcare must overcome a unique reverse tragedy of the commons to enable long-term investment in pro-health activities, including primary and preventive care, chronic disease management, integrated behavioral health services, and health promotion.
- Medicare Advantage, dual-eligible programs, and CMMI's AHEAD program are examples of how governments are using their purchasing power to drive better care outcomes at lower costs. While constructive, governments must do much more to drive transformation by becoming better buyers of healthcare services.

This completes our analysis of the relentless macro forces pressing down on the U.S. healthcare system, demanding change. There's nothing the system can do but accommodate the demographic realities unfolding in real time. More effective resource distribution of healthcare's massive expenditures can relieve the funding pressure on the overall economy and reverse the rampaging spread of chronic disease. Technology and enlightened governance are tools reformers can and will use to drive transformation.

The necessary changes that are coming to healthcare may be messy, but they also should be revitalizing. Revolutionary healthcare is at our fingertips. We can feel the tingling. It provides light and hope for a brighter day.

The second half of this book explores how new value-based business models are reconfiguring the healthcare marketplace from the bottom up. Innovative companies are placing enormous economic pressure on entrenched value-depleting business practices.

Feeling the strain, enlightened incumbents are adapting their business models to decentralize delivery of whole-person health. Liberated data and level-field competition are prerequisite conditions for innovative start-up and established companies to develop products and services that deliver kinder, smarter, and more affordable healthcare for all Americans.

PART

II

Market Forces

Introduction:
It's Complicated

In a speech to the National Governors Association on February 27, 2017, then President Donald Trump made the following observation about his efforts to repeal the Affordable Care Act (the ACA or Obamacare):

I have to tell you, it's an unbelievably complex subject. Nobody knew that health care could be so complicated.

With due respect to the former president, those who have wrestled with reforming the U.S. healthcare system going back to the Truman administration and beyond have appreciated its complexity. As articulated by the Institute for Healthcare Improvement (IHI), the "Quintuple Aim" goals of healthcare reform are clear and logical:

1. Improve population health
2. Enhance the care experience
3. Reduce costs
4. Address clinician burnout
5. Advance health equity

The path to achieving these goals, however, is treacherous. It requires balancing competing interests within a highly regulated practice environment with differential pricing for identical services while serving very large and extremely diverse populations. By most measures, the U.S. is at best treading water or even regressing in meeting the IHI's Quintuple Aim objectives. As a result, the U.S. has become an increasingly frail and unhealthy nation.

The profound weaknesses and strengths of the U.S. system were on full display during the COVID pandemic. Relative to other national health systems, the U.S. underperformed on testing, developing care protocols, distributing protective gear (PPE) for medical professionals, providing equitable treatment access, and distributing vaccines. As a result, COVID-related morbidity and mortality were disproportionately high in the U.S.

Concurrently, U.S.-led innovation created effective COVID vaccines in less than a year using newly developed messenger RNA (mRNA) technologies under Operation Warp Speed. Imagine how much higher pandemic deaths would have been without the vaccines.

Our book's defining conclusion is that concurrent macro and market forces are sufficiently powerful to transform the massive healthcare industry, which until now has mightily resisted and forestalled change. In many ways, identifying the macro forces is the easier task. They are like a series of massive comets streaming through outer space. Almost anyone can see them if they choose to look up.

By contrast, transformative market forces are more elusive to categorize, sequence, and illustrate. The authors know this to be true because we have spent countless hours debating how best to present and discuss the strategic positioning of innovative ideas and companies seeking competitive advantage within a dynamic healthcare marketplace.

Albert Einstein astutely observed that "things should be as simple as possible, but not simpler." Not all frameworks are created equal. We've done our best to create one that captures the scope and complexity of healthcare's economic activities without overly simplifying business models, market dynamics, and/or regulatory modulation.

Despite the complexity of synthesizing and explaining these powerful market forces, we believe that America can have its cake and eat it too in healthcare – that a pluralistic U.S. system can leapfrog highly centralized national health systems in achieving the IHI's quintuple aims while cultivating and sustaining innovation.

To achieve Quintuple Aim–level transformation requires the U.S. healthcare ecosystem to overcome some daunting challenges. Below we identify five structural flaws embedded with the current healthcare ecosystem. Each incorporates one of the following single bolded, all-caps words: Cheaper, Better, Balanced, Easier, and Empowered. Each represents a core value-creating strategy. We have encapsulated the five strategies in the acronym $\mathbf{CB^2E^2}$.

- **An immature organizational configuration** that relies on high-cost, centralized delivery mechanisms to provide largely predictable and routine services is too expensive and unwieldy. Healthcare service delivery must become **CHEAPER** without compromising quality or customer experience.

- **Fragmented service delivery** frustrates both caregivers and consumers with excessive administrative burden, transaction friction, over-treatment, undertreatment, and poor customer experience. Even when delivered in the right setting, healthcare service delivery must develop much **BETTER** care protocols and administrative practices to deliver whole-person health.

- **Underinvestment in vital primary, preventive, and promotive care services** exacerbate the expansive spread of chronic disease and declining life expectancy now occurring in the U.S. Achieving whole-person health requires far more than disease management. Even as it improves healthcare service provision, the health system must achieve greater **BALANCE** between vital primary care services and acute care delivery to reduce the incidence of acute disease and improve the nation's overall population health.

- **Inadequate and inconvenient consumer access** to personalized health information, care navigation, and service provision unnecessarily complicates individual care journeys, leads to sub-optimal medical decision-making, and generates significant waste. The U.S. healthcare system must become much **EASIER** for consumers to manage their healthcare needs efficiently at affordable and transparent prices.

- The failure of **underperforming caregivers and disengaged consumers** to unite in joint medical decision-making compromises care delivery and care outcomes. Working in unison, **EMPOWERED** caregivers and consumers will align to personalize care delivery, engage in whole-person health, and improve its health outcomes.

The acronym **CB²E²** provides a shorthand mechanism for categorizing potential solutions for addressing healthcare's structural flaws, i.e., does a particular strategy/business model make healthcare cheaper, better, more balanced, easier, and/or more empowering for caregivers.

In Part I, we identified five macro forces (demographics, funding fatigue, chronic pandemics, technological imperatives, and pro-consumer/market reforms) pushing top-down on the U.S. healthcare system, demanding change. They are indiscriminate and unrelenting. Their collective power is sufficient to kill Healthcare Inc., the massive healthcare industrial complex that over-consumes societal resources while underserving the American people.

Part II looks forward. It describes the rebirth of U.S. healthcare through the decentralized and democratized delivery of whole-person health (3D-WPH- **D**emocratized and **D**ecentralized **D**istribution of **W**hole-**P**erson **H**ealth). While also relentless, the five market forces described in Part II are emerging bottom-up through well-organized and laser-focused companies that deliver **CB²E²** healthcare solutions.

Collectively, CB²E² companies are eviscerating entrenched, inefficient, and ineffective business practices. Healthcare's future belongs to them. Our individual market force chapters described below detail how this reshaping and improvement of healthcare's supply–demand dynamics is unfolding in real time:

- *Force #6: Whole Health* explores strategies for expanding investment in pro-health activities that reduce acute interventions and total-care costs. Investments in this type of "whole-person" care when amplified by "healthy multipliers" enhance health status among distinct populations. Capitated payment models are critical for balancing resource allocation between health-oriented and treatment-oriented activities.
- *Force #7: Care Redesign* describes the initiatives that innovative companies are undertaking to advance whole-person health. Greater use of value- and risk-based payment models by payers support this transformational redesign of care delivery.
- *Force #8: Care Migration* describes the marketplace bets that companies are making to decentralize care delivery in ways that advance whole-person health. Care Redesign and Care Migration represent a one-two knockout punch aimed directly at status-quo healthcare practices.

Force #9: Aggregators' Advantage investigates how innovative companies are assembling a holistic and comprehensive suite of health and care services within a seamless, cohesive, and holistic customer-friendly platform. These "one-app-covers-the-map" companies will become the trusted partners for consumers in managing their whole-person health needs. In the process, they will take control of healthcare's supply–demand service relationships in ways that reward providers that deliver higher-value services.

Force #10: Empowered Caregivers examines business strategies that innovative companies are using to unleash untapped human potential among caregivers. No other investments generate equivalent returns as those that empower employees/caregivers to go the extra mile for their customers/patients. This type of purpose-driven "people power" is unstoppable.

In his book *The Origin of Wealth*, author Eric Beinhocker brilliantly applies Darwin's theory of evolution to marketplace dynamics. In nature, successful mutations emerge, adapt, and amplify into the general population. In this bottom-up way, nature's "fittest" creatures survive and multiply in response to changing environments. As Darwin himself famously observed,

It is not the strongest of the species that survives, not the most intelligent that survives. It is the one that is the most adaptable to change.

Beinhocker postulates that the same bottom-up evolutionary mechanisms apply in the marketplace. Successful business ideas emerge, adapt, and amplify to establish their "market fitness." Companies create, develop, and sell innovative products and services to customers who find value in their offerings. Effective buyer–seller signaling within competitive markets enables efficient resource allocation that optimizes value creation.

The powerful macro forces described in Part I collectively have created the need and conditions necessary for the equally powerful market forces described in Part II to cultivate **CB²E²** health and healthcare business models, adapt them to changing consumer needs, and amplify their presence through value creation.

Like in nature, market evolution embodies fierce competition for survival with clear winners and losers. Based on Marxist economic theory,

Austrian economist Joseph Schumpeter described this type of market reordering as "creative destruction" in his 1942 book, *Capitalism, Socialism, and Democracy*. Healthcare Inc. has blocked the creative destruction of the industry's business practices for decades. This explains why the pressure for transformation now is so pervasive and persistent.

Together, these 10 macro and market forces are bringing the antiquated and bloated U.S. healthcare ecosystem into the modern era. The rebirth of U.S. healthcare cannot occur without the demise of Healthcare Inc. Without fully realizing its vulnerability, Healthcare Inc. is now in its death throes. A new, transformed, more equitable, and uniquely American healthcare system is rising from its ashes. It will dazzle the world and turbocharge U.S. productivity.

6 | Whole Health

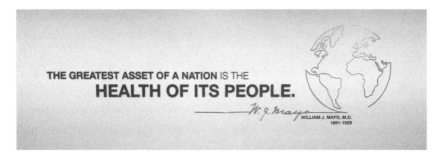

THE GREATEST ASSET OF A NATION IS THE
HEALTH OF ITS PEOPLE.
WILLIAM J. MAYO, M.D.
1861-1939

Figure 6.1

As currently configured, the U.S. healthcare system cannot contain the damage caused by the rampant spread of chronic diseases. Despite trillions of dollars in annual expenditure, the U.S. healthcare system is simply over-matched. The bodies are piling up.

More than all other factors, failure to address the nation's chronic disease pandemics is causing the decline in life expectancy. Massive overinvestment in sick care and massive underinvestment in whole-person health is a uniquely American problem. As a nation, the U.S. must achieve greater balance between the two.

Competing to improve health is very different than competing to improve healthcare. In Chapter 5, we suggest that U.S. healthcare suffers from a "reverse tragedy of the commons" problem. Economists describe individual overuse of a public good as a "tragedy of the commons."

Accordingly, societies develop rules to limit use of public goods to sustain their availability and utility.

U.S. healthcare reverses the tragedy. Relative to other advanced economies, the U.S. underinvests in pro-health programs (a very public good) that generate high societal returns through greater individual and community wellbeing, enhanced productivity, and reduced healthcare spending. Overcoming this economic "tragedy" will require a major societal resource shift away from "sick-care" management into pro-health or whole-health activities that elevate health status, extend life expectancy, and reduce inequality.

We deliberately chose the word "inequality" to end the last sentence. During a 1966 press conference in Chicago, Martin Luther King observed, "Of all the forms of inequality, injustice in health is the most shocking and inhuman because it often results in physical death." Notice that King says "health" not "healthcare" and "inhuman" not "inhumane." King was exactly right. It is unequal investment in health that underlies the "shocking and inhuman" "death gaps" that proliferate in the U.S.

The inequality in healthcare investing can be breathtaking. The Austin neighborhood on Chicago's west side is among the city's most impoverished communities. Its population of 100,000 has a median household income of $40,000 and life expectancy of 69 years. Affluent Lake Forest, a suburban community north of Chicago, has a population of 20,000 with a median household income of $200,000 and life expectancy approaching 85 years.

With billions of dollars on its balance sheet, nonprofit Northwestern Medicine received approval from the Illinois Health Facilities and Services and Review Board in May 2023 for an almost $400 million expansion of its relatively new 201-bed Lake Forest Hospital. Northwestern Lake Forest's new hospital opened in 2018 at a cost of $400 million. Its five interconnected pavilions sit within a 160-acre tree-filled campus that includes 116 acres of open space, a six-acre pond and ample bike/walking paths. The expansion and modernization program will add nearly 100 new beds. Northwestern Lake Forest has a five-star quality rating from the Centers for Medicare and Medicaid Services (CMS).[1]

By contrast, Austin has only one hospital for a population that is five times larger and much sicker than Lake Forest's. The 177-bed Loretto

Hospital opened in 1923. Its website celebrates an $8.2 million capital expansion program completed in 2009. Due to a lack of information, CMS does not list a star-quality rating for Loretto. At 69 years, Austin's life expectancy is roughly 15 years lower than Lake Forest. Should we be surprised?

What's truly remarkable is that American society tolerates this level of inequitable healthcare investment with barely a shrug. *The Washington Post* reporter Dan Diamond makes this point in a compelling December 28, 2023, commentary titled "America has a life expectancy crisis. But it's not a political priority." Diamond notes that America was already trailing other high-income countries in health status before COVID. Despite the dire trend, there appears no political will to counteract it.[2]

Declining life expectancy and increasing death gaps in America's low-income communities are relatively recent phenomena. They are part of a broader, decades-long decline in the connectedness and resilience of American society.

I-WE-I

Robert Putnam is among America's foremost sociologists. He came to prominence in 2000 with the publication of his highly acclaimed book *Bowling Alone*. In it, Putnam explores the decline of social capital in America since the 1950s. The book's title comes from Putnam's research that found many more bowlers in 1990s America but many fewer bowling leagues. That trend of less participation in civic organizations has continued and fuels an increasing surge in social isolation and loneliness.

Addressing the public health challenge of social isolation in the strongest terms possible, Surgeon General Vivek Murthy issued an advisory in May 2023 like one issued in 1964 by Surgeon General Luther Terry warning the public against the dangers of smoking tobacco. Titled "Our Epidemic of Loneliness and Isolation," Murthy details the corroding impact of increasing social isolation within American society while cataloging "the healing effects of social connection and community."[3]

Back to Putnam. Now well into his 80s, Putnam enjoys sifting through old and obscure data sets looking for patterns and insights. It was this exercise that led to a remarkable discovery. When viewed over the 120-year period from 1895 to 2015, economic, political, social, and cultural trends followed

Economic, Political, Social and Cultural Trends 1895-2015

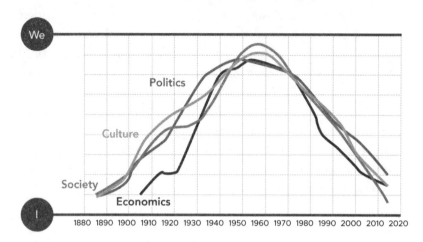

**Figure 6.2   The Gilded Age lives: Economic, political, social, and
cultural trends, 1895–2015.**

Source: Adapted from Heather McGowan, *Data from the Upswing* (Putnam) with
permission of Heather E McGowan.

the same inverted-U pattern (see Figure 6.2). In 2020, Putnam and co-author
Shaylyn Romney Garrett published *The Upswing* to detail this phenomenon.

1895 America was a time of ostentatious wealth and great economic dis-
parity. It also was a time when there was little compromise in politics, limited
cohesion in social life, and almost no cultural affinity. From the early 1900s
through much of the 1960s, American society migrated upward across all four
dimensions. The authors make this point persuasively:

> . . .*on the heels of the first American Gilded Age came more than six decades
> of imperfect but steady upward progress toward **greater** economic equality,
> **more** cooperation in the public square, a **stronger** social fabric and a **growing**
> culture of solidarity.*
>   . . .*By the time we arrived at the middle of the twentieth century, the
> Gilded Age was a distant memory. America had transformed into a more egal-
> itarian, cooperative, cohesive and altruistic nation.*[4]

After peaking in the mid-1960s, the inverted-U curve begins a downward trajectory into the current day. The turning point occurred in the late 1960s and early 1970s, a period of remarkable social, political, and cultural tumult. The authors describe the inverted-U curve as an "I-We-I" pattern where the United States moved from a highly individualistic society to a highly communitarian one and then all the way back again to a highly individualistic one. There is sadness in their account of the downturn:

> . . .*in the mid-1960s the decades-long upswing in our shared economic, political, social and cultural life abruptly reversed direction. Between the 1960s and today. . . we have been experiencing **declining** economic equality, the **deterioration** of compromise in the public square, a **fraying** social fabric and a **descent** into cultural narcissism.*
>
> *As the 1960s moved into the 1970s, 1980s and beyond, we re-created the socioeconomic chasm of the last Gilded Age at an accelerated pace. In that same period we replaced cooperation with political polarization. We allowed our community and family ties to unravel to a marked extent. And our culture became far more focused on individualism and less interested in the common good.*[5]

Unfortunately, the "I-We-I" pattern has also shaped healthcare policy during the same 120-year timespan – first to increase healthcare service access and improve health outcomes, then to diminish access and tolerate declining health outcomes.

Healthcare's Up- and Downswing

First the upswing. As part of his attempt to reclaim the U.S. presidency in 1912, candidate Teddy Roosevelt and his Progressive Party made comprehensive social and health insurance part of their platform. Roosevelt lost the election but the momentum for a national health insurance program continued. In 1915, The American Association for Labor Legislation (AALL) published a draft bill for compulsory health insurance. Initially, the American Medical Association (AMA) supported the bill but then reversed its position in 1920.

During the Great Depression, President Franklin Delano Roosevelt included national social and health insurance as part of his proposed New

Deal legislation. The AMA threatened to mobilize its nationwide network of doctors to block enactment of the law. Responding to the threat, FDR dropped health insurance from the Social Security Act of 1935, which enabled the bill's passage. FDR continued to advocate for national health insurance but could not generate enough support in Congress for a new bill as enthusiasm for big government programs waned and the nation began mobilizing for World War II.

During the 1948 campaign, President Harry Truman was a full-throated supporter of a national health insurance program. After his surprise victory over Thomas E. Dewey, passage of his signature policy seemed within reach. It was not to be. Despite Truman's vigorous efforts, special interests (including the AMA) ultimately blocked passage of the enabling legislation. In his memoir, Truman acknowledged that failure to gain national health insurance for all Americans was his biggest disappointment as president.

Healthcare continued to ride the broader national upswing into the 1960s and 1970s. Bi-partisan problem-solving expanded FDR's Social Security Act by creating Medicare and Medicaid (1965) and by providing universal federal funding for dialysis treatments (1972).

Both parties sought to go further. In February 1974, President Nixon declared that "comprehensive health insurance is an idea whose time has come in America." His administration proposed health insurance for all Americans either through employer-based insurance, assisted health insurance (for lower income populations) and an enhanced Medicare program. Nixon's program received support from the AMA as well as hospital and health insurance associations.

The U.S. appeared on the cusp of passing legislation to provide universal healthcare insurance. History, however, snatched defeat from the jaws of victory. The Vietnam War, Watergate, the oil embargo, and stagflation derailed the bill's passage.

Now the downswing in healthcare policy. As the 1970s unfolded, healthcare policy debate shifted from universal access to controlling costs. Despite this economic focus, healthcare costs continued to rise at highly inflated rates and consume higher percentages of the overall U.S. economy through the 1980s, 1990s, and early 2000s.

As the healthcare industry grew ever larger, the numbers of uninsured Americans also spiraled upward, peaking at 18% in 2010 just before passage of the Affordable Care Act (ACA).[6] Concurrently, obesity and related chronic disease became an increasing concern as the standard American diet, lifestyle, and environment (SADLE) compromised individual and community wellbeing.

SADLE'd and Quartered

Consistent with the upswing's conclusions, Gilded Age levels of inequality are the root cause of America's declines in health status and life expectancy. *The Washington Post* spent a year investigating and reporting on the "nation's crisis of premature death." Their work culminated in an investigative report in 2023 about chronic illness.[7] The report's in-depth analysis focused on adults aged 35–64 and their final judgment on the U.S. healthcare system is harsh:

> *The portrait that emerged shows a nation beset with chronic illness and saddled with a fractured healthcare system that, compared with its peers, costs more, delivers less and fails at the fundamental mission of helping people maintain their health.*

Accompanying their investigative report, *The Post* had a separate article identifying their report's seven core findings.[8] We reprint them here in full to illustrate the full scope of the societal challenges the U.S. must overcome to rejoin the community of healthy nations. *The Post's* summary findings explain why America has become so enfeebled, but they also point toward an obvious solution. As a nation, we need to invest more in health, so that we can spend less on healthcare. Here are *The Post's* findings:

- **Chronic diseases are killing us:**
  The role of opioids and gun violence in claiming American lives has garnered considerable attention, but **it is chronic illness that looms as the paramount threat to Americans in their prime.** *The Post* analysis reveals that those diseases kill far more people aged 35 to 64 than drugs and guns. In fact, chronic diseases erase more than twice as many years of life among people younger than 65 as all the overdoses, homicides, suicides, and car accidents combined. And it is those health woes that create the chasm in life expectancy between the United States and its peers.

- **Gaps between poor and wealthy communities are growing:**

    Today, **the divide in life expectancy between the nation's poorest and wealthiest communities is dramatically wider than it was in the 1980s**, *The Post* analysis shows. But that finding masks another sobering reality: People in wealthy communities in the United States live shorter lives **than their peers in Canada, France and Japan.** The same is true for people in the poorest communities.

- **U.S. life expectancy is falling behind its global peers:**

    Forty years ago, the United States was in the middle of the pack among nations with advanced economies when it comes to life expectancy. **Now, the nation is lagging – and falling further behind.** Experts in peer nations are confounded by the paradox of sagging life spans in a country that spends more than any other on healthcare.

- **The seeds of this crisis are planted in childhood:**

    In recent years, disease trackers and doctors have witnessed the **emergence of a condition rarely seen before in children**, nonalcoholic fatty liver disease. Now that malady is believed to be as prevalent in children and adolescents as asthma. It comes against the backdrop of years of increases in obesity and diabetes in the young. Sweeping changes in the food we eat – the proliferation of ultra-processed food that has supplanted fresh vegetables and fruits – are cited by experts as one potential culprit. That is evident in the schoolhouse, where **packaged meals crafted to conform with controversial federal nutrition guidelines** are served to hungry students.

- **American politics are proving toxic:**

    Decisions made years ago by elected officials are complicit in the nation's life expectancy crisis. Cigarette taxes, seat belt laws, public health spending: Policies on those and other issues help determine rates of chronic illnesses such as lung cancer. A *Post* examination of three counties strung along the shore of Lake Erie shows in stark relief how state policies in Ohio, New York, and Pennsylvania can shorten or lengthen lives.

- **Our bodies are weathering from stress:**

    The damage happens at a microscopic level: Inside us, the wages of American life – inflation, violence, politics, race relations – are **weathering our bodies from the inside out**. Stress is a physiological reaction, hard-wired in the body, that helps protect against external threats. But stress can also do harm, causing illness, disability, and shorter lives. Inside us, **unremitting stress exacts a devastating toll, causing the gears of life to spin too fast** and, eventually, to malfunction.

■ **Answers can be found across the ocean:**

It doesn't have to be this way: *The Post* traveled to **Portugal to explore why that country of 10 million ranks among the nations with the best population health outcomes.** It wasn't always this way. But Portugal's embrace of a wide-ranging health network – built on a foundation of primary care – offers a structural and philosophical road map for reaching at-risk residents early and tackling chronic illnesses. Experts say devoting more resources to primary care in the United States – and **emphasizing health rather than the treatment of illness** – could make for a more robust nation.

The Post's most startling finding is that the death gap, not the income gap, is the most accurate measure of inequality in America today. In 1980, people living in America's poorest 10% of counties died at a 9% higher rate than those in the nation's 10% wealthiest counties. By 2020 – 40 years later– that percentage had increased to 61%, an astonishing 570% increase. The income gap only grew 39% during that same 40-year period.

Digging deeper, *The Post* found that deaths in 1980 among adults aged 35 to 64 were roughly equivalent in urban and rural communities. Since that time, deaths in small cities and rural towns for that same age cohort have increased at an alarmingly higher rate. People aged 35 to 64 in rural areas are now 45% more likely to die than those in the largest cities.

Although they are related, declines in health status more than income disparities are hollowing out of rural America. For this age cohort as a whole, deaths from kidney disease, obesity, diabetes, hypertension, and liver disease are increasing markedly. This is an alarming development.

It's becoming crystal clear that the land of the free and home of the brave is well on its way to becoming the land of the sick and the home of the frail. *The U.S. cannot recapture its greatness without fixing healthcare.* To rejoin the first family of nations, this nation must prioritize health over healthcare. In Chapter 1, we introduced the acronym SADLE as shorthand for the unhealthy Standard American Diet, Lifestyle and Environment. To get back in the saddle and become among the family of healthier nations, the U.S. must overcome and improve its SADLE.

TIME TO CHANGE TACTICS

The year 2024 marks the 50th anniversary of boxing's most entertaining and unusual title bouts, the "Rumble in the Jungle" (Figure 6.3). Staged at 4 a.m. in Kinshasa, Zaire (now the Democratic Republic of the Congo), on October 29, 1974, the legendary Muhammad Ali knocked-out the undefeated heavyweight champion George Foreman to regain his crown. As many as a billion people worldwide watched the event live. They got their money's worth.

Going into the match, nobody gave the 32-year-old Ali a chance against the much younger (25) and heavily muscled Foreman. Of Foreman's 40 wins, 37 had been by knockout. It took Foreman just two rounds to KO both George Frazier and Ken Norton, the only two boxers to defeat Ali up

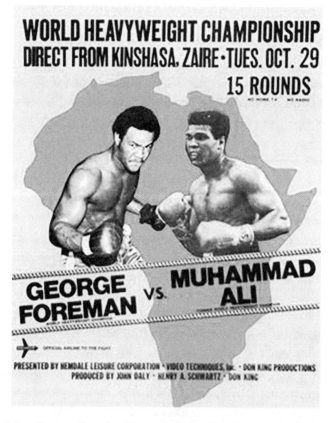

Figure 6.3   Poster for the "Rumble in the Jungle," 1974.

Source: https://en.wikipedia.org/wiki/The_Rumble_in_the_Jungle

to that time. Oddsmakers made Foreman a going-away 4–1 favorite to win the match and retain his title. It turns out that the "smart money" wasn't safe once the two men entered the ring.

Ali had a "secret plan" that he had bragged about to his fans and perfected with his trainer Angelo Dundee. He knew he couldn't beat Foreman in a slugfest. He also worried that dancing away from Foreman ("floating like a butterfly") would deplete his energy and make him vulnerable to a later-round knock-out punch.

Instead, he and Dundee devised an ingenious "rope-a-dope" strategy that turned the tables in his favor. Rope-a-dope exploited Foreman's brutal strength, ferocity, and overconfidence. The idea was to wear Foreman out in earlier rounds as he pounded away at Ali.

Rope-a-dope worked precisely as planned. Beginning in the second round, Ali leaned backward against the ropes and taunted Foreman to attack him. Foreman wailed away with punches to Ali's body and arms. Ali had prepared his body for Foreman's brutal onslaught through rigorous training.

By the sixth round, momentum shifted to Ali. An exhausted Foreman stumbled through two more rounds until Ali landed a devastating left-right combination that sent him crashing to the canvas. After a 10 count, the referee called the match.

Great champions almost always change tactics to stay at the top of their game. New tactics enabled Ali to regain his heavyweight championship title.

Healthcare can learn a valuable lesson from Ali's approach to the Rumble in the Jungle. Rather than continue a losing slugfest with chronic diseases, the U.S. system must change tactics. It can embrace whole-person health. Rather than reactively treating the symptoms of advanced chronic diseases, the system can proactively strive to prevent and/or diminish their lethal impact.

There are two key tactics required to implement this winning strategy:

1. Develop widespread access to integrated primary care services; and
2. Identify and engage vulnerable individuals before their chronic diseases debilitate them.

Other nations like Portugal already do this. The U.S. doesn't need to invent a new rope-a-dope strategy to battle the chronic disease pandemic on more equal terms. It must, however, have the courage and wherewithal to undertake systematic reform to achieve appropriate balance between promoting health and treating disease.

Portugal's Playbook

An article in *The Washington Post* series mentioned above profiled the health journeys of two Portuguese sisters, 63-year-old Lucilia living in Lisbon, Portugal, and 66-year-old Lurdes living in Union, New Jersey. Both suffer from chronic rheumatoid arthritis (RA), a crippling and complex disease that attacks the body's immune system. People suffering from RA often require care from multiple specialists. Despite their many similarities, the sisters' treatment regimens are remarkably different:

> *Almost all the care that Lucilia, 58, receives is carefully coordinated through Portugal's Serviço Nacional de Saúde – the National Health Service – which puts a premium on universal access to primary care.*
>
> *Her sister Lurdes, 66, has cobbled together her treatment in the United States, paying some doctors out-of-pocket or showing up at the ER when her symptoms flare, and sometimes returning to her native Lisbon for more-affordable care.*[9]

Unlike the U.S., Portugal devotes significantly more of its healthcare expenditures to primary care service. In Portugal there are 57 doctors per 10,000 people with roughly half practicing general medicine. By contrast, there are 27 doctors per 10,000 residents in the U.S. The vast majority of U.S. doctors practice as specialists.

Relative to the U.S., Portugal's healthcare bang for the buck is extraordinary. Its 2022 per-capita GDP[10] was less than a third of that of the U.S. ($24,515 versus $76,329). It spends one-fifth of the U.S. per-capita cost on healthcare. Despite these economic discrepancies, Portugal's life expectancy at birth in 2021 is almost five years longer than that of the U.S. (81.1 versus 76.3 years) and rising.

The backbone of Portugal's national healthcare system are accessible health centers embedded within local communities. Overhauled in 2005, these centers include multidisciplinary care teams of family doctors, nurses, and clinical secretaries that focus their attention on at-risk individuals like Lucilia.

These teams also conduct health education, undertake disease surveillance, and collect outcomes data. They feed this information into a central database in real time to guide development and application of treatment protocols.

Like most Americans, Lurdes must cobble together her own care teams that lack access to her entire health record. Fragmentation rather than coordination characterizes her care delivery. Plus, the out-of-pocket costs for Lurdes' care, not surprisingly, are orders of magnitude greater than her sister's.

For these reasons, Lurdes has decided that she will move back to Portugal to be closer to her sister and have access to coordinated whole-person care. There will be many things that Lurdes will miss about living in New Jersey. The U.S. healthcare system will not be one of them.

This chapter began with a quote from William Mayo, M.D. Figure 6.4 captures Dr. Mayo's full quote. William and Charles Mayo founded the Mayo Clinic on the principles of personalized and coordinated care delivery. That foundation of collaborative, team-based care infuses all aspects of Mayo's operations.

In this way, Mayo avoids the fragmentation that plagues other healthcare institutions. It applies a single standard of care universally to all its patients. That translates into standardized protocols informed by interdisciplinary and integrated care teams. Therefore, Mayo care avoids unnecessary treatments, makes fewer medical errors, and improves outcomes.

As Dr. Mayo incisively observes, however, individualism and competitive medicine are root causes of the rampant dysfunction plaguing U.S. healthcare.

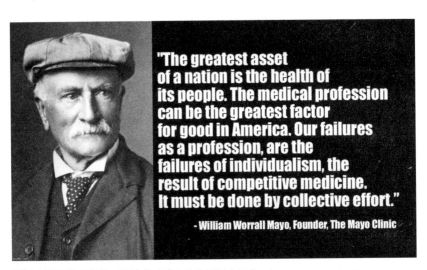

"The greatest asset of a nation is the health of its people. The medical profession can be the greatest factor for good in America. Our failures as a profession, are the failures of individualism, the result of competitive medicine. It must be done by collective effort."

- William Worrall Mayo, Founder, The Mayo Clinic

Figure 6.4   An American dilemma.

Source: WayneBreivogel / Imgflip LLC / https://imgflip.com/i/36m82v

Relentless optimization of perverse payment incentives results in too much healthcare delivery and not enough health promotion and preventive care. Mayo's strong culture supports appropriate care delivery that balances treatments and wellbeing.

Indeed, Dr. Mayo's quote emphasizes that a nation's overall health depends on the health of its people. In this respect, Mayo echoes the timeless wisdom of the Roman poet Virgil who observed over 2,000 years ago that "the greatest wealth is health."

As the Portugal case study makes perfectly clear, delivering exceptional primary care services is not rocket science. There are pockets of U.S. healthcare that embrace whole-person health and that provide cohesive, integrated primary care services. They, however, are the exception rather than the rule. That must and will change. The U.S. is bankrupting itself by not investing enough in preventative, non-emergent care.

Additionally, as an aging country beset by chronic disease, the United States requires a long game to transform its healthcare system. Reform cannot be a one-and-done proposition. Achieving better population health requires reframing and a wider definition of what constitutes appropriate health and healthcare service delivery.

Good population health requires whole-person health, not just isolated, one-off clinical care treatments. Addressing all dimensions of whole-person health in a consistent and comprehensive manner manifests in significantly healthier populations.

The core challenge for U.S. policymakers isn't what to do, it's how to overcome the monumental institutional, cultural, political, and economic barriers that currently block rational system redesign. Overcoming these barriers is prerequisite to achieving the right balance (the second "B" in "CB^{2}E^2") between primary and specialty care, between prevention and treatment, between whole health and healthcare.

The macro and market forces described in this book will force the U.S. to transition to systems that generate better health and healthcare outcomes. It's not a question of whether this will occur, but rather when and how. Given Healthcare Inc.'s current operating profile and historic resistance to change, this transformation will be disruptive, not accommodative, to incumbents. The transformation itself will be exponential, not incremental, in nature. It will be revolutionary, not evolutionary, in impact.

Given the certainty of coming system-wide transformation, we encourage policymakers to stoke the reform fire. They must think outside the proverbial box and exploit opportunities to speed better health outcomes/status at lower costs through appropriate and personalized care delivery and related "health multiplier" investments.

Health-multiplier opportunities are hiding in plain sight. Here's the secret for finding them: Identify communities and programs where focused pro-health investment can meaningfully displace status-quo sick-care delivery. Achieving appropriate health–healthcare balance is the goal.

How can we stimulate more whole-health investment within existing healthcare markets? To answer that question, we consider two real-life pro-health policy opportunities where co-author Dave has taken a visible advocacy role. The first is in his current hometown of Chicago. The second is in his birth state of Minnesota.

REVITALIZING INNER-CITY HEALTHCARE ON CHICAGO'S SOUTH SIDE

The U.S. healthcare system struggles and mostly fails to address the daunting inner-city health and healthcare problems borne out of innate social inequities. Effective solutions are few and far between. One initiative on Chicago's South Side launched just before the COVID pandemic encapsulates the potential and perils of pro-health system restructuring.

In that distant January of 2020, four Chicago safety-net hospitals almost pulled off a miracle. Mercy Hospital and Medical Center, St. Bernard Hospital, Advocate Trinity Hospital, and South Shore Hospital overcame their parochial interests and tried to form a cohesive community health network for their South Side communities.[11]

This was a made-for-Hallmark movie moment wrapped within the cruel realities of inner-city healthcare. Hope and cynicism intermingled as proponents sought to redirect monies away from antiquated hospitals into more distributed, holistic, and community-based care delivery. The question was whether the healthcare system could improve the lives of the South Side's beleaguered residents.

Even as the pandemic raged, the transformation plan gained momentum and widespread political backing for the $520 million in state funding required to cover implementation costs. Then, with the funding bill on the cusp of passage, disaster struck.

Worried about hospital closures and without specific knowledge regarding replacement investments, key South Side legislators withdrew their support on the last day of the legislative session that May. The big transformation program died a quick death. A smaller state-funded transformation collaborative replaced it. Two months later, Mercy announced its intent to close.

Resurrecting and perhaps expanding on the original transformation plan may be Chicago's best chance for improving lives and livelihoods on the South Side. In the process, South Side healthcare could become a model for revitalizing inner-city health and healthcare nationwide.

The Fierce Urgency of Now

The need for healthcare transformation in Chicago's disadvantaged neighborhoods is even greater today than it was in 2020 (Figure 6.5). COVID became a grim reaper in South Side neighborhoods whose residents suffer disproportionately from chronic diseases. Limited access to healthcare services added to the death toll. The human costs of disfigured, disrupted, and lost lives are incalculable.

In his book *The Emergency*, University of Chicago ER doctor Thomas Fisher chronicles the "healing and heartbreak" of treating patients from the South Side during COVID's intense first year. His seething anger and frustration come through in this remarkable passage from a fictionalized letter he writes to a patient named Robert. Suffering from kidney disease, Robert celebrated his 25th birthday in the ER with a gunshot wound in his leg:

> *Families on the South Side have less education, income and wealth, which contributes to diminished access to goods, services and legal protections. . . As a result, Black people, who densely populate the South Side, are forced to endure a gauntlet of health risks: jobs that maim, food that sickens, air that chokes and guns that kill.*
>
> *This would be a simple story of winners and losers, except there is no competition — not a fair one, at least. The contest was decided at birth, and this tournament trades in the most important of human endowments — our health.*[12]

Fisher's anger is justifiable. Far too often, the U.S. healthcare system is unfair, inequitable, uncaring, and unaccountable. Healthcare disinvestment in highly segregated, low-income communities mirrors the broader societal disinvestment in these communities.

The impact of this structural disinvestment on individual and community wellbeing is catastrophic. The ambitions, productivity, and health of those on the losing end of this high-stakes "tournament" wither. As a consequence, South Side residents live shorter, harsher lives. The difference in

Inequity of life expectancy in Chicago

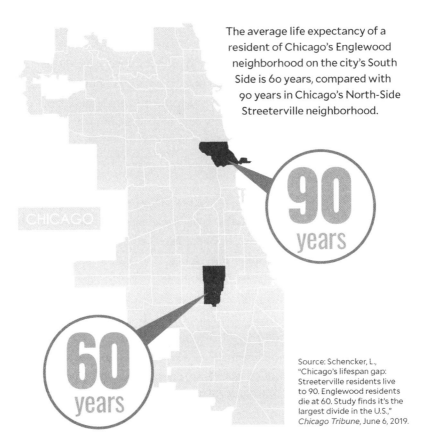

The average life expectancy of a resident of Chicago's Englewood neighborhood on the city's South Side is 60 years, compared with 90 years in Chicago's North-Side Streeterville neighborhood.

Source: Schencker, L., "Chicago's lifespan gap: Streeterville residents live to 90. Englewood residents die at 60. Study finds it's the largest divide in the U.S.," *Chicago Tribune*, June 6, 2019.

Figure 6.5   An unacceptable "death gap" in Chicago.

Source: Healthcare Financial Management Association.

life expectancy between the impoverished Englewood and the affluent Chicago Loop (just 8 miles away) is 30 years, the largest such "death gap" in the country.[13]

Fighting against gravity to preserve an inadequate status quo, the state of Illinois spends hundreds of millions of dollars each year through very complex funding arrangements to support safety-net hospitals. It's wasteful and the equivalent of putting Band-Aids on open wounds. It's a policy that sacrifices community-wide health to protect hospital beds and jobs.

As a nation, we already spend enough on healthcare. We need to spend the money we have more wisely. St. Bernard Hospital's CEO Charles Holland said as much in January 2020 when he observed, "We recognize that it doesn't make sense to keep pouring millions of dollars into aging, outmoded, out-of-date healthcare facilities."

More of the same approach will yield more of these same dismal results. It's time to think bigger and act differently. Incremental improvements aren't enough. The system requires exponential, not incremental, change. Post-COVID, America has a moral imperative to reimagine inner-city healthcare. Why not start on Chicago's South Side?

Health Over Healthcare

In May 2023, Chicago elected Democrat Brandon Johnson as its mayor. "Treatment Not Trauma" became his signature campaign issue and propelled him to victory in a close race. Mayor Johnson now faces the challenge of translating his campaign promises into policy.

The headline from Mayor Johnson's first "Treatment Not Trauma" budget was a modest $4.8 million allocation (out of a $16.6 billion total city budget) to expand mental health services. Imagine how much more "treatment" Chicago could provide by redirecting safety-net hospital funding into vital primary and preventive care services. This type of health-first investment would constitute a galvanizing paradigm shift.

For the uninitiated, the state of Illinois has enacted Hospital Assessment Legislation to bring an additional $250 million in federal dollars to fund "safety-net hospitals" in low-income communities.[14] To generate this funding, Illinois taxes all the state's hospitals to gain access to federal matching funds, which it then redistributes disproportionately to safety-net hospitals.

Most of this incremental funding occurs in lump-sum payments. This is problematic because federal regulations call for phasing out of non-claims-based payments to all hospitals by 2027. This will compromise Illinois' ability to provide ongoing funding to prop up the shaky finances of its safety-net institutions.

Rather than patching up antiquated facilities with low-quality scores to dispense uneven and fragmented care, Chicago and Illinois could align care provision with resident needs. That approach would promote expansive investments in pre- and post-natal care, chronic disease management, and mental health and health promotion services. This policy shift would not only save money, it would dramatically improve health outcomes.

As discussed above, there's already a good transformation plan on the books from 2020. With the exception of Mercy, the original organizations are still there. Put the band back together, dust off that plan, sharpen it up, invite others to participate, and market it aggressively to South Side residents.

Earning South Siders' trust is difficult and can only be won with deeds, not words. This is what "Health Over Healthcare" investment looks like:

1. Build appropriatelysized new hospitals and aligned facilities before closing or repurposing existing institutions.
2. Promise jobs to all existing employees in the new community health network. Healthcare workers are in short supply. It makes sense to redeploy those already employed.
3. Recruit and train an army of people from the community to fill new positions as health coaches, nutritionists, physical therapists, social workers, aids, and technicians.
4. Celebrate the new approach to South Side health and wellbeing expansively.
5. Create health champions within each South Side neighborhood.

When the dust settles, there will be appropriate and sufficient healthcare facilities and services on Chicago's South Side. Overall healthcare spending will decline. Individual and community health and wellbeing will improve. In the process, the City of Big Shoulders will lift up rather than push down its South Side residents.

SENSE AND NONSENSE IN MINNESOTA

In a textbook political move, Minnesota Governor Tim Walz launched a task force in October 2023 to study the University of Minnesota's education and training programs for healthcare professionals. Governor Walz assembled this blue-ribbon panel of experts to respond to the University's ambitious and controversial MPact Health Care Innovation proposal, which calls for the state legislature to fund the multibillion-dollar cost of acquiring, building, and operating a revitalized academic medical enterprise at the University.

The incongruence of the University's MPact proposal is staggering. Minnesota struggles with rising rates of chronic disease and inequitable healthcare access for low-income urban and rural communities. The idea that a massive governmental investment in centralized, high-cost academic medicine will "bridge the past and future for a healthier Minnesota," as the MPact tagline proclaims, is ludicrous.

Like the rest of the country, Minnesota is experiencing declining life expectancy.[15] Despite spending more than double the average per-capita health-care cost of other wealthy countries, the U.S. scores among the worst in almost all health status measures.[16] Spending more on high-end academic medicine won't change these dismal health outcomes in Minnesota or other states. Addressing social determinants of health (what we call "health multipliers") could.

Managerial guru Peter Drucker once observed, "If you want something new, *you have to* stop doing something old." If Minnesota truly wants to improve the health of its residents, it needs to redirect funding away from hospital-centric care into vital, community-based care services that actually improve health status. Such services would include preventive care, health promotion, chronic disease management, and behavioral health services.

The billions saved by not underwriting the University's massive capital plan, for example, could fund "UP4C" (universal primary, pre-natal, post-natal, and palliative care) for several years. Imagine the uptick in health status this type of pro-health investment could achieve in Minnesota's low-income rural and urban communities.

Improving the health of the state's residents will lower Minnesota's total healthcare costs. It also will increase productivity, expand human potential, reduce inequity, and improve individual wellbeing. As with other states and the nation, Minnesota's long-term economic prosperity and wellbeing depends upon its residents' health, not the grandeur of its academic healthcare system.

This debate regarding the University of Minnesota's healthcare enterprise has national ramifications. This won't be the last time we witness a battle to use public funding to prop up unsustainable clinical enterprises. Minnesota can say "no" to more unnecessary expansion of hospital-centric care models and "yes" to a thoughtful, comprehensive, and modern redesign of the University's educational programming and facilities. Putting health first should be the guiding principle in deciding how and where to allocate precious public resources.

Let's hope Minnesota seizes this opportunity to chart a pro-health course of action. As a nation, we need to spend far more on population health infrastructure and far less on acute care facilities. It's really not that complicated. Remember Portugal.

CONCLUSION: A HEALTH-PROPELLED "UPSWING"

What our Portugal, South Side Chicago, and Minnesota case studies have in common is that they stop feeding Healthcare Inc. and amplify pro-health investments. Most importantly, all three resoundingly say "yes" to health. They illustrate how cost-effective pro-health programming can generate expansive human and financial returns.

There are no bigger bangs for the buck than extending individuals' health spans and optimizing their human potential. It's within our power to make the U.S. a pro-health nation again and generate expansive benefits for the nation.

Whole Health is the first of our 5 market force chapters. We placed it up front because it is our North Star. It informs and guides the other four market forces. The organic interconnectedness of the 5 market forces reflects the comprehensive nature of revolutionary healthcare reform. It cannot be done piecemeal. The whole of health must be greater than the sum of healthcare's aggregate interventions. The component parts must work in unison to drive better population health.

Answering whether specific governmental policies or business investments improve the whole health of targeted populations can inform prudent decision-making and resource allocation. Let's revisit this chapter's two case studies.

Should the State of Illinois redirect public monies to create integrated care networks that advance community-wide health on Chicago's South Side? We believe the answer is a resounding, "YES!"

Does spending billions of public dollars funding an academic medical colossus at the University of Minnesota advance community-wide health? The answer is an equally resounding, "NO!"

Maybe, just maybe, with enough pro-health investment, Americans can unite to become healthier together. In the process, we can end a decades-long downswing in our collective health that has made the U.S. population increasingly sick and frail. Viewed from this hopeful perspective, Whole Health can become a force for creating a more just, equitable, and productive nation for all Americans.

As former Cleveland Clinic CEO Toby Cosgrove asserts, "The state of our nation depends on the state of our health." Let's act like our lives and our country's future depend on embracing Whole Health because they actually might.

KEY INSIGHTS ON WHOLE HEALTH

- Consistent with a long-term downswing in societal connectivity, care access and quality gaps within U.S. healthcare have widened considerably. These gaps are contributing significantly to worsening health status among lower-income populations and declining national life expectancy.
- Chronic diseases are killing Americans at record levels. More of the same expensive treatment-centric approach to care delivery will not reverse this trend.
- Despite several attempts and unlike other high-income countries, the U.S. has not been able to secure universal health insurance that provides appropriate access to care services for the American people.
- The U.S. healthcare industry needs to change tactics to deliver better outcomes. Other countries, like Portugal, offer integrated and community-based primary and social care services. As a result, they achieve better health status for their populations at significantly lower expenditure levels.
- Policymakers and investors can accelerate the transition to whole-person health by redirecting resources away from acute care facilities and into pro-health activities. Chicago and Minnesota case studies illustrate ways in which this could occur.

7

Care Redesign

Powerful incumbents rarely transform of their own accord. Complacency creates a static managerial mindset. Once-great companies built on innovation and value-creation retrench. Most, once they become entrenched incumbents, use their scale and leverage to inflate sales and optimize profitability rather than using their advantages to build and deliver better products and services for customers.

Consequently, disruptive change almost always comes from the outside. Agile competitors with new energy, ideas, and value-creating business models challenge status-quo thinking. Not bound by legacy investments, products, and practices, these new competitors offer exciting new value propositions to customers. Underestimated at first, disruptive companies gain traction gradually and then steal market share suddenly. Too often, entrenched incumbents are blindsided. They fail to respond effectively to these emerging and often existential competitive threats.

As documented in this book's introduction, U.S. healthcare operates in much the same disease-, physician-, and hospital-centric manner that it has for the last century. Healthcare's share of U.S. GDP has grown from 7% in 1970 to 18% today even as adult obesity and the chronic disease it triggers has grown from 15% to 43% of the population. Rather than transform to meet the chronic disease pandemics, Healthcare Inc. has resisted change, expanded status-quo business practices, and optimized profitability to the detriment of U.S. society.

Too often, Americans forgo vital care to save money or can't get access to services they desperately need. Managerial arrogance and complacency predominate. Despite abundant rhetoric to the contrary, U.S. healthcare does not provide value-based services. Only disruptive innovation can save U.S. healthcare from itself.

There are numerous parallels between the U.S. healthcare industry today and the then-dominant U.S. auto industry of the 1970s. A toxic managerial mindset led Detroit's Big Three automakers to pursue ill-informed, short-term, profit-oriented strategies that ultimately backfired and brought the industry to its knees.

Incumbent healthcare companies are falling into the same managerial trap. Too many ill-advised strategies by healthcare incumbents are setting the stage for system-wide failure.

We focus our editorial lens on the Ford Motor Company to illustrate the larger story of how value-driven competitors disrupted slow-footed incumbents. The transparent message for healthcare leaders is don't pursue short-term profits at the expense of longer-term value creation. This strategy can and will lead to ruin.

FORD'S BETTER IDEA?

Just before the hammer fell on the U.S. auto industry, Ford commissioned its long-time advertising partner J. Walter Thompson (JWT) to design a new

Figure 7.1   Ford's 1968 advertisement.

campaign to lure baby boomers into buying Ford vehicles (Figure 7.1). Launched in 1968, JWT's "Ford has a better idea" marketing campaign continued throughout the 1970s. JWT embellished its new slogan visually by substituting a light bulb for the "o" in Ford. The authors still remember the catchy "better ideas" commercials featuring smiling boomers enjoying their new Ford cars and trucks.

Irony can be cruel and great advertising never compensates for bad product designs and flawed business practices. It was during the 1970s that the U.S. auto industry surrendered its global leadership position to higher-quality vehicles imported from Europe and Japan.

For decades, oligopoly manufacturers General Motors, Ford, and Chrysler (the "Big Three") had devalued quality and safety to maximize profits. They incorporated "planned obsolescence" into vehicle designs and used their political clout to minimize regulatory interference. These proverbial chickens now came home to roost for the Big Three.

Short-sighted corporate behaviors ultimately brought this bedrock U.S. industry to its knees. During congressional testimony in 1953, General Motors CEO Charles Wilson proclaimed, "As goes GM, so goes the nation." At the time, GM was the world's largest corporation by a wide margin. In 1956, the Big Three ranked 1, 3, and 5 on the "Fortune 500" list.[1] U.S. manufacturing dominated the global economy.

Hubris aside, the U.S. auto industry was so big and powerful that few questioned the accuracy of Wilson's declaration. The bigger they are, the harder they fall. And no industry today is bigger or has farther to fall than U.S. healthcare.

Government bailouts have kept the American auto manufacturers and its suppliers intact. It's taken decades for GM, Ford, and Chrysler to regain their competitive footing. Today, Volkswagen and Toyota are the global leaders in auto manufacturing. Ford and GM rank 4th and 5th respectively. Chrysler is now part of the European conglomerate Stellantis.

Pinto Malevolence

Going back to the 1970s, the saga of the Ford Pinto and the decline of U.S. auto manufacturing serve as a cautionary warning to healthcare incumbents who place secondary importance on quality, safety, and value and who believe U.S. healthcare is impervious to disruption.

Beset by higher fuel costs triggered by inflation and the oil embargoes, American consumers began buying sub-compact vehicles in record numbers during the 1970s. Racing to respond, American manufacturers pushed new sub-compact vehicles into production. In short order, Ford's Pinto became America's most popular small car. In all, Ford sold over three million of these vehicles. Ford's profits on Pintos were astronomical but ultimately went up in flames.

In its September/October 1977 issue, *Mother Jones* published an in-depth investigative report titled "Pinto Madness." From the beginning, Ford knew that rear-end collisions ruptured Pinto fuel tanks and risked incinerating the cars' occupants.

Ford conducted 11 secret crash tests on the Pinto prior to the car's sales launch in September 1970. The tests averaged 31 miles-per-hour on impact. The fuel tanks ruptured in 8 of the 11 cars. Minor, low-cost modifications on the remaining three cars kept their fuel tanks intact. Nonetheless, Ford sold new Pintos to an unsuspecting American public without modifying its flawed fuel tanks.[2]

On average, Ford required 43 months to take a new vehicle from concept to production. Ford's then-president, Lee Iacocca, who subsequently became Chrysler's CEO and flirted with running for U.S. president, shortened the Pinto's development span to 25 months. That required Ford to "tool up" its Pinto assembly lines as it finalized the car's design, making subsequent design changes more expensive to execute.

Meanwhile, Iacocca set stringent guidelines that the new Pinto could not weigh more than 2,000 pounds nor cost more than $2,000. Following Iacocca's mandate, Ford's "bean counters" rejected adding a one-pound $11 plastic insert that prevented gas tank punctures as too expensive and too heavy.

Almost immediately, fiery Pinto crashes began killing and maiming people inside the vehicles. In response, JWT dropped the final line from a radio ad that proclaimed, "Pinto leaves you with a warm feeling." Seemingly indifferent to the human carnage, Iacocca frequently observed, "Safety doesn't sell." He continued to push Pinto production and sales levels higher without fixing its fuel tank glitch.

Ralph Nader came to prominence in the 1960s with the publication of his book, *Unsafe at Any Speed.* His advocacy led to the passage of the Motor Vehicle and Traffic Safety Act (MVTSA) in 1966. That legislation created the National Highway Traffic Safety Administration (NHSTA) to regulate vehicle safety.

As exploding fuel tanks killed more and more Americans, "Nader's Raiders" lobbied aggressively for better regulation governing rear-end collisions (Federal Motor Vehicle Safety Standard 301). Implementation of Safety Standard 301 would have required Ford to undertake a massive and expensive vehicle recall program to fix the Pinto's defective fuel tanks. Ford decided to fight its promulgation.

No one resented regulatory interference more than Ford's chairman, Henry Ford II, the eldest grandson of Ford's legendary founder of the same name. This Henry Ford fought tooth-and-nail against the MVTSA. When it became law, Ford employed armies of lawyers and lobbyists to delay and water down new safety regulations.

It took eight long years to implement Safety Standard 301, which went into effect for model-year 1977 vehicles. During that time, rear-end Pinto collisions needlessly devastated thousands of lives.

Ford's most effective delaying tactic was cost-benefit analysis. Under industry pressure, the NHSTA determined in 1972 that the cost of human lives killed and maimed in traffic accidents was $200,725 and $67,000 respectively.

With this information, Ford successfully argued that the benefits derived from fixing Pinto's design flaw (hundreds of lives saved from death and injury) did not justify the $11-per-vehicle cost. It was better, evidently, to accept the preventable deaths and injuries. Henry Ford II continuously thundered that implementing Safety Standard 301 might force Ford "to close down."

The final paragraph of the *Mother Jones* Pinto article notes that the draft Motor Vehicle Safety Act included criminal sanctions for manufacturers who willfully sold unsafe cars. The auto industry lobbied those provisions out of the final legislation. The article ends with this provocative sentence: "One wonders how long the Ford Motor Company would continue to market lethal cars if Henry Ford II and Lee Iacocca were serving 20-year terms in Leavenworth for consumer homicide."

Hitting Bottom and Repositioning

Lawsuits, operating losses and declining sales ultimately caused Ford to shift its strategic orientation. When all else fails, do the right thing. Reeling from a sullied public image, Ford changed tactics. Under new leadership, the company embraced "Quality is Job 1" as its organizational mantra in 1981. There would be no more planned obsolescence or frivolous cost-cutting. In making this pivotal strategic shift, Ford put consumers back in the driver's seat.

Ford commercials of that era feature line workers extolling their personal commitment to manufacturing high-quality vehicles. A sign above proclaims, "Build it as though you're going to buy it." This campaign marked the beginning of Ford's long comeback to respectability and profitability as it worked to regain the public's trust.

Current healthcare operations mirror the dysfunction, greed, and intransigence exhibited by the U.S. auto industry in the 1970s. The level of physical, emotional, and financial harm inflicted on ordinary Americans by a callous healthcare system today, however, is orders of magnitude greater than that inflicted by the Big Three automakers at their worst.

It took a crisis of confidence for the U.S. auto industry to regain its bearings and organize itself to deliver consistent high-value products and services to its customers. U.S. healthcare now confronts an equivalent crisis of confidence. Business as usual is no longer working. It's time to do the right thing. It's time to make value "Job 1."

Better outcomes at lower costs with great customer service (i.e., value) is a timeless business strategy. Following this strategy, the most innovative healthcare companies today are designing their service platforms to achieve CB^2E^2 outcomes. They pose the same type of competitive threat to healthcare's outdated business practices today that foreign automakers posed to Detroit's Big Three in the 1970s.

As it was in the 1970s, the writing is on the wall today for healthcare incumbents. Disruptive change, like winter, is coming. They must either pivot toward value or lose market relevance.

VALUE'S DISRUPTIVE ONE-TWO COMBINATION

There is a growing realization that good health requires a "whole-person" focus. Healthcare in America is sick care. Practitioners apply a clinically driven approach to treating disease and illness. It patches up damaged people without addressing the root causes of their disease.

The human and financial toll of high-cost centralized care is triggering a crisis of confidence in U.S. healthcare. Healthcare Inc.'s monochromatic view that healthcare only works in delayed and expensively whiplashed ways compromises its ability to treat the whole person. Reactive care of an aging and increasingly sick population results in worse health outcomes and higher costs. Like the U.S. auto industry in the 1970s, U.S. healthcare today needs better ideas.

After World War II, it was Japanese, not American, automakers that developed and executed "better ideas" for building cars and trucks. In the process, the term "Made in Japan" shifted from meaning shoddy manufactured goods to the highest-quality products.

Management guru Peter Drucker exercised outsized influence on the Japanese industry. His theories for optimizing industrial production emphasized teamwork and employee empowerment. He recommended putting workers into "quality circles" to minimize manufacturing errors and enhance efficiency. Drucker preached that continuous performance improvement achieves higher-quality outcomes by eliminating wasteful practices. Japanese business leaders were great students.

Producing efficient, high-quality cars supported by excellent customer service transformed Toyota, Honda, and Nissan into global leaders. As sales of their cars increased, Japanese auto manufacturers producing lower-cost, higher-quality vehicles became an existential competitive threat for Detroit's Big Three automakers. It became a "do or die" time for Ford, GM, and Chrysler.

Like U.S. car companies in the 1970s, traditional U.S. healthcare companies confront an existential challenge from new competitors and new business models. These disruptors, however, are home-grown on American soil. Their disruptive "better ideas" promote expansive primary care services within an integrated "whole-person" framework that practices continuous performance improvement.

"Advanced" or "enhanced" primary care promotes health, prevents disease, and manages chronic conditions proactively. Organizations practicing continuous performance improvement strive for consistently better outcomes, lower costs, and enhanced consumer engagement.

This one-two combination of enhanced primary care and improved care delivery are at the center of value-based business models that are challenging and disrupting entrenched and outmoded healthcare business practices. Care redesign focuses on expanding primary and social care services to promote whole-person health. Care migration addresses improved care delivery through more appropriate and efficient resource allocation throughout an expanded care-delivery continuum.

An individual's health is not simply a function of excellent clinical care, even though that's where the U.S. healthcare system devotes most of its effort and funding. Rather, health and wellbeing encompass a much broader spectrum of activities than clinical diagnoses and treatments. Addressing broader health needs through late-stage clinical care means the system is intervening too late to meaningfully improve health status.

The Commonwealth Fund's "Mirror, Mirror" analysis periodically compares the U.S. healthcare system across these five categories with health systems in 10 other high-income countries: Care Access; Care Process; Administrative Efficiency; Equity; and Healthcare Outcomes.[3] Its last assessment was in 2021. The results were not good.

The U.S. system finished second in Care Process and last in the other four measures. As a result, the U.S. system's composite ranking was last by a wide margin (see Figure 7.2) even though we spend over two times as much per capita as comparable nations on healthcare expenditure.

Health Care System Performance Compared to Spending

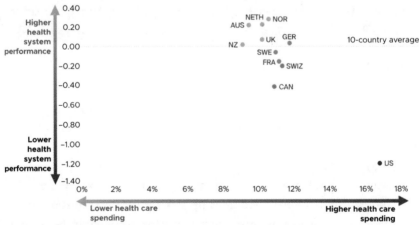

Note: Health care spending as a percent of GDP. Performance scores are based on standard deviation calculated from the 10-country average that excludes the US. See How We Conducted This Study for more detail.

Data: Spending data are from OECD for the year 2019 (updated in July 2021).

Source: Eric C. Schneider et al., *Mirror, Mirror 2021 – Reflecting Poorly: Health Care in the U.S. Compared to Other High-Income Countries* (Commonwealth Fund, Aug. 2021). https://doi.org/10.26099/01DV-H208

Figure 7.2   Negative outlier: U.S. healthcare system spends more and performs worse.

Source: Reproduced with permission of the Commonwealth Fund.

Here is the report's concise conclusion:

Four features distinguish top performing countries from the United States: 1) They provide for universal coverage and remove cost barriers; 2) They invest in primary care systems to ensure that high-value services are equitably available in all communities to all people; 3) They reduce administrative burdens that divert time, efforts, and spending from health improvement efforts; and 4) They invest in social services, especially for children and working-age adults.

How can the U.S. healthcare system close the gap between it and those found in other high-income countries? The answer is really quite simple – by pursuing value-based services that "solve" health and healthcare "jobs-to-be-done." By accomplishing this, U.S. healthcare will become cheaper, better, balanced, easier, and empowering (CB^2E^2) for American consumers.

Combining whole-person health with consumerism is the path by which the U.S. can improve the overall health status of its people. Unleashing the American innovation engine to enhance outcomes and improve health status is how the U.S. can catch up and even surpass the performance of healthcare systems in other high-income countries. That journey begins with, and must encompass, an expansive approach to whole-person health.

WHOLE-PERSON HEALTH

The overarching conclusion from Part I ("Macro Forces") is that more of the same narrow, last-minute, acute treatment–centric approach to tackling the nation's declining health status is a recipe for financial and social disaster. The overarching solution to addressing the U.S. healthcare crisis is achieving greater balance between the nation's investments in health and healthcare. Practicing whole-person health achieves that balance. Delivering whole-person health at scale is the unifying concept around which the healthcare marketplace is reorganizing.

While the concept of whole-person health has ancient historical roots, its modern incarnation originated within the Veterans Administration (VA) in 2011 under the leadership of Dr. Tracy Gaudet. Faced with an aging and chronically sick population, Gaudet created the "Circle of Health" (see Figure 7.3) to guide the VA's individualized approach to care delivery.

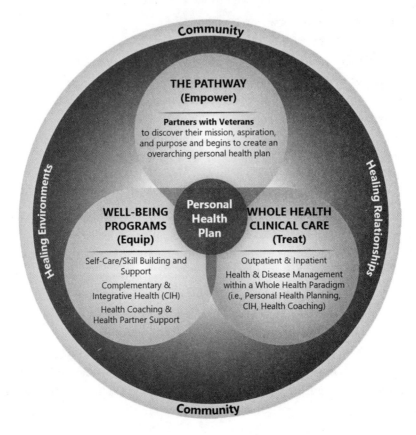

Figure 7.3   Veteran's Administration's "Circle of Health"
Source: Created by Dr. Tracy Gaudet.

Gaudet's approach emphasizes community- and relationship-based care conducted in partnership with veterans within healing environments. The VA describes its Whole Health program as follows:

> *Whole Health is VA's approach to care that supports your health and wellbeing. Whole Health centers around **what matters to you**, not what is the matter with you. This means your health team will get to know you as a person, before working with you to develop a personalized health plan based on your values, needs, and goals.*

Every whole health medical visit includes these two questions for patients: What is most important to you, in your life, right now? What is the thing that you would be willing and able to do today or tomorrow to move closer to that? Answers to these two core questions shape individualized care plans.

Shifting focus to whole health has enabled the VA to proactively address health-related issues, such as homelessness, mental health challenges, loneliness, and food insecurity, that historically were beyond their service mandate. The results have been remarkable. The VA achieves better care outcomes with a sicker population at two-thirds of Medicare's per-beneficiary cost.

The rest of the healthcare industry is taking notice. The VA's pioneering work on whole-person health is influencing the design of other risk-bearing care management payment models, including many Medicare Advantage and Medicaid managed care programs.

For our purposes, whole-person health has the following four components (see Figure 7.4): (1) Clinical Care; (2) Behavioral Care; (3) Activities of Daily Living (ADLs); and (4) Social Determinants of Health (SDoH or Health Multipliers). Particularly for chronically ill people, integrating these four components into individualized care plans stabilizes and improves their overall health.

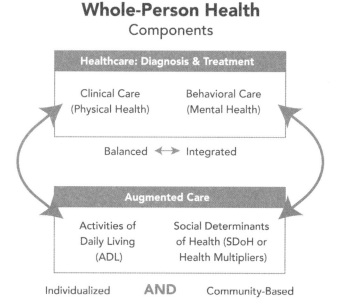

Figure 7.4 Whole-person health requires a comprehensive approach.

This type of integrated care delivery represents CB^2E^2 care in action. It not only improves health outcomes for patients, but also costs less and places less stress on the system, patients, and caregivers.

Clinical care encompasses diagnosis and treatment activities for physical impairment to the body from disease and injury. Behavior care integrates with physical care to treat mind and body together. One without the other compromises care outcomes and health status, particularly for individuals with chronic conditions.

Augmented care is vital non–clinical care that increases independence and improves wellbeing. Attending to ADLs enables compromised individuals to function independently in their environments of choice. SDoH/ Health Multipliers seek to understand and address environmental factors that detract from an individual's health status and life quality.

Components of Whole–Person Health

There are obvious correlations among these four elements of whole–person health that drive individual wellbeing. The essence of clinical and behavioral care is diagnosis and treatment. The benefits of great clinical care are obvious. The U.S. excels at diagnosing and treating clinical ailments.

Fragmented, undertreatment and underfunding of mental health conditions, however, has alarmingly high and costly consequences. Optimal care delivery integrates physical and behavioral health therapies.

However, diagnosis and treatment of clinical and behavioral conditions constitute only half of the equation for delivering whole-person health. ADL and SDoH are components of augmented care. Less understood and applied, augmented care services incorporate the individual and community-based context in which providers deliver care. Proper delivery of augmented care services is often the difference between achieving good and poor health outcomes.

Following care plans becomes impossible for individuals with cognitive and/or physical limitations, particularly if they reside in communities that lack access to products and services that amplify health status. Ignoring these obstacles to optimal care delivery compromises life quality and shortens life spans.

As with behavioral care, there is growing appreciation that appropriate augmented care enhances health outcomes. Accordingly, governmental and private payers are implementing new programs with financial incentives that improve the individual and community context in which healthcare companies deliver care. The good news is that proactive augmented care delivery generates both improved health outcomes and positive financial returns by reducing subsequent need for acute treatment interventions and institutionalized care.

Sidney Katz first identified the ADLs in 1950 to identify a person's functional status by measuring their ability to complete basic self-care tasks. There are five core ADLs: eating, bathing, toileting, dressing, and transferring (being able to get out of bed or a chair). Loss of any two usually triggers insurance coverage for personal care services from licensed health aids. ADL service provision can occur at home or within institutions.

A September/October 2023 report in the *American Journal of Occupational Therapy* states that "greater functional ADL impairments. . .were significantly associated with worse outcomes." Adding, "Lower ADL function (toileting, bathing, grooming, etc.) on admission exhibited a longer length of stay, had an increased risk for hospital-acquired conditions, and were more likely to discharge to a post-acute facility instead of going home."[4]

There is strong correlation between loss of ADL independence and declines in mental health. Centers for Disease Control and Prevention (CDC) research finds that it is important to "initiate preventative (ADL) measures" concurrent with the onset of chronic illness.[5]

Social determinants of health – SDoHs, or what we term as "health multipliers" – constitute the final component of whole-person health. The CDC defines social determinants of health as "Life-enhancing resources such as food supply, housing, economic and social relationships, transportation, education and healthcare, whose distribution across populations effectively determines length and quality of life."

The U.S. Department of Health and Human Services identifies the following five broad SDoH categories:

1. Economic stability
2. Educational access and quality
3. Healthcare access and quality
4. Neighborhood and built environment
5. Social and community context

Together, these factors powerfully influence health quality and care access. As expected, poor and rural communities rank lower on these criteria. A 2018 Kaiser Family Foundation report indicated that, to the extent it exists, Medicaid funds much of the nation's SDoH programming.[6] Not surprisingly, the report further notes that individuals living in communities with poor SDoH experience higher levels of stress, which contributes significantly to mental and physical decline.

Nutrition and Loneliness

Two important health multipliers that deserve specific mention are improving nutrition and reducing social isolation because they are powerful triggers for the onset of debilitating chronic conditions. Addressing these "root-causes" of disease in a proactive and thoughtful manner is implicit within whole-person health. Tackling these challenges effectively marries social care with healthcare service provision to enhance individual and community wellbeing.

Co-author Paul serves on the board of PurFoods, a company that provides healthy meals to people with food insecurity. Delivered mainly as a Medicaid benefit, PurFoods helps reduce malnutrition and unhealthy food consumption, which foster the onset of chronic disease and related treatments. Additionally, PurFoods prepares disease-specific menus for individuals with diabetes, kidney disease, cancer, and other conditions. Food really is medicine. Research has demonstrated that proper nutrition dramatically improves health outcomes.

As discussed previously, social isolation and loneliness are becoming a major public health concern. Author Jeremy Nobel, M.D., the founder and president of Project UnLonely, has found that improving social connection translates into better health outcomes.

An innovative personal care company named Papa proves Nobel's contention. As Papa's website (papa.com) proclaims, the company "helps health plans and employers connect members and their families to real people for help with companionship, everyday tasks, transportation, and more. It's vital human connection, right to the front door."

Indexing Whole Health

Having actionable data to predict and apply the components of whole-person health is prerequisite to achieving better outcomes. This is easier said than done. Many companies are working diligently to collect, analyze, and apply personalized clinical and social data to create individualized care plans. These data sets are massive and often require significant "cleansing" to become accurate and actionable.

Importantly, big data analytics accelerates providers' ability to address consumers' specific health and healthcare "jobs to be done" within a whole-person health service model. Not only does data-driven whole-person care deliver the right clinical care delivered at the right time in the right place at the right price, but it also facilitates more expansive preventive care and health promotion. The result is better health outcomes and fewer acute episodes.

The elegance and potential of whole-person health is what inspired Dr. Katie Kaney to write *Both/And: Medicine and Public Health Together* (published in 2023). Kaney's research establishes that individual health outcomes derive from the following four factors: behavior, genetics, social/environmental factors, and clinical care.[7] These factors interact with one another to trigger positive and negative health outcomes. Kaney's research supports our earlier observation that focusing exclusively on clinical care is woefully insufficient to improve the public's health.

Building on her research, Kaney has developed a Whole Person Index that collects and analyzes data in these four categories. Her model is predictive, where it "prioritizes areas for intervention to prevent demise and promote stability" (see Figure 7.5). Like many similar tools, Kaney's Index exemplifies how innovative companies are using data to proactively advance individual and community health.

Consistent with Kaney's research, the Bipartisan Policy Center has found that clinical care accounts for only 10% of an individual's length of life and quality of life.[8] Social and economic factors, health behaviors, and the physical environment account for the other 90%. Other studies peg the percentage of clinical care's contribution to overall health as high as 20%.[9] Whatever the actual percentage, non-clinical factors drive most of the health status.

As a consequence, the U.S. needs to expand beyond clinical health services to enhance individual and community wellbeing. In this race to achieve improved individual and community wellbeing, payers appear to have a competitive edge over providers in advancing whole-person health. Figure 7.6 illustrates how some commercial health insurers are reconfiguring their strategies and operations to amplify the benefits of providing whole-person health services to their members.

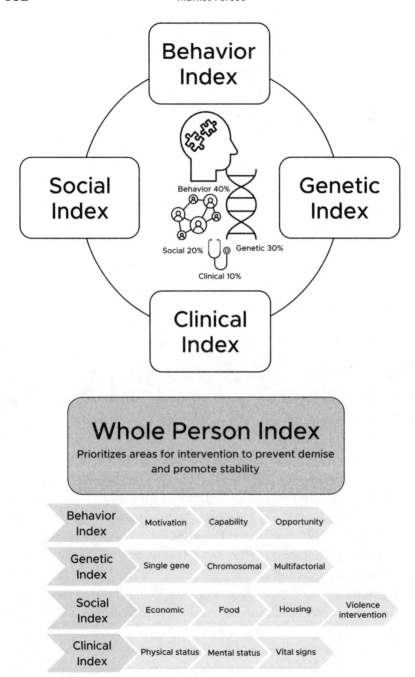

Figure 7.5   Whole-person index: Clinical, social, behavior, and genetic components.

Source: Katie Kaney.

Payers Migrating Toward Value

Like the VA has done, commercial and other governmental payers want to reduce wasteful and preventable hospital admissions. They are finding ways for their members to receive care, when appropriate, in more convenient and lower-cost settings.

Toward this goal, many are building and/or contracting with delivery networks to provide clinical procedures outside hospitals. Their investments have propelled increases in the numbers of outpatient clinics, ambulatory surgery centers, specialty hospitals and facilities, rehab facilities, and outpatient physical therapy centers.

Beyond acute care services, payers are assembling post-acute networks with skilled nursing facilities (SNFs), inpatient rehabilitation facilities (IRFs), assisted-living facilities (ALFs), and home health services to transfer their members out of hospitals more quickly into lower-acuity, lower-cost facilities, including the home. Additionally, payers (and at-risk providers) are testing and deploying technologies – such as telehealth, remote monitoring, and wearable monitors – to track their members' health and identify emergent issues. The goal in all these endeavors is, whenever possible, to triage and care for members outside hospitals.

Co-author Paul spearheaded care redesign efforts for Humana, a large commercial insurance company. Humana became an early market leader in Medicare Advantage, which requires more active care management for beneficiaries under capitated contracts. This commitment to care management was the underlying reason that Humana chose to exit the group commercial health insurance market in February 2023.[10]

After querying members' service preferences and identifying its competitive strengths, Humana invested in the following four areas to buttress its Medicare Advantage service offerings: home healthcare, primary care, pharmacy benefits, and clinical informatics.

Humana's investments in these four service lines improved the quality and reliability of their members' care while expanding Humana's revenues. During Paul's five-year tenure (2009–13), Humana also started to acquire clinical data tools that tracked and predicted changes in members' health status and calculated future clinical trajectories.

Like Humana, the UnitedHealth Group (UHG) and its huge $71 billion subsidiary, Optum, have been the industry leaders in vertically integrating their risk and care management activities to improve care outcomes and

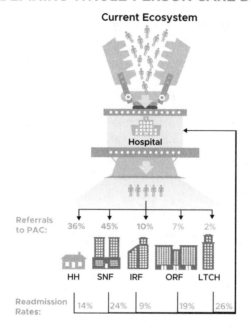

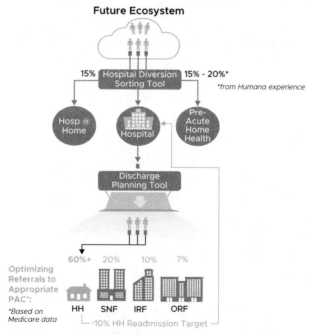

Figure 7.6 **A payer's journey: Migration from fragmented, treatment-centric care to whole-person health.**

Source: Paul Kusserow and Nick Muscato.

efficiency. With over 70,000 physicians in 2,200 locations, Optum is now the nation's largest employer of physicians. Optum assembles care management assets to help its client health plans optimize their members' care. This expansive platform diversifies UHG's revenue mix and enhances their capacity to retain and attract plan members.

The capital markets – as measured by stock prices – favor the payers' competitive positioning over publicly traded health systems that have not redesigned operations to deliver whole-person health. Whether payer or provider-led, companies that can coordinate and monitor individuals within comprehensive care plans are well-positioned to gain market relevance.

Among providers, only general practitioners, internal medicine doctors, and nurse practitioners have the training and experience to monitor patients longitudinally and manage their long-term-care risk. Interestingly, these are exactly the types of care professionals that payers are aggressively acquiring and bringing into their care networks.

Acquired by CVS in 2023, Oak Street Health is among the new breed of advanced primary care companies that deliver efficient and superior care to complex patients. Founded in Chicago, Oak Street Health locates primary care clinics in working-class neighborhoods to serve Medicare Advantage and dual-eligible Medicare-Medicaid beneficiaries (basically old, poor, and often very sick individuals). Co-author Paul formerly served on Oak Street Health's board.

Oak Street Health's business model centers on developing strong personal relationships with their patients/members for whom they accept full financial risk. As a result, Oak Street Health often provides services where other providers have not and emphasizes Augmented Care services. Keeping their members as healthy as possible improves health status, reduces hospitalizations, and lowers total care costs.

These case studies and factoids suggest that healthcare's future belongs to those payer and provider organizations that can manage the care for individuals and distinct populations under fixed payment arrangements. This is as it should be.

Putting It All Together

Whole-person health works. Addressing individuals' total health and healthcare needs pays off in better health outcomes and lower overall healthcare expenditures. Whole-person health prevents unnecessary hospitalizations and delays or negates the need for institutionalized care.

Companies like Oak Street Health that practice whole-person health deliver superior care for 65 to 75 cents on the dollar. Equivalent application of whole-person health at scale will generate better health outcomes and cost billions of dollars less. This is why the payers, like Humana and UHG, are acquiring and contracting with as many risk-taking physician groups as they can find. Their members become healthier and happier even as it costs less to manage their care.

Individual health reflects multifaceted clinical and non-clinical factors. This should surprise no one. Tailoring health and healthcare services to the totality of individual needs and preferences makes eminent sense. It's why all other high-income countries already do this. By contrast, fee-for-service payment models fund piecemeal care without the obvious benefits of holistic care delivery.

The beauty of value-based payment models is that they incentivize providers to address patients' clinical and non-clinical needs. They're also more effective at curbing chronic illness and limiting acute episodes.

A uniquely American model of whole-person health is getting traction in Columbus, Ohio. Let's get under its hood.

AHOY COLUMBUS: HEALTHCARE'S NEW-FOUND TERRITORY

The first line of Shakespeare's Sonnet 116 is among the most provocative in English literature, "Let me not to the marriage of true minds admit impediments." In Columbus, the "two minds" are JP Morgan Chase & Co. (JPMC) and Apree Health. JPMC is the nation's largest commercial and investment bank. Apree is a whole-person health company that is reinventing "the way patients access and engage with care, the way providers deliver care, and the way employers and other purchasers pay for care."

There are no "impediments" (i.e., intermediaries) in the JPMC-Apree "marriage" (i.e., contractual relationship). JPMC contracts directly with Apree for their services, and Apree has performance guarantees tied to patient outcomes and population health measures. Sticking with English poetry, John Keats might describe the JPMC–Apree relationship as "a thing of beauty and a joy forever."

No Safe Haven

Our Columbus story begins with a press release on January 30, 2018, that sent thunderbolts into the healthcare marketplace. On that day, JPMC's CEO Jamie Dimon joined with Jeff Bezos of Amazon and Warren Buffett of Berkshire Hathaway, to announce a partnership "to address healthcare for their U.S. employees with the aim of improving employee satisfaction and reducing cost."[11]

These three titans of industry further announced the creation of a yet-to-be-named new company to provide "simplified, high-quality and transparent healthcare at a reasonable cost." Market reaction to the announcement was immediate. Stock prices for publicly traded healthcare companies tumbled. UHG, CVS, and Anthem shares lost more than 7% of their value.

In the press release, Buffett described ballooning healthcare costs as a "hungry tapeworm on the American economy." Bezos emphasized that success would require "talented experts, a beginner's mind and a long-term orientation." For his part, Dimon was both granular and grandiose when he observed:

Our people want transparency, knowledge and control when it comes to managing their healthcare. The three of our companies have extraordinary resources, and our goal is to create solutions that benefit our U.S. employees, their families and, potentially, all Americans.

Amid much fanfare and under intense scrutiny, the new company became Haven and hired the prominent surgeon and author Atul Gawande as its CEO. Dimon, who originally conceived the venture and sold the concept to Bezos and Buffett, was the only one of the three CEOs to participate actively in advancing Haven's pilot projects.

Haven, however, failed to realize its massive potential. It ceased operations in January 2021. Commentators cited data inadequacy, bureaucracy, inadequate market leverage, payer resistance, an overly ambitious agenda, and the partners' competing priorities as reasons for Haven's demise.

Morgan Health

Disappointed, but wiser and still committed to making U.S. healthcare better and more affordable, Dimon went back to the drawing board. On May 20,

2021, just four months after the Haven shutdown, JPMC launched a start-up business unit named Morgan Health and seeded it with $250 million. The new company combines a sizable venture fund with a big media platform and a "laboratory" (JPMC's 285,000-plus insured U.S. employees and dependents) to test new tools and approaches to managing the health and healthcare needs of self-insured populations.

Dimon selected Dan Mendelson, a seasoned healthcare operator, investor, and policy wonk, to assemble the Morgan Health team and get the new company up and running. Mendelson had worked on the Balanced Budget Act of 1997 and the Children's Health Insurance Program (CHIP) in the Clinton administration, was an operating partner at Welsh Carson Stowe & Anderson, and was the CEO/founder of Avalere, a large and influential healthcare consulting and advisory company.

Under Mendelson's leadership, Morgan Health has established an ambitious strategy: "Our mission is to improve the quality, equity and affordability of employer-sponsored healthcare in the U.S."[12] In essence, Morgan Health wants to enable self-insured employers to become better buyers of healthcare services.

That is sweet music to your co-authors' ears. Our biggest disappointment in U.S. healthcare has been the inability and/or unwillingness of self-insured employers, who pay premium prices for health insurance coverage, to realize greater value for their healthcare purchases.

Mendelson believes that it is vital for Morgan Health to work closely with commercial health insurers to drive industry transformation. He believes that payers have the distribution networks necessary to amplify the impact of the innovations that Morgan Health's portfolio companies are developing to improve employer-sponsored healthcare services.

The Morgan Health team has been busy. As of February 2024, Morgan Health has invested $155 million of its allocated capital with companies focused on advanced primary care, navigation, quality-of-care analytics, affordable health plan alternatives, and fertility. Perhaps Morgan Health's first and largest venture investment to date is its most interesting and promising. On August 5, 2021, Morgan Health invested $50 million in Vera Whole Health, a pioneering advanced primary care company. The company is now managing the care for JPMC's 36,000 employees and dependents in and around Columbus, Ohio.

Free to Be Apree

On September 12, 2022, Vera Whole Health closed an all-cash merger with Castlight Health. Days later, the new company rebranded as Apree (see Figure 7.7) and hired former Cerner President and self-professed "data geek" Don Trigg as its CEO. From Trigg's perspective, Apree combines Vera's advanced primary care (APC) services with Castlight's digital and care navigation platform to create a powerful and personalized vehicle for managing the care of commercial populations.

Like Mendelson, Trigg is a policy wonk and serial entrepreneur. He co-authored *The New Health Economy: Ground Rules for Leaders* (published in 2022). Trigg likes to say that he "has spent the last two decades waking up at the intersection of healthcare and IT." Trigg's experience and orientation align perfectly with Apree's mission to "reimagine how we deliver and pay for care."

Among his many duties at Cerner, Trigg managed the network health and value-based care strategies for the company's self-insured employees and dependents. As he assumed his new responsibilities, Trigg asserted that Apree had the unique "opportunity to deliver an end-to-end strategy for digital navigation, advanced primary care and member risk management."

Apree works with health insurance plans and self-insured employers in multiple markets throughout the country, but it's staking its biggest claim with JPMC in Columbus.

Chasing Healthcare's Holy Grail

Before diving into Apree's business model and performance, let's first consider how and why this remarkable configuration of talent, technology,

Figure 7.7

capital, and expertise has assembled in Columbus. Scalable, data-rich, tech-enabled platforms that personalize and optimize health outcomes have always been just over the horizon in U.S. healthcare. Dozens of companies have crashed and burned in pursuit of this "Holy Grail" platform play. Healthcare's innate complexity, pluralistic service delivery, cultural variation, data fragmentation, and artificial economics have been too daunting for that vision to become reality.

Castlight is one such example. Morgan Stanley took the company public in 2014. So great was its promise to bring rationality to healthcare pricing through data transparency that its valuation soared to $3.5 billion, 107-times revenue and almost 10-times more than its 2022 valuation.[13] Castlight's battle scars inform Apree's understanding of what technology can and cannot do to advance care outcomes and population health.

Continuing the theme, lessons learned from Haven's failure have informed JPMC's design for Morgan Health and its insistence that any investments must work first and foremost for JPMC's employees and their families. That's why the firm's HR department is Apree's client, not Morgan Health. Vera Health's early success in developing integrated networks for delivering whole-person health has demonstrated that advanced (and independent) primary care clinics are essential to engaging members in pursuit of their health and healthcare goals.

The pieces of the puzzle are now in place for Apree to scale whole-person health that can deliver the goods (better outcomes, lower costs, great service, customer satisfaction) for a large commercial population. JPMC's Ohio population is a big enough Petri dish to prove its hypothesis and potentially fulfill the quest for delivering healthcare's Holy Grail to the masses.

Without belaboring the point, the JPMC/Morgan Health/Apree enterprise illustrates how disruptive innovation gains marketplace traction. A promising idea emerges. Entrepreneurs experiment with business models to realize its potential. They act on marketplace signals. They learn from failures. They amplify success. The successful few, like Amazon, Apple, and Google, break through and rewire the marketplace's existing supply–demand dynamics.

Let's be perfectly clear. JPMC, Morgan Health, and Apree are on a mission. They want to rewire healthcare's supply–demand dynamics in ways that drive better health outcomes at lower costs with better customer experience.

The Secret Sauce

In our interviews with Mendelson, Trigg, Kevin Wong (Apree's chief medical officer), and Marla McLaughlin (Apree's associate chief medical officer), all emphasized the importance of independent advanced primary care clinics, easy-to-use technologies, risked-based payment models, and performance metrics to build trust, engage members, and create value.

Trigg emphasized the point with a David Ogilvy (the "father" of advertising) quote: "It's impossible to save souls in an empty church." Members have to buy in for the platform to succeed.

Apree describes the three pillars of its operating model as "Total Engagement," "Whole Health," and "Total Outcomes." In pursuit of these goals, Apree's integrated health network focuses on four principles, listed here from their website:

- **Know the person:** We put the person at the center, leveraging the industry's richest data foundation to understand a person's unique health profile and needs.
- **Manage whole health:** We offer an advanced primary care model built around an integrated care team that includes navigators, coaches, and behavior health specialists.
- **Integrate all care:** We integrate the fragmented delivery system to create a single connected care experience regardless of where a person receives their care.
- **Align to value:** We align incentives across purchasers, providers, and patients to prioritize health outcomes and deliver value.

Of course, none of these principles mean anything without appropriate financial incentives and superior execution. Apree's business model and risk-based contracts achieve a "Goldilocks" balance between payment and services that uniformly delivers appropriate care. For JPMC, Apree platform successes translate into better care outcomes, happier employees, and lower costs.

As the healthcare marketplace learned the hard way in the 1990s, capitated payments are not enough to guarantee better care outcomes. Unscrupulous health maintenance organizations (HMOs) used gatekeepers to restrict care delivery independent of outcomes. That's what turned the American public against them.

The demise of managed-care contracting in the early 2000s triggered a broad expansion of fee-for-service payment and steep medical inflation. Given that reality, it is imperative to link financial incentives with desired health outcomes for whole-person health programs to succeed.

JPMC, Morgan Health, and Apree understand the importance of aligned financial incentives. Rigorous documentation and performance measurement are hard-wired into Apree's contractual relationship with JPMC. Here is a partial list of performance metrics that the principals employ to determine payment rewards and penalties:

- Net Promoter Scores
- Utilization/engagement with high-value, advanced primary care (APC) networks
- Responsiveness to appointment requests
- HEDIS (Healthcare Effectiveness Data and Information Set) measures
- Biometric screens
- SDoH screens
- Emergency Department (ED) visits
- Hospital admissions
- Cost savings

JPMC benchmarks Apree's performance against a control group of their employees without active care management. Where possible, the parties measure performance on the total population (36,000 members) and not only those receiving services. JPMC's and Apree's shared belief is that coordinated whole-person care will generate better outcomes and lower costs. Each side benefits when this occurs.

If successful, the JPMC–Apree business arrangement solves healthcare's "reverse tragedy of the commons" (underinvestment in vital primary services) discussed previously. Done well, whole-person care will generate abundant savings that can accrue to both self-insured employers and at-risk providers.

Properly incentivized, Apree proactively engages with members to identify at-risk individuals for earlier and more effective care interventions. Their goal is to match resource deployment (digital, virtual, in-person clinical) to perceived risk levels through evidenced-based protocols. Health coaching is an integral feature of member engagement, so individuals and the care teams together can execute better medical decision-making.

Apree's business model requires independent primary care providers as well as easy and timely access to care services. In Columbus, Apree meets the first requirement through a partnership with Central Ohio Primary Care (COPC), the largest physician-owned primary care group in the United States.

With over 350 internists operating in almost 90 offices, COPC is an ideal partner for Apree to manage JPMC's covered lives in central Ohio. Apree has made it even easier for these members to access care services by augmenting its robust digital and virtual care platforms with five new clinics staffed by COPC professionals on or adjacent to JPMC's Columbus offices.

Apree began its direct contracting relationship with JPMC in Columbus on October 24, 2022. While still early in the relationship, performance metrics suggest Apree is improving health outcomes and could lower JPMC's total-care costs curve while providing an improved customer experience.

Apree's Net Promoter Scores are in the mid-80s. HEDIS scores are trending into top-decile performance. There's been a 90% increase in utilization of Apree's high-value physician/provider network. Over half of those screened positive for hypertension have received follow-up care. The wait for the third available video appointment is only 0.5 days. Twenty-three percent of JPMC's members have engaged with either COPC or Apree since the beginning of 2023. Two-thirds of members presenting for ER care received appropriate treatment in lower-cost and more convenient facilities. The list goes on.

The key takeaway from this case study is that whole-person health works at scale with aligned financial incentives and appropriate resource allocation. In Columbus, Apree is delivering improved access, quality, and member experience at lower costs for JPMC. Traditional providers and payers should be afraid. Very afraid.

CONCLUSION: RECKONING AND REDEMPTION

In 1986, Pulitzer-prize winning author David Halberstam published *The Reckoning*, a 752-page history of the post-WWII industrial competition between the United States and Japan. It took him five years to write and was the third book in his trilogy on America's power centers, following *The Best and the Brightest* and *The Powers That Be.*

The Reckoning details how Japan exploited American weaknesses and emerged as an industrial powerhouse in the 1980s. Halberstam illustrates the larger economic, political, and cultural narrative by examining two leading automakers, Ford in the U.S., and Nissan in Japan. Ford's Pinto debacle, market decline, and subsequent recommitment to manufacturing high-quality vehicles are core elements of that history.

Noted economist John Kenneth Galbraith titled his *New York Times* book review "When Nissan Had a Better Idea," playing on the iconic Ford advertisement referenced at the beginning of this chapter.[14] A review by Sam Quinones relates the story of a 1980s conversation between a politician and GM's CEO Roger Smith regarding a land purchase or exchange where GM had closed an auto plant. In the middle of their conversation, Smith observed, "We're [GM] not in the business of making cars; we're in the business of making money."[15]

Smith's quote captures the rot that develops in industries where corporate purpose shifts from serving customers to optimizing profits. Short-term thinking replaces long-term strategic positioning. Value creation and customer satisfaction become secondary considerations. The *Chicago Tribune*'s review describes the U.S. auto industry at mid-century as "wallowing in narcissism." It ends with this remarkable passage:

> *All this having been said, it must be added that David Halberstam has done something unique and valuable in "The Reckoning." He has penetrated two cultures, one in Tokyo and the other, scarcely less foreign, in Detroit. Out of the conflict between two nations he has fashioned a cautionary tale that makes us understand why we weep for America at the same time that we buy Japanese.*[16]

Pause for a moment on the last phrase, ". . .we weep for America at the same time we buy Japanese." Some may wonder why a book on healthcare reform devotes so much explanation to a decades-ago story of another industry's decline and subsequent repositioning. There is a method to our madness.

The U.S. auto industry in the 1970s and 1980s is the closest equivalent we could find to the market dynamics and strategic turmoil currently confronting U.S. healthcare. Then, like now, a dying but still powerful status quo is clinging to sclerotic business practices that generate enormous profits while undercutting longer-term market relevance.

U.S. healthcare is headed for an even deeper and more disruptive reckoning than the auto industry experienced 50 years ago. Make no mistake. The adoption of whole-person health at scale represents revolutionary transformation. It will purge value-depleting enterprises from the healthcare ecosystem.

Like what happened to the auto industry, healthcare's disruption and transformation will come "outside-in" from external competitors. It's inevitable. The real question is how leading healthcare organizations will respond to this disruptive threat. Will they fight or welcome industry transformation? Time will tell.

What we can say with certainty is that leaders of America's great healthcare organizations have a choice. They can continue their decades-long pursuit of volume-driven, fee-for-service medicine that has plundered societal resources, eroded the public's confidence, and weakened our national wellbeing.

Alternatively, they can choose to embrace value-based care delivery and the movement to whole-person health. This is the courageous choice. It means risking organizational failure while attempting to rewire established and counterproductive business behaviors. Change is never easy and it's going to be exceptionally difficult for an industry that still largely operates with a 1970s-era managerial mindset. The clock, however, is ticking.

Japanese industrialists, as mentioned previously, closely followed the teachings and advice of managerial guru Peter Drucker. Healthcare's leaders should as well. Drucker draws a critical distinction between management and leadership. For him, "management is doing things right." There's an abundance of that by-the-book, we've-always-done-it-that-way activity in U.S. healthcare. Leadership goes farther. It has moral character. For Drucker "leadership is doing the right thing."

Another Drucker maxim is "If you want to do something new, you have to stop doing something old." Bringing these two Drucker insights together, American healthcare needs much more right-thinking leadership with the courage to stop doing old things so their companies can start doing new things.

KEY INSIGHTS ON CARE REDESIGN

- U.S. healthcare is on a parallel path with the U.S. auto industry in the 1970s. At that time, the Big Three automakers prioritized short-term profitability over longer-term value creation for customers. This made the auto industry ripe for disruption from outside competitors. As a result, the U.S. auto industry lost its global leadership position.

- As a national system, the performance of U.S. healthcare ranks last among health systems operating in other high-income countries. Far too many incumbent healthcare companies are pursuing short-term profit optimization at the expense of longer-term value creation. This makes them vulnerable to disruptive innovation.

- The emergence of whole-person health at scale is the disruptive innovation that imperils the current U.S healthcare system. Whole-person health encompasses Clinical Care (physical and behavioral care delivery) and non-clinical Augmented Care (Activities of Daily Living and Social Determinants of Health/Health Multipliers).

- The U.S. Veterans Administration has been a pioneer in advancing whole-person health. It achieves superior care outcomes at significantly lower costs with a very sick population.

- The integration of clinical and social care service delivery tailored to individual patient/customer needs is the strategy that will differentiate winning companies within the broader healthcare ecosystem.

- The partnership between JP Morgan Chase & Co. and Apree Health to manage the care for JPMC's 36,000 employees and dependents in Columbus, Ohio, illustrates how whole-person health is emerging into the commercial healthcare marketplace. The Apree model employs personalized advanced primary care services to diagnose disease earlier, manage care delivery proactively, and promote overall wellbeing.

8

Care Migration

Care Redesign (emphasizing whole-person health) and Care Migration (emphasizing decentralized delivery) constitute the mechanical components of the organic, disruptive, and revolutionary overhaul that is currently occurring within the healthcare industry. The democratized and decentralized delivery of whole-person health (3D-WPH) is the principle around which the marketplace is reorganizing to improve outcomes, advance health, tame rampaging chronic disease, and lower costs.

In the previous chapter, we compared the strategic and managerial mindsets of Healthcare Inc.'s leading companies with those of the U.S. auto industry in the 1970s. In both cases, the bean counters reign supreme. Misplaced emphasis on revenue optimization and profit maximization translates into suboptimal product development and service provision. In both cases, value-oriented competitors challenge and disrupt sclerotic business practices to deliver greater value to consumers.

It was better foreign cars that disrupted the automakers in the 1970s. Today, value-based, whole-person health is the disruptive innovation. It is the first punch of a one-two combination aimed squarely at the jaws of traditional healthcare companies.

The second punch is democratized and decentralized delivery (3D) of whole-person health (WPH) within a digitally connected and humane ecosystem. Care Redesign and Care Migration go together like thunder and lightning. Their ascendance is pre-ordained. The only remaining questions relate to how painful the transition to 3D–WPH will be for healthcare incumbents and society writ large.

It is audacious to compare 2020s healthcare to 1970s auto manufacturers. What we are about to do next is even more audacious. The best historical comparison we can find for Care Migration is the Great Migration of Black Americans out of the Jim Crow South into the industrialized North. As a historical event, the Great Migration began in 1915 and continued until 1970.

While not a business example, the Great Migration captures the idiocentric character of bottom-up societal change. It is through these types of individualistic investments that health companies are striving to decentralize care delivery in ways that deliver value to customers. Their collective power is formidable. After centuries of repression and worse, the Great Migration became a massive, spontaneous, and hopeful expression by Black Americans of their intense desires for freedom and better futures. By sheer magnitude of numbers, individual leaps of faith became a collective movement.

After decades of stagnation, fragmented delivery, and declining health status, the transformational promise of delivering whole-person health expansively is spurring enough investment by innovative companies for the Care Migration movement to achieve critical mass. Individual decisions are creating enough collective strength to topple a still potent but decaying status quo.

GOING NORTH

In her book *The Warmth of Other Suns*, Pulitzer prize–winning author Isabel Wilkerson describes the Great Migration as "the biggest underreported story of the 20th century." Here's the full passage containing this remarkable observation:

> *Historians would come to call it the Great Migration. It would become perhaps the biggest underreported story of the 20th century. It was vast. It was leaderless. It crept along so many thousands of currents over so long a stretch of time as to be difficult for the press truly to capture while it was under way.*

The movement to whole-person health is perhaps healthcare's biggest underreported story. Pushing our analogy further, the organic, bottom-up way in which healthcare is transitioning along "thousands of currents" resembles the Great Migration's defining characteristics. Leaderless change unfolding on a vast canvas takes decades to reveal itself.

Individual healthcare companies seeking market tractions make strategic bets. Most of these "bets" aim to succeed within a decadent and dysfunctional status quo. An increasing number, however, are daring to bet that the future will not mirror the past, that outcomes and value will become the industry's dominant currency. These progressive companies are fueling Care Redesign and Care Migration from the bottom up. They are the ones seeking a true North in U.S. healthcare.

Like the Great Migration, U.S. healthcare is leaderless. It grows of its own accord. There are no healthcare luminaries with enough gravitas and influence to guide the nation into whole-person health. Healthcare lacks the likes of Steve Jobs and Bill Gates, who brought technology to the masses. Momentum toward whole-person health emanates from the many, not the one.

As documented in this book's introduction, healthcare encompasses four of the nation's largest businesses (hospitals, drug wholesaling, drug manufacturing, and health insurance). In this sense, healthcare has competing factions. Leaders of these factions are visible, vocal, and powerful. They act like warlords protecting their share of the realm. Their interests do not align with those of the American people.

Given U.S. healthcare's size and fragmentation, there are few potential leaders with sufficient credibility and influence to demand and direct system transformation. Surgeon General Vivek Murthy has used his bully pulpit to elevate and advance behavioral health into healthcare's mainstream.

CEO Jamie Dimon of JP Morgan Chase & Co. (JPMC), whom we profile in the Apree case study, is a non-healthcare leader making a difference. Under Dimon's leadership and in partnership with Apree, JPMC is pursuing decentralized whole-person care in Columbus, Ohio. Dimon and JPMC have the stature, pocketbook, and market presence in Columbus to bend the system to provide value-based services in that market. Bravo. At the same time, there's only so much Dimon can do. His day job is running the world's largest bank.

In *The Warmth of Other Suns*, Wilkerson chronicles the movement's demographics, politics, economics, and sociology, but then goes further. She also tells the powerful and intimate stories of specific individuals as they leave the South and settle into an uncertain future in new and strange places. She does this to bring coherence to a movement so massive and varied that it defies easy explanation.

The scale and complexity of U.S. healthcare also make it difficult to comprehend in its totality. That is why individual narratives are so crucial to healthcare's transformation (remember Keith and Maria from the Force #3 chapter – both suffered from debilitating and preventable diabetes).

A profound appreciation for the on-the-ground impact of policy and investment decisions must accompany system-wide transformation. The U.S. healthcare system touches every American community. The system's benefits are considerable but so is the harm it causes. Improving the total population's health happens one individual at a time.

To achieve the right balance between resource allocation and desired outcomes, between health and healthcare, requires both a macro under-standing of the forces propelling organizational behaviors and a micro ap-preciation for how the system interacts with individuals and within communities. Oscar Wilde observed that "the truth is rarely pure and never simple." Nowhere is that truer than in U.S. healthcare today.

Competing narratives and interests shape a tumultuous national debate. Grounding health policy deliberations in value, outcomes, and societal well-being is the only way forward. Getting the formula right is difficult.

Americans today are on a healthcare pilgrimage that echoes the vastness and ambiguity of the Great Migration. As this customer and consumer-led revolution gains momentum, the healthcare industry and country will change in profound and beneficial ways.

The movement to whole-person health through distributed service provi-sion requires rewiring almost 20% of the U.S. economy. We believe healthcare's reformation also creates momentum for broader, constructive societal change.

The movement toward a more equitable and effective healthcare system can help repair the societal fabric that binds individuals and communities together. Rather than being a flashpoint for discord, whole-person health can become a unifying force; one where we all get healthier together; where all Americans can lead healthier, happier, and more productive lives.

STAGING DECENTRALIZATION

In 2009, Harvard Business School professor and disruption guru Clay Chris-tensen published *The Innovator's Prescription* with co-authors Jerome Gross-man and Jason Hwang. Christensen's brilliance lies in his ability to discern patterns within chaotic and tumultuous markets, distill their implications, and apply them proactively. In *The Innovator's Prescription*, Christensen applies his theories of disruptive innovation to healthcare.

A consistent theme is the interplay between centralization and decentralization as industries grow and mature, as they move from producing unique high-cost items in centralized facilities to producing low-cost commodity items in decentralized facilities. Christensen characterizes the "disruption" process that fuels this migration from centralized to decentralized production over time as follows:

> . . .*In the beginning stages of nearly every advanced industry, the initial products and services are complicated and expensive. Disruption then "democratizes" these, by making products and services that are simpler and more affordable.*

Staging is an essential component of Christensen's centralization–decentralization framing. Stage Zero occurs in analog environments where people complete tasks by hand. Examples of Stage Zero production include writing letters by hand, using slide rules for computation, and making copies with carbon paper.

Modern technologies bring quantum improvements in the quality, cost, and speed of production. This is when industries experience Growth Wave One. The investments in technology and expertise to achieve these quantum-level improvements are expensive. Consequently, it is more efficient and cost-effective to centralize production.

Over time, industry products and services standardize, even commoditize. Disruptive innovators attack the high costs and inconvenience of centralized operations. In Growth Wave Two, industries begin to decentralize to lower costs, increase efficiency, and improve customer experience. Growth Waves Three and beyond incorporate advances that lower costs, increase efficiency, and improve customer experience even more. These advances activate even more production decentralization.

Applying these growth waves to the shopping experience over time illustrates the centralization–decentralization dynamic in action:

- **Stage Zero:** Customers went from store to store to purchase what they needed.
- **Growth Wave One:** Downtown department stores like Macy's brought a comprehensive range of goods into a central location. Customers go downtown for a "one-stop" shopping experience.

- **Growth Wave Two:** Suburban shopping malls replicate the one-stop shopping experience in locations closer to where customers live.
- **Growth Wave Three, etc.:** Internet retailing enables consumers to shop from the convenience and comfort of their homes. More efficient logistics enables fast and accurate shipping of those purchases directly to homes or convenient pick-up locations.

Christensen also applies these growth waves to medical care to illustrate how healthcare decentralization is occurring (see Figure 8.1):

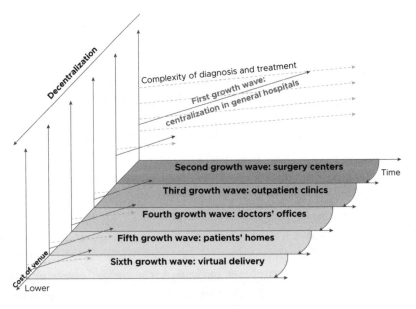

Centralized to Decentralized Care Delivery (Circa 2024)

The waves of growth through centralization and decentralization correspond to disruptive business model innovations.

Figure 8.1   Migration from centralized to decentralized care delivery (c. 2024).

Source: Adapted from C. Christensen, *The Innovator's Prescription*.

- **Stage Zero:** Doctors, nurses, and families took care of the sick in homes.
- **Growth Wave One:** Patients go to general hospitals where doctors and nurses provide care.
- **Growth Wave Two:** Procedures that once required hospitalization can be performed in ambulatory clinics and surgery centers.
- **Growth Wave Three, etc.:** Procedures that once required going to an ambulatory clinic or surgery center can be done in doctors' offices.

What's unusual about healthcare is the extent to which the industry's growth activities have stalled within centralized Growth Wave One. Movement of surgical procedures to lower-cost ambulatory surgical centers (ASCs), doctors' offices, and even the home has occurred and does reduce costs. According to a 2019 report from Bain and Company, ambulatory surgery centers can "offer surgical procedures at rates 35–50% lower than hospitals."[1]

Equally importantly, the Centers for Medicare and Medicaid Services (CMS) has approved more than 300 formerly inpatient-only procedures (IOPs) for treatment in ASCs. This movement of IOP surgeries to ASCs removes a significant percentage of activity from hospitals' most profitable service lines. This is why the publicly traded hospital management company Tenet, where co-author Paul was once chief strategy officer, has shifted its facility portfolio dramatically to include more ASCs and fewer hospitals.

However (and this is a big one), health systems insist on receiving higher hospital-based payments for procedures delivered in lower-cost settings, including ASCs and physicians' offices. Their lobbyists are fighting against site-neutral payment legislation that would require the same payment for equivalent services administered in hospitals, ASCs, doctors' offices, or other venues.[2] Health systems argue they require the incremental compensation to support the 24/7 costs of hospital operations and the community benefit hospitals generate.

Health systems' opposition to site-neutral payment reflects a managerial mindset that feels under pressure to justify high-cost centralized operations when there are better alternatives. This value-depleting managerial orientation will continue until payment models and financial incentives reward value through 3D-WPH.

Like Growth Wave One conglomerates of old, hospitals are high-cost centralized production locations with abundant expertise that endeavor to be all things to all patients. Unless supported by favorable hospital-based payment rules, they resist decanting care delivery to more convenient and lower-cost treatment modalities.

Given the degree of commoditization that has occurred within healthcare, its level of decentralization should be and will become much greater. Irrespective of payment rules, providers should actively be asking themselves what procedures and treatments they can and must decentralize. The list would be long.

The knee-jerk response from industry apologists is that healthcare is different. Healthcare requires centralization to deliver the best outcomes for patients. This assertion represents willful ignorance. The industry has known since the 1970s, for example, that hospital-at-home and home-based dialysis are more effective and are lower-cost treatment options for most patients.

Technological advances in medical procedures make the case for medical decentralization even more apparent and compelling. For example, the massive application and success of telemedicine during COVID illustrate the power, reach, effectiveness, and scalability of virtual care modalities.

Another feature of stunted Growth Wave One healthcare today is the artificial limitations it places on healthcare professionals to practice at the top-of-license. Technological advances in Growth Waves Three and beyond enable lesser-trained professionals to deliver higher-level medical services less expensively with greater consumer convenience. Regulatory and licensing barriers should not impede the advent of these value-creating improvements in care delivery.

Democratization of technological advances can dramatically expand individual capabilities. For example, drone pilots don't require flight training to be effective. Video gaming skills are usually sufficient to master the job's requirements.

Healthcare is ripe for this type of "democratizing" human–machine collaboration. Co-author Dave made this point in an HFMA commentary, "Right-Sizing Physician Training? The Case for Surgical Mechanics," where he questioned the extended surgical training required for doctors to perform routine procedures.[3]

The minimum amount of training required to become a surgeon in the U.S. is 13 years. This makes no sense for specialists or sub-specialists who continuously perform routine procedures, like angioplasties or endoscopies. It's the equivalent of training bicycle mechanics with the same intensity as jet engine mechanics.

With appropriate oversight and safety back-ups, individuals with good hand–eye coordination could perform these procedures effectively with the equivalent of professional training that master electricians receive. Imagine how this type of staffing paradigm could improve delivery efficiency and reduce treatment costs.

Table 8.1 is from *The Innovator's Prescription*. Remember, *The Innovator's Prescription* was published in 2009. The growth potential for medical procedures to advance into Growth Waves Four and beyond with the assistance of generative AI and other path-breaking technologies is far greater today than it was then. New Wave-adding, tech-enabled capabilities like remote surgeries and wearable medical devices represent the proverbial tip of the iceberg.

The world lost one of its greatest business theorists when Clay Christensen died too soon at age 67 on January 23, 2020. Just a few months before, Christensen endorsed co-author Dave's previous book, *The Customer Revolution in Healthcare: Delivering Kinder, Smarter and Affordable Care for All.*

Dave's book applies Christensen's theories of sustaining and disruptive innovation as well as dual transformation to healthcare business practices. Christensen's endorsement came only after his chief of staff reviewed the entire book's manuscript for accuracy.

In awe of Christensen's strategic acumen, we refer to Table 8.1 for insights into how growth waves will shape healthcare's future. With this as inspiration, we'll now get more granular and discuss how decentralized growth is manifesting in "wave-shifting" fashion as healthcare moves expansively into the home.

HOMEWARD BOUND

Samuel Johnson, the famous eighteenth-century man of literary letters, once said, "Home is the ultimate result of all ambition, the end to which every labor and enterprise tends. . . ." In healthcare today, mimicking Johnson's wisdom, home appears to be the destination. There is an accelerating

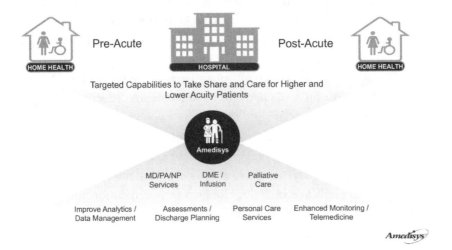

Figure 8.2   **The delivery of healthcare services is transitioning rapidly to lower-cost and more convenient settings, including the home.**

shift in care delivery from institutions into home, community-based, and virtual modalities.

For ease of reference, we term this broader decentralization of care delivery as home-based care. Consumers and payers want alternatives to expensive, inconvenient, and often ineffective care in hospitals, nursing homes, and other healthcare institutions.

The drivers of care decentralization are very clear. The movement to whole-person care relies on the monitoring and treatment of chronic illness in non-acute settings. Consumers, most notably aging baby boomers, increasingly want personalized care delivery in their homes. Post-COVID, new technologies and changing regulations permit higher-acuity care in the home. Increasingly, home is where the health is.

Co-author Paul spent 13 years in the home care business. He's witnessed this transformational care shift first-hand. As Amedisys' CEO, Paul ran the nation's largest and most diversified home care business.

Prior to Amedysis, he managed Humana's buildout of alternative and non-institutional care models. As Humana pivoted to embrace whole-person health, Paul led the effort to acquire physician practices capable of managing the complex care of chronic patients with multiple co-morbidities.

Table 8.1 Cycles of Centralization and Decentralization in Medical Procedures

Stage Zero	Wave One	Wave Two	Wave Three etc.
Doctors examined blood samples through microscopes in their offices.	Blood samples are sent to central labs, where high-speed multi-channel machines run the required tests. Results are then sent back to the doctor.	Tabletop and hand-held diagnostic devices such as Istat brought testing to the physician's office.	Home testing equipment and mail-order services enable patients to monitor their own blood chemistries without having to see a doctor.
Patients have heart attacks, seemingly at random. They recover or die.	Cardiac surgeons perform bypass surgeries in academic medical centers, and later, general hospitals.	Cardiologists perform angioplasty in hospitals, but a cardiac surgeon must be waiting in the wings in case something goes wrong.	Equipment enables cardiologists to safely perform these procedures in ambulatory clinics, without needing a surgeon-in-waiting.
Many doctors' offices had basic X-ray machines.	Patients go to general hospitals' radiology departments, where experts use CT, MRI, and PET scanners to look inside our bodies.	Stand-alone imaging centers bring these machines closer to the neighborhoods in which we live. Trucks even take this equipment into areas that cannot support a permanent center.	Portable, affordable CT and MRI machines are in VAP clinics, operated by surgeons, and integrated into the patient process flow.

(Continued)

Table 8.1 (*Continued*)

Stage Zero	Wave One	Wave Two	Wave Three etc.
Doctors intuited problems by listening through stethoscopes and feeling for lumps.	Ultrasound machines production in radiology departments of hospitals enabled radiologists to see soft tissues in motion.	Smaller, cart-based ultrasound machines became available in many obstetrics and cardiology practices.	Hand-held ultrasound devices are allowing doctors in intensive care units, emergency departments, and primary care clinics to take a "quick look" to help guide diagnoses.
Patients died of kidney failure.	Patients with renal failure were hospitalized, where they underwent dialysis on massive machines.	Ambulatory dialysis centers closer to home are staffed by nurses and technicians.	Small in-home dialysis machines can be operated by patients and family members.
Doctors diagnosed diabetes by tasting whether patients' urine was sweet.	Machines in hospital labs could measure the amount of glucose in a patient's blood. Nurses drew the blood, orderlies carried it to the lab, and technicians operated the machine.	Chemical reagent strips were developed for use in endocrinologists' offices. Nurses drew the blood and compared the color on the strip against a template to estimate glucose levels.	Patients take portable meters – the size of pocket calculators – with them wherever they go. They prick their own fingers and apply a drop of blood onto a reagent strip.

Table 8.1 (*Continued*)

Stage Zero	Wave One	Wave Two	Wave Three etc.
Surgical skill depended on dexterity, among other things. Patients often travel long distances to find the best surgeon.	Surgical robots enable surgeons to perform intricate, minimally invasive procedures with much better outcomes. Only the largest hospitals can typically afford these million-dollar robots.	Remote surgery, in which surgeons control robots from a different site, allows patients to access some of the best surgeons closer to home.	Some surgical robots, such as modern LASIK machines, have become self-contained operating rooms.

Source: Adapted from Clay Christensen, 2016.

Decentralized whole-person health is essential to enabling individuals to age in place affordably and with dignity. AARP research has found that almost 80% of American adults aged 50 and older want to remain in their homes for as long as possible.[4] They are only willing to receive institutionalized care when there are no other viable alternatives.

Consistent with the AARP findings, survey research by the National Institute on Aging (NIA) found that 85% of seniors are confident they can age comfortably in their homes.[5] They prefer to age in place for logical reasons, most notably to stay in homes they like and to be near friends and family.

After hundreds of home visits while at Amedisys, co-author Paul can confirm that patients fight to remain in their homes regardless of how difficult and grim their situations may appear. Absent serious concerns regarding their personal safety, almost all patients elect to receive home-based rather than institutionalized care.

The good news is that technological advances and improvement in care delivery models, including ADL (activities of daily living) and social determinants of health (SDoH or Health Multipliers), make whole-person care available to almost all who want to age-in-place. A trip to Boston illustrates the power of home and home-based care to enrich the lives of both patients and caregivers.

Boston Strong

Elderly patients often build fragile but effective care mechanics for themselves. As they become frailer, they lean more heavily on improvised structures that often appear quite fragile. We disrupt these structures, however, at great risk. While appearing unstable, they usually hold tight when called upon. Paul discovered this on a home visit to an advanced diabetic patient in a working-class neighborhood outside of Boston.

Let's call her Martha. Then in her 80s, she had outlived her husband as most women do. Her house had not been updated in over 30 years. Nothing worked particularly well. The rehab costs to make it safe and livable for an elderly woman on a fixed income were prohibitive. Medicare and Medicaid will pay for scooters, handrails, and stair lifts but not for meaningful home modifications. The logistics of arranging for covered improvements can be daunting. Her son-in-law did Martha's home improvement work himself and cursed the government.

A village of caregivers surrounded Martha. Her family and neighbors stopped by all the time. Her daughter visited daily and helped coordinate her care. Martha's doctor knew her health history and when to activate needed interventions. The local pharmacist explained medication changes to her daughter who made sure Martha took her medications.

As necessary, Amedisys provided homecare services. The Amedisys nurses enjoyed Martha's company. They got to know her well enough to fine-tune their service provision.

Despite her frailty, it became apparent to all that Martha's care network and infrastructure were allowing her to age in place with grace. Whenever the care team discussed moving her into institutionalized care, Martha balked at the idea and said it would "kill her" to leave home. Everyone believed her.

Home Tech

Home-based care costs far less than institutionalized care. On average, home care is a sixth the cost of a hospital, a fourth the cost of an assisted living facility (ALF), a third the cost of a skilled nursing facility (SNF), a third the cost of an inpatient rehabilitation facility (IRF), and much cheaper than buying into a continuing care retirement community (CCRC).

Technology is making home-based care better and more available. Falls are a significant health issue for seniors. PERS (personal emergency response systems) have been available for decades. They are wearable devices that trigger external assistance with the push of a button.

Older readers may remember the Life Alert ads, "Help, I've fallen and I can't get up!" More advanced patient monitoring devices measure gait and balance. They accurately predict when a senior is at risk of falling, enabling caregivers to intervene proactively.

Remote patient monitoring (RPM) devices use existing internet connectivity to monitor a patient's movements and vital signs. Over time, accumulated RPM data creates individualized patient profiles that can detect pattern variation and activate appropriate interventions. RPM not only predicts and detects falls, it also can monitor drug adherence and identify worrisome changes in eating, sleeping, and other routine behaviors.

Going beyond RPM, prominent companies, including Best Buy, Phillips, Google, and Comcast, are creating "smart homes" wired to optimize safety and wellbeing for aging seniors. Powered by digital connectivity these healthier homes are in everybody's future. Telehealth and virtual services will seamlessly integrate into daily life.

Although available for decades, virtual care came of age during COVID when people self-quarantined and the healthcare system halted non-emergent, in-person care. McKinsey and Company found that telehealth visits were 38 times higher on average during COVID.

Even with moderating post-COVID usage, McKinsey estimates that virtual care could replace up to $250 billion of in-person care. It is a particularly effective modality for delivering behavioral health services. Many of the most innovative digital tech companies, including One Medical, apply a virtual-first operating model. This enables personalized 24/7 coverage and access.

Complex At-Home Care

Under co-author Paul's leadership, Amedisys acquired the comprehensive-care-at-home company Contessa and launched a high-acuity home care division within the company. Contessa has three basic service lines: hospital at home; SNF at home; and palliative care in the home. The Contessa delivery platform enables patients with lower-acuity conditions to receive home-based care when they initially present at the ER or have stabilized in the hospital.

Providing hospital-quality care in the home reduces care costs by approximately 30-40% while delivering equivalent or better outcomes. As a result, health insurers contract with Contessa for hospital-at-home care and encourage their members to access Contessa's services. Contessa also partners with the hospitals seeking more cost-effective delivery of care services.

Hospitals often lose money treating low-acuity patients and many welcome their transfer. Most importantly, patients prefer hospital-at-home care. Contessa's Net Promoter Score (NPS) numbers are in the high 80s or low 90s, much higher than scores for hospital-based care. Everybody wins.

Like its hospital-at-home service, Contessa's SNF-at-home service enables patients to receive lower-cost skilled nursing care at home. Contessa's palliative care at home service uses interdisciplinary care teams to optimize life quality for patients with end-stage chronic conditions and minimize their suffering. Like its other two service lines, Contessa's palliative care at home limits or eliminates the need for subsequent institutional care.

Next to the birth of a child, a good death is perhaps the most powerful of human experiences for all involved. Important conversations occur. Transition occurs naturally but the costs of end-of-life care can be astronomical.

Hospice and personal care in the home (PCH) are the remaining two types of home-based care. According to the *Journal of American Medical Association*, a quarter of all Medicare spending occurs in the last year of life.[6] Aligned NIH (National Institutes for Health) research found, "Medicare expenditures increase sharply in the last few days of life, particularly for patients who die in a hospital."

Even with its high costs, or perhaps because of them, most end-of-life care is simply wasteful. At its worst, it increases suffering and leads to earlier deaths.

Hospice and palliative care are growing businesses. Over half of all deaths now occur in hospice. Fifteen years ago, that percentage was approximately 27%. Nine out of 10 patients want to die at home. Hospice and palliative care offer higher-quality end-of-life care at lower costs.

The timing of hospice activation shapes outcomes and total care costs. Patients who enter hospice without taking heroic and usually futile care measures to prolong their lives not only cost less to treat, but they also live longer and experience better life quality. High Net Promoter Scores confirm this.

PCH is non-clinical, home-based care that enhances delivery of ADLs and SDoH/health multiplier services. PCH delivers low-cost, high frequency, eyes-on care that enhances patients' stability and independence. PCH caregivers usually earn just $15 to $20 per hour. Beyond ADLs they help patients in myriad small ways (e.g., preparing meals) and provide meaningful human connection.

Traditional Medicare underpays for vital non-clinical services like PCH. By contrast, Medicare Advantage (MA) plans are beginning to use PCH caregivers to enhance their service provision. Having PCH caregivers in their members' homes provides an additional set of eyes to monitor and report on a patient's health. Integrated PCH services enable earlier and more effective interventions. They enhance whole-person health.

Innovative home care companies are also incorporating PCH services into their whole-person health delivery models. For example, Boston-based CareForth where co-author Paul is executive chairman uses Medicaid funding to employ patients' family and friends to provide PCH care services and monitoring. How smart is that?

As Amedisys CEO, co-author Paul invested in Medalogix, a health tech company that individualizes care planning and improves resource allocation without sacrificing quality. ConnectRN optimizes caregiver scheduling to create more opportunities for nurses to work while maintaining appropriate work–life balance.

As the value of home care service provision has become more apparent, interest in acquiring home care companies has increased. MA plans have acquired the top three home health companies in recent years. At the time of this book's writing, UnitedHealth Group (UHG) is acquiring Amedisys, having already bought the LHC Group, while Humana has acquired Kindred At Home. Together, these three acquired companies represent roughly 20% of the home health market.

UHG and Humana clearly appreciate the incremental benefits that home health services provide within at-risk care management programs. By acquiring industry-leading home care companies, they have locked in access to an undervalued yet vital service. These companies already know what the rest of the industry will undoubtedly learn – that delivering efficient and cost-effective whole-person care requires robust home care capabilities.

THE UNDER-USED AND
OVER-APPRECIATED HOSPITAL

On the Sunday before the start of the 2014 JP Morgan Healthcare Conference, co-author Dave toured the Stanford Medical Center in Palo Alto, California, with a group of Chinese pharmaceutical executives. Being Sunday, the facility was largely empty.

The Chinese executives were dumbfounded. They peppered the tour guide with questions, wanting to know where all the doctors, nurses, and patients were. They couldn't conceive of an expensive healthcare facility not running 24/7. Neither can we.

The underutilization of high-cost hospitals is a uniquely American phenomenon. Other nations run their hospitals much more intensely than U.S. hospitals. They often do this to distribute facility costs over a more expansive patient mix.

The financial profligacy doesn't stop there. Not only are U.S. hospitals less utilized than those in other countries, but they are also more expensive to build. Luxurious facilities with all the bells and whistles drive per-bed construction costs into the millions of dollars.

Chapter 6 chronicled the billions of dollars required to revitalize the University of Minnesota clinical enterprise and the hundreds of millions of dollars to expand Northwestern Lake Forest Hospital. These are just two among dozens of current examples of high-cost healthcare facility investments either in planning or under construction as we write in early 2024.

Despite its massive facility investments or perhaps because of them, healthcare is an outlier among U.S. industries in its limited use of capital-intensive assets. Other industries use their capital-intensive assets almost around the clock. Not surprisingly, manufacturing has a metric for measuring its capital and operational efficiency: production capacity.

The MRPeasy website (MRPeasy.com) describes production capacity as follows:

> *Production capacity is the maximum output of a production facility, measured in finished products over a given period of time. It shows the potential output i.e., the theoretical upper limit of goods able to be produced with production machines, labor, and resources.*

In practical terms, companies measure their actual production against a theoretical maximum production. Here's a common example. There are 168 hours in a week. Production capacity would measure what percentage of those hours a company's production lines are up and running.

Production capacity calculations incorporate time allocated to staffing breaks and retooling. Production capacity percentages in the high-80s and low-90s reflect efficient manufacturing operations.

Operating rooms (ORs) are very expensive to build. A 2022 *Becker's* article reported that cost to be $1.4 million for ASCs.[7] It is even higher for hospitals. Given off-hours and block-scheduling for surgeons, a generous estimate of used OR capacity in typical hospitals and ASCs is 50 hours per week. That translates into a production capacity percentage of just 30%.

Production capacity percentages measure supply. In basic economics, supply and demand intersect and influence one another. When production capacity is greater than demand, companies have surplus or excess production. When this happens, companies reduce their production capacity to meet demand. When there is insufficient production capacity to meet demand, shortages occur until companies can expand their capacity to produce the desired goods.

Based on healthcare's dismal production capacity metrics, there is a massive over-supply of OR capacity. This is true even before incorporating reduced demand for hospital-based care as procedures migrate to lower-cost venues.

Hospitals have a strategic-positioning problem. Rushing to attract patients with higher-paying commercial insurance policies. Health systems are investing in attractive new acute facilities and running them inefficiently even as the demand for those facilities is diminishing.

Hospital apologists will cite staffing shortages for the existence of unused OR capacity, but that doesn't explain the continued boom in OR construction nor does it realistically consider how using technologies and more enlightened staffing protocols (e.g., having healthcare professionals practice at top-of-license) could improve productivity.

Rather than fight Care Redesign and Care Migration, health systems that wish to remain competitive should embrace production capacity as a performance metric. It will lead them to pursue "focused factory" surgical facilities that run longer hours and achieve greater efficiency, better outcomes, and lower costs.

Once again, the answers to healthcare's operating challenges require value-based care delivery. When value is the performance goal, quality becomes "Job 1" and eliminating waste becomes the path to achieving better outcomes.

The market dynamics actually get even worse for hospitals and ASCs when buyers of healthcare services execute better demand management.

DEMAND MANAGEMENT AND DISINTERMEDIATED PROVIDERS

In Chapter 2 we referenced an observation by Intermountain's CEO Rob Allen on hospital utilization. Based on documented research, Allen asserted that 52% of the healthcare services delivered in the U.S. are either preventable or wasteful.

Any movement to value-based care delivery should tackle this overconsumption first and foremost. Providers are doing some of this work by reining in costs. Likewise, payers are more aggressively using payment denials (providers would say too aggressively) to reduce unneeded care.

Self-insured employers have the most to gain by managing total care costs more effectively. One promising strategy employs virtual and non-acute care providers to address lower-acuity medical conditions. Nowhere is this strategy more apparent than in orthopedics.

Orthopods' Dilemma

The OrthoForum is the premier convening and advocacy organization for large, independent orthopedic physician groups. In March 2022, co-author Dave gave a keynote address at the OrthoForum's Annual Conference in Orlando, Florida. Attending the conference at the posh Grande Lakes Ritz-Carlton gave him a front-row seat to the economic forces reshaping orthopedic care in the United States.

In terms of money and prestige, orthopedic surgeons are at the top of medicine's totem pole. Average compensation exceeded $630,000 in 2021.[8] Physician partners at large orthopedic practices earn millions of dollars. However, the emergence of pesky musculoskeletal (MSK) companies are making it harder. MSK companies don't compete directly with orthopedic practices, but they care for increasing numbers of consumers with pain and mobility complaints.

Right after Dave's keynote address, as if on cue, an investment banker and a lawyer took the stage. They invited OrthoForum members to participate in a cooperative MSK company. This initiative represented the OrthoForum's competitive response to the emergence of venture-funded MSK companies, like Hinge Health and Sword Health, that provide virtual and digital physical therapy services. Typically, MSK companies contract with self-insured employers to offer their digital products and related services as an employee benefit.

Back, joint, and muscle complaints plague half of American adults.[9] MSK companies can cure the vast majority of these complaints through their digital platforms and services. Consumers love the service. They reward MSK providers with Net Promoter Scores in the high 80s and low 90s. Employers have embraced MSK offerings because they avoid the costs and disruption caused by unnecessary orthopedic interventions and their employees like the service.

The OrthoForum is right to worry about the disruptive threat posed by MSK companies. Only a small percentage of individuals with MSK conditions require surgery. It's not a stretch to envision a not-distant future where trusted MSK providers guide where and on what terms their customers receive orthopedic surgeries. In this brave new healthcare world, orthopods become highly trained surgical mechanics.

Used to being on top, orthopedic practices confront a vexing strategic dilemma. They're unsure how to sustain competitive advantage. Nontraditional competitors are disrupting their cozy and profitable economic model. Adapting to changing market dynamics requires scale, expanded service offerings, and solid execution. There is little room for error. There will be winners and losers.

Either way, orthopedic practices that wish to remain competitive must adapt to these changing market realities and accept that MSK companies could disrupt their surgical referral channels. Orthopedic practices must up their game, exploit their competitive advantages, and expand their service offerings to win consumers' loyalty and sustain market relevance.

Demanding Management

Orthopods' Dilemma is part of a larger dynamic unfolding within the healthcare marketplace. Providers historically have controlled access to and prices for their service offerings to commercially insured patients. Aligned primary care doctors make initial diagnoses and refer patients to specialists for treatment. This approach amplifies specialists' income but also leads to unnecessary utilization and even profiteering.

The marketplace is organizing to shift demand management for health-care services to entities outside the traditional payer–provider ecosystem. As this shift in referring patterns gains momentum, demand for specialty care will migrate to higher-value providers. In orthopedics, expect fewer overall surgeries occurring in higher-volume, lower-cost, higher-quality focused factories. This is a logical and beneficial outcome that rewards companies delivering high-value care services.

The potential reduction in acute admissions caused by 3D-WPH and better overall demand management by healthcare buyers poses a massive disruptive threat to hospitals and specialists. It gets worse.

Advances in diagnostics are on the cusp of identifying life-threatening chronic conditions before they manifest and negate previously required hospitalizations. Pre-emptive diagnosis paired with effective interventions offer the potential of healthier futures for all Americans. Their ascendance, however, will further eviscerate patient volume for hospitals and specialists.

PRE-EMPTIVE DIAGNOSTICS

In the 1986 movie *Star Trek IV: The Voyage Home*, the starship *Enterprise* travels back in time to San Francisco in the mid-1980s. Its mission is to transport humpback whales into the twenty-third century to redirect a space probe heading to destroy earth. It's a complicated story.

While trying to escape police custody, crewmember Pavel Chekov falls and seriously injures his head. An ambulance transports Chekov to a trauma center where surgeons are about to drill into his head to relieve pressure on his brain.

Afraid of placing Chekov "in the hands of twentieth-century medicine," Captain James T. Kirk and Dr. Leonard "Bones" McCoy break into Chekov's operating suite. McCoy, who compares contemporary medical practices to the Dark Ages, tells the surgeons to put away their butcher knives so he can treat Chekov. The good doctor uses a twenty-third-century tricorder scanner to precisely diagnose and cure an arterial tear in Chekov's brain.

This futuristic movie scene has relevance to today's twenty-first-century medicine. Advancing genetic knowledge combined with big-data analytics is giving medicine the capacity to diagnose diseases much earlier. Before long, medicine will be able to prevent or slow disease progression through less invasive, more personalized, targeted, and effective treatment interventions.

Pre-emptive diagnostics isn't science fiction. Ten years from now, physicians will require fewer surgical knives, poisonous therapies, and toxic medications to treat their patients. Over the next decade, pre-emptive diagnostics will change medicine as we know it. The healthcare industry will dedicate far more resources to prevention and far fewer resources to acute care treatments. Health systems must adapt or risk losing market relevance.

Keeping millions of Americans healthy will enable the nation's providers to create sustainable business models that truly put patients first. As Ben Franklin first observed, "An ounce of prevention is worth a pound of cure." With reduced reliance on expensive hospital-based technologies and treatments, health systems will achieve better outcomes at lower costs. Value-based care will become a reality, not just a dream.

Many diseases either combine a genetic predisposition with environmental stimuli or are entirely caused by environmental factors. For example, individuals without a predisposition for lung cancer can still contract the disease by smoking multiple packs of cigarettes per day.

Environmental factors trigger humanity's most virulent and deadly chronic conditions – heart disease, stroke, COPD, most cancers, diabetes, arthritis, cirrhosis, and Alzheimer's disease. Whole-person health must treat both genetic and non-genetic disease origins. This is where pre-emptive diagnostics is riding to our rescue.

The Mechanics of Pre-Emptive Diagnostics

As discussed in Chapter 4, the twenty-first century's two biggest scientific breakthroughs thus far involve big-data analytics and biological mechanics. Pre-emptive diagnostics combine these advances to sift through massive biometric data sets to uncover early signs of impending disease. Due to its prowess in very early disease detection, pre-emptive diagnostics will trigger more timely and effective therapeutic responses tailored to each individual's genetic and epigenetic profile.

In its purest form, pre-emptive diagnostics identify specific pre-disease markers that come with targeted interventions. This is new. Current medicine diagnoses disease when symptoms present, not at disease onset. For chronic conditions, including most cancers, disease onset usually occurs years before symptoms manifest.

The mechanics for discovering these pre-disease markers are uniform across biometric sampling (e.g., blood, imaging, device signaling). They combine longitudinal collection of biometric data with machine-learning (ML) to identify pattern changes and their correlation with risk stratification (low, medium, high, very high) to specific diseases. We use the word *pre-emptive* to convey the ability of very early diagnosis to stop disease essentially before it starts.

Industry Pioneers in Pre-Emptive Diagnostics

Already, pre-emptive diagnostic companies have begun to pursue earlier and more accurate disease identification through differing biometric markers. While the companies' approaches have much in common, it is their differences that expand pre-emptive diagnostics' therapeutic potential.

Recently acquired by Standard Bio Tools, SomaLogic in Boulder, Colorado, has developed the ML-driven capability to measure changes in the ways proteins express themselves in real time. As basic building blocks of life, proteins adapt as individuals' genomes interact with environmental factors. Measured properly, proteomic signaling enables researchers to identify recognizable patterns of protein expression that correlate with an individual's future risk (high, medium, low) of contracting a disease or a condition.

As SomaLogic's former CEO Roy Smythe observes, "The machines see patterns of disease progression that humans cannot. The development of clinical proteomics will disrupt healthcare delivery and improve life quality. Who doesn't want that?"

New York–based Ezra uses full-body MRIs and artificial intelligence to detect minute changes in the body's organs indicative of cancer or other diseases. It is the first comprehensive diagnostic methodology to screen for the range of cancers. To date, Ezra has conducted scans on more than 5,000 individuals and discovered actionable diagnoses of disease in 13% of them.

To make MRI preventive screenings more widely accessible – and achieve its mission to "detect cancer early for everyone in the world" – Ezra has lowered the cost of full-body MRIs from $10,000 to $1,350 by meaningfully decreasing the time required for scanning and interpretation while increasing the accuracy of its predictive algorithms.

Ezra announced in June 2023 that it had received Federal Drug Administration 510(k) clearance for an AI application that enhances MRI image quality, enabling the company to launch the world's first 30-minute, full-body MRI.[10]

A third company, Egnite, in Aliso Viejo, California, uses pre-emptive diagnostics to close gaps in cardiovascular care, improve outcomes, reduce healthcare costs, and enhance lives. Egnite collects and interprets data transmitted by implanted devices. Their platform is device-agnostic with the ability to receive data continuously from any cardiac implant. Egnite also uses AI-driven algorithms to uncover disease signals through progressive and retrospective pattern recognition.

Don Bobo, corporate vice president of strategy and development at Edwards Lifesciences (which developed and spun out Egnite), stressed that cardiac disease is often misdiagnosed as a byproduct of aging. Such misdiagnoses lead to unnecessary follow-up care and needless patient suffering. Bobo believes predictive disease algorithms will become more accurate and actionable over time. This will enable people to lead longer, better, and healthier lives.

An Ounce or Pound of Prevention

The U.S. allocates a higher percentage of its national healthcare expenditures to prevention than most other wealthy nations.[11] A study published by the Peterson-KFF Health System Tracker found in 2018 that the U.S. tied for third with Germany at 2.9% for spending the highest percentage of its national health expenditure on prevention (see Figure 8.3).[12] That's the good news.

The bad news is that the vast majority (over 97%) of healthcare expenditure goes to treat rather than prevent diseases. That is about to change.

Some consider data to be the "oil" for the digital economy.[13] Like oil, data requires refining to provide productive value. For the first time in human history, our expanded knowledge of the human body's mechanics combined with advancing digital technologies give medicine the understanding and the tools to spot and expunge disease at or near its inception.

Preventive care spending by government/compulsory schemes as a share of total national health expenditures, 2018

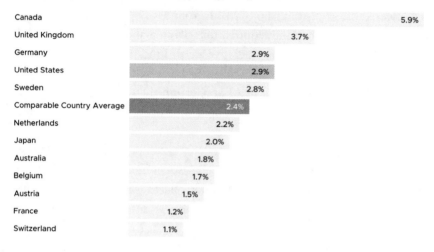

Note: Preventive care includes "any measure that aims to avoid or reduce the number or the severity of injuries and diseases, their sequelae and complications" (OECD). Data for Australia and Japan are from 2017.

Source: KFF analysis of OECD data

Peterson-KFF
Health System Tracker

Figure 8.3

Source: Peterson-KFF.

Medicine is at the dawn of a new era. Today, it is often too late to reverse disease progression once symptoms present. Imagine a not-distant future where pre-emptive diagnosis uncovers disease while there's time to reverse its course. This is game changing.

The question we have to ask ourselves is: How much higher a percentage of total healthcare expenditure will prevention constitute a decade from now? Will it be 10%, 15%, 20% or more? Whatever that percentage, preventive care aided by big-data and synthetic biology will disrupt and revolutionize healthcare delivery. Data will fuel these biological and healthcare revolutions. Humanity will be their beneficiary. In *Star Trek* terms, we will all "live longer and prosper."

The combined impact of 3D-WPH, improved demand management, and pre-emptive diagnostics spells doom for the overbuilt, inefficient, and reactive acute care sector. While beyond the scope of this book, we believe that government should take proactive steps to right-size the nation's excessive acute-care footprint. Failure to act sooner will require more dramatic intervention later. Healthcare's disruptive avalanche is already falling. It's time to take corrective measures to limit its damage.

CONCLUSION: DECENTRALIZED, DEMOCRATIZED, AND DELIGHTED

Part One of *The Warmth of Other Suns* carries the title "In the Land of the Forefathers." Wilkerson ends the section with a remarkable quote about the motivation of the millions of Black Americans who comprised the Great Migration:

> *They did what human beings looking for freedom, throughout history, have often done.*
> *They left.*

Using the Great Migration as context, this chapter explores the migration of healthcare service delivered from the land of its forefathers (a centralized, fragmented, and failing status quo) to a better, newer model of personalized, decentralized whole-person health (3D-WPH) delivered wherever and whenever needed.

As Care Redesign and Care Migration gain momentum, more and more Americans are saying goodbye to a system that fills them with fear and frustration. With some trepidation, consumers in ever-growing numbers are gravitating to companies with whole-health service platforms that facilitate their ability to lead healthier, happier, and more productive lives.

With individuals at the center of whole-person health, the nexus of care shifts to the home and integrates seamlessly into daily life. Achieving whole-person health is a continuous process. Advances in technology make the pursuit of whole-person health achievable today in ways never thought possible before. Advances in diagnostics offer the promise of much earlier disease detection and pre-emptive interventions to negate disease spread. The need for hospital-based and specialty care will diminish. The potential for healthy futures will magnify.

Healthcare "migrants" who embrace 3D-WPH leave behind a health-care system that will struggle to retain market relevance. Hospitals will not disappear but there will be many fewer; the ones that remain will become focused procedure factories and specialized "solution shops" for those managing complex, late-stage diseases. End-of-life care will be more humane and adhere to informed individualized preferences.

The one-two punch of Care Redesign and Care Migration will push the nation to achieve better balance between health and healthcare. 3D-WPH at scale will cost less and deliver better outcomes. It will liberate resources from healthcare to fund other societal needs.

Everyone wins except Healthcare Inc. U.S. healthcare today is less than the sum of its parts. It's time to break up the whole and reassemble the parts to create a better, higher-functioning system. As the pace of transformation accelerates, innovative companies are reconfiguring the healthcare ecosystem in constructive ways. New companies are emerging with breakthrough products and services that consumers love.

Some incumbents are rewiring their platforms to remain relevant. Cracks in the existing system have appeared and are widening. Disintermediation awaits those that cannot deliver value-based care. Growth Waves Four and beyond that Clay Christensen imagined in 2009 are already here or just around the corner.

The time for revolutionary healthcare in America has come. It's time for healthcare revolutionaries to seize the mantle of transformation. Paraphrasing Hillel the Elder, If not now, then when? If not by us, then by whom?

KEY INSIGHTS ON CARE MIGRATION

- The slow migration of care delivery from hospitals into lower-cost, more convenient facilities resembles the decades-long migration of Black Americans in the South in search of greater freedom and economic opportunity. Both movements are vast, leaderless, organic, multidimensional, and epoch changing.

(continued)

(continued)

- In combination with Care Redesign, Care Migration is the second punch in a one-two combination that is disrupting U.S. healthcare. Democratized and decentralized delivery of whole-person health (3D-WPH) is the disruptive innovation that is fundamentally altering supply–demand dynamics within the U.S. healthcare marketplace.

- As described by Harvard Business School professor Clay Christensen in *The Innovator's Prescription*, centralization and subsequent decentralization of production is the universal pattern through which industries modernize to deliver greater value to customers. Industries initially centralize production to improve upon pre-industrial organizational models. Disruptive innovation triggers decentralization of production through sequential growth waves.

- Hospitals emerged in the early 1900s as centralized production facilities for the delivery of medical services. They replaced a disorganized system of licensed and unlicensed practitioners delivering largely unproven home-based remedies. U.S. healthcare has remained largely stuck in this "Growth Wave One" centralized operating model.

- Decentralized care delivery is an essential feature of whole-person health. It increases convenience, lowers costs, and improves outcomes. Technological advances enable delivery of hospital-level care in the home where necessary.

- Hospitals continue to expand in hopes of securing greater funding. This massive investment in centralized delivery has become an albatross and increases health systems' and specialists' vulnerability to disruptive innovation.

- Some providers are experimenting with new, value-driven delivery models to maintain market relevance.

- New value-based business models are emerging to challenge healthcare's status-quo business practices.

- Pre-emptive diagnostics offer the promise of disease prevention, earlier diagnosis, and more effective interventions.

9 | Aggregators' Advantage

In November 2016, Fairview Health Services announced the hiring of James Hereford from Stanford Health Care as its new CEO. An operations wunderkind, Hereford wanted to understand Fairview's underlying workflows and approach to performance improvement through process standardization. As an initial test, he asked his senior team to count the number of phone numbers through which patients could contact the system. The answer was over 600.

At $5.3 billion in annual revenues, Fairview is Minnesota's third-largest health system with 36,000 professionals working in almost 150 locations. By the time Hereford arrived, Fairview had grown both organically and through acquisition into a very large academic and community-based delivery network with a patchwork of legacy communications systems.

Hereford's assessment was that Fairview's customer experience was at best uneven and nowhere near where it should be. He immediately set out to upgrade Fairview's customer connectivity. Stealing a phrase from Stanford's then-CEO Amir Rubin, Hereford insisted, "One call does it all!"

With great fanfare, Fairview's new operations center opened in 2019. Powered by QVentus technologies, the new center combines data, analytics, and dynamic system monitoring to reduce transaction friction and improve resource allocation.

The results were spectacular: enhanced patient connectivity and care navigation; streamlined operations; fewer bottlenecks; and lower costs. While the ops center's consolidation work continues, one call really can do it all. Thousands now call 1-855-Fairview every day to schedule appointments, ask questions, and/or get directed to a specific service provider.

This improvement in Fairview's operation illustrates the two "*Es*," Easier and Empowering, of our CB^2E^2 acronym. Of course, most customer engagement today occurs on digital platforms, so we've updated Rubin's and Hereford's catchy slogan from "One Call Does It All" to "One App Covers the Map." The concept remains the same. Omni-channel connectivity makes it much easier for consumers to engage proactively in pursuit of their individual health and wellness goals.

While simple in concept, achieving seamless consumer engagement has proven elusive for healthcare payers and providers. Clunky websites and lack of customer trust compromise their ability to create long-term, "sticky" customer relationships that engender true brand love.

Where there is challenge lies opportunity. Health companies that aggregate services within seamless, easy-to-use platforms that solve consumers' health and healthcare problems (their "jobs to be done") will differentiate and increase their market penetration. They will drive an Aggregators' Advantage within a consolidating healthcare marketplace. These aggregators will create and unleash healthcare's Holy Grail: cohesive apps that empower consumers to manage their healthcare needs and improve their health through "one-stop shopping."

Many organizations aspire to become consumers' one true source for health information, guidance, and services, but only a few will prevail. Fortunately, other industries have already made this journey and developed the playbook for success.

HEALTHCARE'S FINAL FRONTIER: ENGAGING CONSUMERS

Healthcare is going retail, fast. Care delivery is democratizing and decentralizing. New interoperability and transparency regulations are making product and service offerings more "shoppable." Informed and connected consumers are assuming more control over healthcare purchasing decisions. They're demanding digital-first experiences and solutions.

New business models are flooding into the healthcare marketplace. Consumerism, competition, and convenience are reshaping supply–demand relationships. The COVID pandemic accelerated movement to virtual, home, and walk-in care modalities. Post-COVID, Care Migration to more convenient and cost-effective settings continue to reshape and invigorate customer experience.

Healthcare companies across the service spectrum confront disruptive, new market dynamics as the landscape for service provision rewires itself. Most incumbents know they are behind the curve and are striving to catch up. The "unbundling" of care services and payment makes it much easier for their customers to purchase better experiences elsewhere. Traditional client acquisition channels cannot sustain demand.

To conquer this new frontier, payers, providers, and manufacturers are seeking out new customers and exploring more enticing ways to deliver services. In short, healthcare is now "boldly going" (catch the *Star Trek* irony) where most industries have already gone before – into full-fledged consumer engagement.

For incumbents, consumerism is a double-edged sword. It provides new channels for building brand loyalty and strengthening market positioning. At the same time, it erodes demand from traditional channels as patients redirect care to alternative vendors. Pricing transparency and data interoperability fuel both trends.

As health information becomes interoperable, consumers' "switching costs" decrease and their choices multiply. Once-secure pathways for channeling customers become less reliable. Particularly for routine care, consumers now shop and purchase services outside traditional network providers based on price, convenience, and customer experience.

From a brand perspective, providers and some payers are best positioned within the ecosystem to capitalize upon healthcare's increasing consumerism. By becoming early adopters in digital health technologies, they can create "stickiness" with customers by personalizing their shopping experiences and by making them more convenient and enjoyable.

Sustaining digital loyalty, however, requires deeper levels of consumer engagement. That occurs as maturing digital platforms learn more about individual preferences and then offer tailored information, guidance, and service access. This personalized engagement empowers consumers to better manage their health and improve their lives.

Traditional hub-and-spoke business models operating within closed proprietary systems are breaking down. They're losing customers because their fragmented and high-cost service delivery isn't addressing vital health-care needs. A new health and consumer-driven paradigm is now emerging to displace the old disease- and hospital-driven paradigm.

Healthcare's Changing Paradigm Changes Everything

With the publication of *The Structure of Scientific Revolutions* in 1962, Thomas Kuhn created the term *"paradigm shift"* to describe how scientific revolutions emerge and amplify through periodic bursts of creativity. Prior to the publication of Kuhn's book, most scientists believed that scientific knowledge grew incrementally. Kuhn argued that sciences advanced through long periods of accumulating knowledge and distinct periods of revolutionary new thinking.

Paradigm shifts ask new questions regarding old problems. They expand the conceptual range of potential solutions. They advance knowledge creation in nonlinear ways. They usher in new-world interpretations and practices. Paradigm shifts are now a universally accepted framework for explaining revolutionary change. Clay Christensen's paradigm-shifting models for disruptive business innovation and dual transformation owe their intellectual origins to Kuhn's work.

As described in our book's introduction, healthcare's last paradigm shift occurred over a century ago. Abraham Flexner's 1910 report put science at the center of medicine, institutionalized the Johns Hopkins medical education model, closed two-thirds of the nation's medical schools and established academic medicine's tripartite mission of education, research, and clinical care. The Flexner paradigm and the fee-for-service (FFS) medicine it perpetuates remains the dominant payment mechanism within U.S. healthcare.

The outdated Flexner paradigm is cracking. Powerful macro and market forces are challenging the sustainability of treatment- and payment-driven business models. In addition to rising consumerism, they include generative AI technologies, genetic knowledge, risk-based payment models, new competitors, and greater emphasis on wellbeing. With abundant investor support, these forces are accelerating the industry's push to democratize and decentralize care delivery.

Consequently, a disruptive consumer-directed paradigm for health is now emerging. Medicine will never be the same. Recalling Peter Drucker's prescient insight, providers and payers who want to do something new must stop doing something old.

As incumbent healthcare organizations embrace consumerism, they must wean themselves off transaction-driven FFS and administrative services only (ASO) medicine. Unfortunately, most find this almost impossible to do.

To the extent that slow-footed providers and payers cling to outdated service and contracting models, they make themselves extremely vulnerable to disruptive innovation. More nimble, asset-light, and consumer-centric competitors are organizing to steal their customers and reduce their market relevance.

Overcoming Old-Paradigm Practices in a New-Paradigm Marketplace

For all the rhetoric regarding risk-based payment and value-based care, transactional FFS and ASO medicine still predominate. According to a Health Management Academy survey, leading health systems made slow but steady progress in raising their percentage of value-based contracting from 15% to 25% of total revenues between 2014 and 2019 (see Figure 9.1).

Shared-savings programs on FFS payment formularies are the most used and least risky form of value-based payment. As such, they are a modified form of FFS payment. Combined with pure FFS payments, they push the FFS percentage of total revenues well beyond 90%.

Channeling our *Star Trek* metaphor, healthcare's prime directive under FFS medicine is to optimize revenues wherever, however, and to the greatest extent possible. Ruthlessly pursuing revenue optimization, however, creates excessive care fragmentation, overtreatment, and overpricing. It also generates enormous waste and alienates consumers.

In their unending quest for payment, the vast majority of healthcare providers and payers rely on FFS and ASO medicine to sustain their operations. Unfortunately, FFS and ASO medicine represent an old math solution to a new math problem. Transactional FFS and ASO medicine, as currently practiced, rewards volume and promotes manipulation of complex payment formulas. Data illiquidity and opaque pricing information limit consumer choice and channel patients into traditional, often inappropriate, treatment venues.

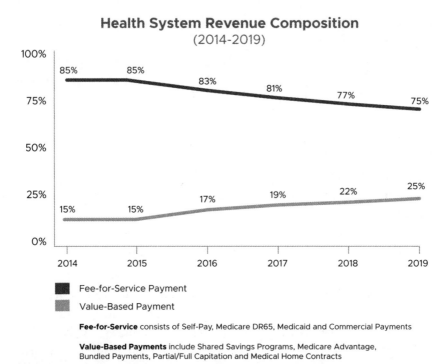

Figure 9.1   Fee-for-service medicine reigns: Health system revenue composition, 2014–2019.

Source: Health Management Academy.

These barriers to greater consumerism in healthcare are under assault and crumbling. Healthcare's "new math" aligns with a new paradigm that emphasizes decentralized delivery of holistic, integrated, value-based care services (see Figure 9.2). Advancing consumerism, however, is not solely dependent on payment reform. Better customer experience creates incremental value within FFS and ASO medicine even as incumbents migrate to risked-based payment models.

As discussed in Chapter 5, new regulatory rules requiring price transparency and data interoperability prevent information blocking, promote information exchange, and enable tighter direct contracting arrangements between payers and providers. Massive amounts of venture and private equity funding have flooded into digital health companies building consumer-friendly care delivery channels.[1] Big retail companies and technology companies also are aggressively expanding their healthcare offerings.

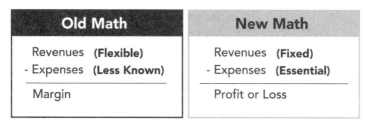

Old Math	New Math
Revenues **(Flexible)**	Revenues **(Fixed)**
- Expenses **(Less Known)**	- Expenses **(Essential)**
Margin	Profit or Loss

Purpose: Getting Paid   **Purpose: Creating Value**

Figure 9.2   Healthcare's "old math" is more difficult to square in a "new math" marketplace.

These progressive market and regulatory forces turbocharge consumerism and value creation. They support care decentralization, coordination, and outcome transparency. They provide solutions to real consumer problems. Delivering value to consumers is the essential feature of healthcare's new paradigm. Creating that value will shape the industry's future.

This paradigm shift goes beyond risk-based payment models. Value-based care amplifies the consumer's role in service design and evaluation. As they do in other consumer-centric industries, customers vote with their wallets. Their purchasing decisions signal the preferences to sellers. To remain competitive, healthcare's "sellers" (payers and providers) must respond with value-based offerings that deliver great customer experiences.

Incumbents understand that the disruptive forces described above challenge status-quo business models and practices. Accordingly, they are prioritizing virtual and asset-lite care modalities, care model innovation, partnerships to expand capabilities, and transparency solutions. However, as a 2021 Kaufman Hall survey of health systems revealed, incumbents' progress in implementing consumer-centric initiatives has been slow (see Figure 9.3).[2]

To address COVID, health systems accelerated their adoption of virtual care services, walk-in clinics, and hospital-at-home capabilities. Under financial pressure, many are regressing back to FFS-based strategies emphasizing acute and specialty care services to optimize revenue generation. Very few have implemented innovative primary care services models that underlie full-risk contracting. Not expanding primary care access poses a substantial risk for health systems as new virtual-first delivery models emerge and "switching costs" decline.

Healthcare Priorities

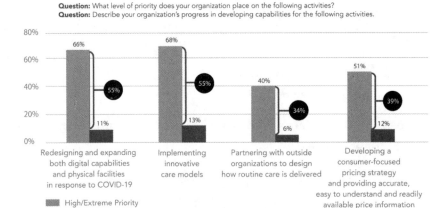

Question: What level of priority does your organization place on the following activities?
Question: Describe your organization's progress in developing capabilities for the following activities.

Figure 9.3　Mistaking articulation for accomplishment.

Source: Kaufman Hall.

Unfortunately, post-COVID workforce and supply-chain challenges have supplanted risk-based contracting as top-of-mind priorities. While necessary, less focus on institutionalizing value-based care makes traditional providers even more vulnerable to disruptive customer-centric delivery modalities. Emphasizing old-math FFS payment and practices makes it harder for incumbents to build and sustain brand loyalty.

A 2022 survey by Jarrard Phillips Cate & Hancock reports high levels of support for healthcare professionals but only tepid support for hospitals. By a substantial margin, most Americans are ambivalent or don't believe their preferred hospital is a good community partner. They also believe their preferred hospital is more focused on its business than its patients.

In essence, hospitals and health systems are losing the battle for consumers' hearts and minds at the very time that consumer healthcare choices are expanding. Addressing service and perception shortfalls requires "one app that covers the map," such as single-site, omni-channel platforms that delight customers with comprehensive offerings, great service, and ease of use.

Improving the digital interfaces first and then expanding service provision to encompass wellbeing are the two prongs propelling greater consumer engagement. Next-generation platforms must automate health-care user experiences to increase their effectiveness. They also must make it easier for individuals to manage their daily health challenges.

Platform solutions will evolve as will consumer preferences. Proactively building best-in-class consumer channels will differentiate winning health-care companies.

Platform Evolution

In response to the 2008 financial crisis, the federal government funded the adoption and meaningful use of electronic healthcare records (EHRs) through the Health Information Technology for Economic and Clinical Health (HITECH) Act of 2009. Up to that point, the inability to standardize health-care data for targeted transmission and analysis diminished care effectiveness and the pace of medical discovery.

Healthcare's digital evolution began with best-of-class point solutions. This was not ideal because these point solutions did not interface well with one another. They often have complicated, rather than simplified, user experiences.

As digitization of health records gained critical mass, many EHR vendors (most notably Epic Health Systems as described in Chapter 5) resisted legislative and regulatory pressure to make EHRs interoperable and available to app developers. Contrary to the government's original expectations, administrative complexity for both caregivers and consumers has increased with the implementation of EHRs. Incremental administrative burden is a profound source of user frustration and caregiver burnout.

Today, even digitally mature health companies rely on patient portals tied to EHRs (e.g., MyChart) as their primary consumer interface. Enterprise-wide EHR apps coalesce patient information but haven't won widespread activation among consumers. They aren't personalized and require users to link to alternative sites for additional information or services.

Despite being available for decades, the uptake of EHR portals typically stalls at 35–40% of patients. The yellow star in the "innovation diffusion" chart (see Figure 9.4) illustrates the current state of consumer adoption of digital health tech applications – stuck among early-majority adopters but poised for widespread adoption.

Other industries have demonstrated the ability to spark widespread digital tech adoption by pairing new capabilities with a modern, consumer-directed

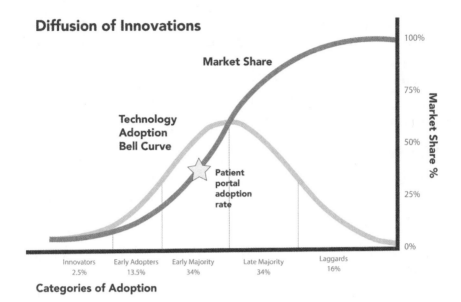

Figure 9.4 Diffusion of Innovations.

Source: Everett Rogers.

UX (user experience). The window for leading the industry into digital health is significant but closing. Motivated companies can differentiate their service offerings, gain customer loyalty, and expand market share by developing omni-channel platforms that enable consumers to manage their health and healthcare needs with ease.

The evolution of digital health solutions no longer requires companies to choose between clunky, data-rich EHR portals and best-in-class consumer engagement. Next-generation interfaces will create an invisible, organic, and native experience that will inform and guide patients to improved outcomes. Make no mistake, EHRs will provide an essential system of record, but they will not be the branded interfaces that healthcare companies present to consumers.

The challenge healthcare faces today is equivalent to the one that aviation confronted as the millennium approached. At the time, the Sabre reservation system owned by American Airlines (AA) was far-and-away the industry's best. But it wasn't consumer-facing. In 2000, AA spun off its ownership of Sabre to facilitate its ability to sell its services to other travel companies and thereby enhance its revenue growth.

As an independent company, Sabre emerged as the travel industry's preferred and fully interoperable reservation system. Individual airlines, hotels, and rental care companies now overlay Sabre with cohesive, user-friendly apps to engage consumers. No consumer-driven travel company would even consider using Sabre as its digital interface to manage customer interactions. So why do health systems do this with Epic's MyChart?

Consumer expectations for digital health and healthcare service provision are accelerating. They do not want a cacophony of disjointed applications and experiences. Consumers want and increasingly expect the consistent, non-obtrusive, and easy-to-navigate experiences they enjoy in their other retail encounters.

Providers' and payers' rudimentary approaches to consumer engagement make them vulnerable to more agile, tech-enabled competitors. As discussed previously, healthcare has a massive intermediary problem. Great software eliminates intermediaries and healthcare is full of them (insurance companies, brokers, navigators, etc.).

Using technology to remove layers of bureaucratic processing will liberate both consumers and caregivers. In the process, healthcare will become cheaper, better, more balanced, easier, and empowering (CB^2E^2 in action).

The broader healthcare ecosystem sees enormous opportunity in healthcare's continued reliance on archaic business practices. Not content with just enabling transactions, tech companies, payers, and retailers are moving aggressively into care delivery (e.g., Amazon, Optum, CVS).

Once established, consumers' digital loyalty and preferences solidify. They become less malleable. Healthcare incumbents are well-positioned to become consumers' preferred suppliers of health and healthcare services. However, this competitive advantage window is rapidly closing as consumerism continues to gain traction and new competitors encroach into care services.

Now is the time for incumbents to make their healthcare offerings more shoppable and enriching for consumers. Differentiated solutions will encompass health as well as healthcare service provision. Voting with their purchases, consumers will establish deep relationships with value-creating companies that help them improve their daily health and wellbeing.

Healthcare to Wellbeing

As discussed earlier, healthcare service provision is stuck in a 1920s Flexner-era operational paradigm that is hospital-centric, physician-centric, disease-focused, and resistant to change. This operating orientation leaves the healthcare ecosystem ill-equipped to address the exploding levels of chronic diseases that are crippling the American people.

According to the University of Wisconsin Population Health Institute, clinical care accounts for only 20% of health outcomes as measured by longevity and life quality.[3] The healthcare ecosystem devotes excessive resources to the 20% and underfunds the remaining 80% (see Figure 9.5). The result is a demographic conundrum where overall American life expectancy is declining while the age 90+ segment is the nation's fastest growing age group.[4]

Americans fully engaged in managing their health already have the knowledge and wherewithal to lead longer, healthier, happier, and more productive lives. The life-or-death challenge for the healthcare ecosystem is to increase the number of Americans who feel empowered to manage their health and healthcare effectively.

To enhance health outcomes, payment models are evolving to reward whole-person social and healthcare delivery. Numerous new business models, most with a retail focus, also are emerging to fill this market need. Over time, resources will shift into preventive care and healthy multipliers that enhance the non-clinical components driving health outcomes. Improving health status broadly requires a greater focus on social determinants of health (SDoH) or what we term "health multipliers."

Health Multipliers

We have never liked the phrase "social determinants of health." Its meaning is not self-evident, so the terminology requires explanation. That's never good.

As language, the phrase "social determinants" is antiseptic. The words mechanistically capture the immense importance of education, housing, food, security, transportation, and other day-to-day living factors in promoting wellbeing and unleashing human potential; however, they fail to stir the blood. Enhancing social determinants can catapult disadvantaged individuals and communities into almost unimaginable happiness and achievement. The terminology should capture that excitement.

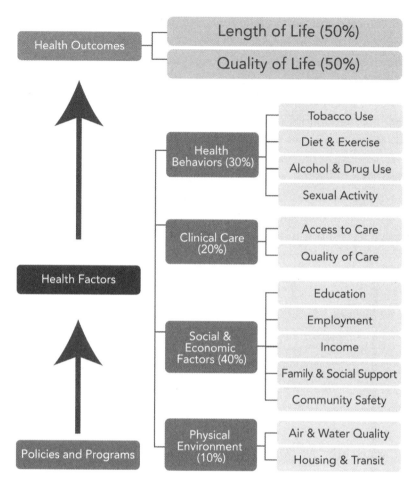

Figure 9.5   Clinical care drives only 20% of health outcomes.

Source: County Health Rankings Model ©2014 UWPHI.

Finally, "social" as a modifier of "determinants" is far too limiting. Figure 9.5 displays the numerous and complex interconnections underlying long, healthy lives. Language describing the pathways to healthy living must be more expansive and invigorating.

As with most great writing, the solution to capturing SDoH's many-splendored characteristics is to simplify language and economize on word choice. With that as our goal, we offer the phrase "health multipliers" as an alternative to "SDoH." As terminology, "health multipliers" is clean, active, and progressive. It captures the essence of what's required for healthy living.

Ultimately, the health of the American people cannot improve without significant changes in lifestyle behaviors. Achieving healthier futures will require a much broader societal embrace of health multipliers. This is not easy but is possible with appropriate policy focus, new technologies, and incentives. For example, the promise of digital health lies in its ability to make healthier lifestyle choices easier and more sustainable for consumers, so they "multiply" their compounding beneficial impact.

According to the Fogg Behavioral Model (see Figure 9.6), motivation, ability, and effective prompts must converge simultaneously for desired behaviors to occur and become habitual.

Competing on health is very different from competing on healthcare. Developing and sustaining healthy behaviors is an ongoing endeavor. Most

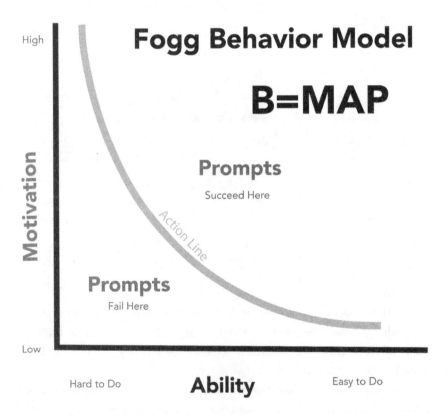

Figure 9.6 Fogg Behavioral Model.

Source: BJ Fogg.

healthcare encounters are episodic. Enhancing motivation, making tasks easy, and prompting desired behaviors appropriately are essential features of productive engagement strategies.

Digital and consumer engagement are one and the same. To fully engage consumers and maintain market relevance, healthcare companies must tailor user experiences to individual preferences and needs through digital platforms. Engagement improves information flow, outcomes, and connectivity. As they do in other industries, consumers will reward healthcare companies that put their interests first. Trust and loyalty will build in unison as consumers choose "partners" to help them manage their health.

The best health companies will meet both consumers' health and healthcare needs through continuous virtual and periodic physical interactions. They will promote individual and community wellbeing within a comprehensive array of services that solve real consumers' problems. Intense ongoing engagement builds durable brand loyalty, feeds customer acquisition, and enhances market presence. It creates value, and value will rule the healthcare marketplace.

User Profiles

The success of digital health platforms and the services they offer depends on the platform's technological prowess and the level of consumer engagement. Even in today's system-centric operating environment, engaged consumers can navigate through fragmented service delivery and independently manage their health.

The challenge for health companies is to simultaneously increase the number of engaged consumers they serve and improve their digital platform capabilities. User experiences will vary depending on the levels of platform capability and consumer engagement.

With that in mind, we've identified the following four user profiles corresponding to current and future digital platforms as well as low and high levels of consumer engagement: burdened, administrative, automated, and empowered.

We've further delineated these user experiences in two ways: occurring first within system-centric and consumer-centric operating models; and secondly occurring between treatment-centric and health-centric interactions. Figure 9.7 uses gray-shaded matrices to display these two user-profile depictions.

The user profiles have the following characteristics:

- **Current State (Burdened):** Disconnected point solutions increase consumer friction and frustration. Rather than make their interactions with the healthcare ecosystem easier, health tech makes them harder.
- **Engagement 1.0 (Administrative):** Enables engaged users to navigate the system with relative ease to complete basic tasks, such as scheduling, registration, bill payment, communication with providers, and receiving test results. Administrative users manage their personal health and wellbeing independent of the healthcare ecosystem.
- **Engagement 2.0 (Automated):** Software enables automated execution of healthcare interactions/transactions through integrated platforms that provide a consistent, non-obtrusive and easily navigable experience. Absent engagement, automated users experience much less friction when receiving health and healthcare services but fail to optimize their health and wellbeing.
- **Engagement 3.0 (Empowered):** This is the Holy Grail. Proactively enables engaged consumers to manage their overall wellbeing as well as their healthcare interactions. As consumers shift from passive to active participants in their health journeys, their service expectations increase, and they migrate to solutions that best meet their needs.

These user profiles are helpful for assessing the level of consumer engagement engendered within specific digital health platforms. Too many incumbents declare victory at engagement level 1.0. Ultimate success, however, depends on automating user experiences and empowering more consumers to engage organically with digital platforms to optimize their health and wellbeing.

Living Longer and Prospering

At their core, the problems plaguing the healthcare ecosystem are structural, political, and/or organizational. They represent tough challenges, but they are solvable. America does not have to accept the lesser of two evils when it comes to providing great healthcare to everyone in the country.

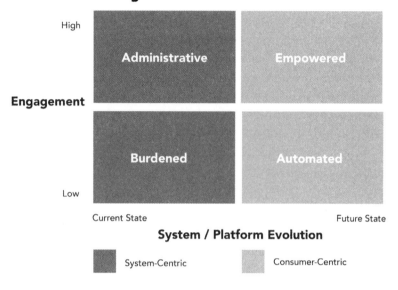

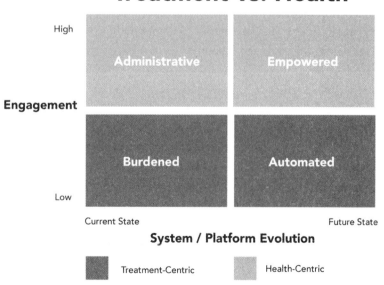

Figure 9.7 User profiles are helpful in assessing the level of consumer engagement.

Paradigm shifts are rare but all-encompassing. U.S. healthcare is undergoing one as the ecosystem searches for new solutions to old problems. Value-driven service provision informed by and tailored to consumer preferences can reverse the negative spiral of higher costs and worsening health status that plagues America. It must. The alternative of skyrocketing costs, excessive waste, and a sicker population is unacceptable and ruinous.

Meta is the Greek word for *beyond*. Incumbents of all types need to go beyond healthcare and seek out new ways to engender health and wellbeing. Metadata is data that describes other data. Digital health is going meta by using data to inform and empower consumers to make smarter purchasing decisions. The aggregation of their individual choices will reinvent the healthcare industry.

Healthcare delivery is rapidly decentralizing and becoming more complex while consumers are demanding increased simplicity and transparency. The ecosystem is reorganizing to meet consumers' health and healthcare needs. Achieving this vision will involve significant dislocation and system redesign. Healthcare's new frontier will be just but demanding. There will be clear winners and losers.

The authors obviously cannot resist *Star Trek* references. Health companies that embrace this new "prime directive" will earn customer loyalty, build brand strength, and gain market share by driving better healthcare outcomes and broader community-wide health. The clearest winners of all, however, will be the American people, who will "live longer and prosper" with longer health spans and a higher quality of life.

THE PERILS AND POSSIBILITIES OF HEALTHCARE APPS

Wanting full-fledged consumer engagement and making it happen are not synonymous. In the best of healthcare times, providers and payers struggle to create cohesive, longitudinal customer experiences that delight consumers with exceptional service. In the worst of healthcare times, customer experience is a labyrinth filled with inadequate guidance, excessive wait times, duplicative administrative procedures, and opaque pricing.

Advancing digital technologies contain the promise of making the complex simple and easing consumers' healthcare journeys. Great technologies, however, cannot by themselves overcome fragmented service delivery and the operational dysfunction that accompanies it. Putting consumers first has to be more than a slogan for healthcare incumbents to sustain market relevance. It must become an operational reality.

Only "apps that cover the map" create the "empowered" 3.0 user experience described above. Lesser apps pale by comparison. Rather than speak in generalities, we illustrate the perils and possibilities of healthcare apps from two February 2023 encounters that co-author Dave had in Chicago.

The first was a frustrating attempt to reschedule a routine dermatology check-up within an academic health system. "Burdened" user experiences leave a bad taste. By contrast, the second was a remarkable response to a COVID diagnosis by an upstart healthcare company. There's nothing quite like the satisfaction and accomplishment that accompany "empowered" user experiences.

An Epic Fail

Co-author Dave requires semi-annual dermatology screening to identify and treat pre-cancerous growths. For over a decade, Northwestern Medicine has provided that service every winter and summer. After each exam, he schedules his next appointment. This appointment system worked well until it didn't.

Like most large health systems, Northwestern uses Epic's MyChart as its digital portal. MyChart incorporates patient information from Epic's EHR to schedule appointments, convey lab test results, advance patient education, and facilitate clinical communications.

Unfortunately, consumers have not flocked to use MyChart. Uptake remains below 40%.[5] MyChart apps are usually not personalized. Unless modified otherwise, they require users to link to alternative sites to retrieve information or access services. In essence, MyChart is a "bolt-on" consumer interface to Epic EHRs, which document clinical activity for subsequent billing.

In early 2023, Dave needed to reschedule his February dermatology screening. Three weeks before the appointment, he accessed MyChart to schedule the new appointment. The first available date wasn't until June, four months beyond the original appointment date. Waiting that long defeats the purpose of a semi-annual screening regimen. This was not acceptable.

Dave first called Northwestern's customer service center to see if they could do better. After lots of back-and-forth, their representative offered the same appointment times available on MyChart. That exercise was a waste of time.

Once more into the breach. Dave returned to MyChart endeavoring to send a message directly to the dermatologist's office requesting the rescheduling. MyChart protocols required a reason for his inquiry. From the drop-down menu, Dave selected "scheduling." MyChart then sent him back to its scheduling page. This was nothing more than circular roulette.

Then what? Being clever, Dave manipulated the message function to guarantee the rescheduling request reached the staff in the dermatologist's office. That effort took some time and creativity but ultimately worked. Unfortunately, the dermatologist's nurse could only offer a new appointment that was just a few weeks earlier than those offered on MyChart – so much for a timely check-up.

Dave had had enough. He found another dermatologist who could see him right away. Their gain was Northwestern's loss. Three months later, Dave received a MyChart message from Northwestern alerting him to the rescheduled dermatology appointment that he hadn't booked. This "alert" only added salt to his gaping customer-experience wound.

A One Medical Miracle

Right after his maddening MyChart app experience, Dave contracted COVID and had to quarantine. This prevented him from traveling to Washington, D.C., where he had planned to meet with his friend and healthcare policy guru Dr. Zeke Emanuel.

After receiving the news, Emanuel wrote this concise response, "Sorry. Get Paxlovid now regardless of symptoms." That seemed like good advice. Dave has been a very satisfied One Medical customer since 2018. Ninety percent of his One Medical interactions are virtual through their personalized and easy-to-use app.

Almost without thinking, Dave accessed the One Medical app to seek a consultation with his primary care physician. Unfortunately, he was on vacation. With a couple more clicks, however, Dave scheduled a video consult regarding Paxlovid with another One Medical physician.

The video chat started within 10 minutes of the request. During the 25-minute session, Dave learned everything he needed to know about

Paxlovid. Based on his age and medical history, Dave and the physician agreed that taking Paxlovid proactively was prudent.

The physician then checked to see whether Dave's local CVS pharmacy had the drug in stock. It did and the good doctor placed the order. An almost-immediate text from CVS pinged Dave's phone indicating the Paxlovid prescription was ready for pick-up.

Wow! This is healthcare as it should be: efficient, convenient, solutions-focused. A feather could have knocked him over. Dave's brand love for One Medical increased exponentially.

TRANSCARENT IS COMING!

Traditional healthcare companies should have felt the ground quake on March 18, 2021. On that day, a Chicago-based business-to-business (B2B) exchange company named Transcarent announced a $40 million fundraise. Transcarent also announced that Livongo's founder, Glen Tullman, would serve as the company's new CEO and executive board chair.

Livongo is a digital health company that employs connected devices and personalized coaching to assist individuals managing chronic diseases, most notably diabetes. Tullman sold Livongo to Teladoc in October 2020 at an agreed-upon valuation of $18.5 billion.[6] At the time, the Livongo sale was the largest digital health transaction in history.

Like Livongo, Transcarent is targeting the lucrative self-insured employer market segment. As such, it poses a greater disruptive threat to status-quo business practices than companies marketing directly to consumers. Transcarent's transparent aim is to make self-insured employers better buyers of healthcare services by enabling their employees to become empowered consumers, able to make smart decisions regarding their personal health and care.

In an interview at the time of the company's launch, Tullman emphasized the need for Transcarent's software to be easy and understandable so that people can use it without assistance:

> *What do people want? They want three things: unbiased information; trusted guidance; and access to needed services . . . Healthcare must create the ability for someone who needs care to navigate the system on their own and book the services they require. That's what we intend to offer our customers and Members.*[7]

Too many healthcare platforms simply assemble services without per-
sonalization. Tullman calls them "link farms." They don't give health consumers the answers they want. They send them shopping. By eliminating
complexity and friction and by providing expert guidance, Transcarent
answers their members' health questions. The platform then empowers
members to select the care they need on their terms.

Transcarent's consumer-directed strategy replicates the business practices
of digital interface or exchange companies like Expedia, and Travelocity that
have disrupted the travel industry. In a nutshell, this is the true aggregators'
advantage. These companies eliminate the middle, removing friction and
cost, while putting consumers in charge of their purchasing decisions. Digital
interfacing is perhaps the most powerful business model ever created.

Exchanges bring suppliers and consumers together to facilitate easier or
better transactions. Pure exchanges have no inventory, do not produce products, and do not curate or deliver services. They facilitate exchanges between
buyers and sellers in ways that increase transaction ease, transparency, and
efficiency.

For example, Hotels.com is a digital exchange that facilitates transactions
between travelers who need rooms and hotels that supply rooms. Notably,
Hotels.com neither owns nor operates hotels. The app simply and elegantly
provides a transparent digital exchange where consumers can select and
reserve a room tailored to their needs, preferences, and budgets. For their
part, hotels gain access to potential customers who reserve rooms with
minimal friction.

Intermediaries Beware

As discussed previously, healthcare is particularly vulnerable to the disruptive "exchange" business model because it has an excessive number of
suppliers offering fragmented, high-cost, high-friction commodity services.
Tullman says, "All we need are 10 major self-insured companies on the
Transcarent platform to disrupt, transform, and optimize healthcare's
supply–demand dynamics."

Three years after its launch, Transcarent is putting the pieces in place to
achieve Tullman's bold vision of becoming "the One Place for Health and
Care." When fully operational, Transcarent will create a high-performing
and efficient health and care marketplace.

Transcarent's app will deliver a more satisfying customer experience
and higher-quality outcomes at lower costs through personalized service

provision. This is the very definition of value. In the process (and this is Transcarent's essential attribute), they'll solve their members' health and healthcare "jobs to be done."

To become "the One Place for Health and Care," Transcarent is attacking employers' three-horned dilemma in providing health insurance coverage to their employees:

- Rising costs, particularly in cancer, without commensurate improvement in access to appropriate care at fair prices.
- Excessive benefit complexity with companies routinely offering over 20 underused digital "point" solutions that confuse rather than improve employees' care.
- Ballooning pharmacy expenditures particularly for "specialty" medications delivered through a maze of profiteering intermediaries, including wholesale distributors, pharmacy benefit managers (PBMs), and pharmacies, often operating under one corporate umbrella.

Adding to the self-insured employers' challenge are tightening federal regulations governing their fiduciary responsibilities to provide cost-effective health insurance plans to their employees. Effective December 31, 2023, employers must attest that their arrangements with third-party administrators, PBMs and other benefit providers contain no gag clauses blocking their ability to receive transparent pricing data. Failure to do so will result in government-imposed fines.

This latest regulatory requirement comes on top of a provision contained in the Consolidated Appropriations Act of 2021. Also taking effect in 2023, the Act mandates that chief financial officers for companies with self-funded health plans must certify that "the healthcare services they buy for their employees are cost-effective, high-quality, and meet mental health parity and pharmacy benefit requirements."[8] This added fiduciary responsibility incentivizes self-insured employers to become even better buyers of value-based healthcare services.

Despite their massive funding of health insurance benefits, self-insured employers still lack the cost and outcomes data necessary to determine whether they're in compliance with their increasing fiduciary obligations. Legislative efforts are underway to improve data transparency, but it's still much more difficult than it should be to isolate specific prices for specific procedures.

As discussed in Chapter 2, there's a reason U.S. healthcare's administrative costs may be as high as 30% of total expenditures. It's simply not in the interests of intermediaries to reveal baked-in transaction costs. As muckraking journalist Upton Sinclair astutely wrote after his failed 1934 campaign for governor of California, "It is difficult to get a man to understand something when his salary depends upon his not understanding it."

Rather than dance exclusively with Healthcare Inc., Transcarent is becoming an Uber-like exchange company that directly links sellers (aka health systems) and users (aka consumers) of healthcare products and services. This enables Transcarent to reduce prices for healthcare services by connecting high-value and high-volume providers with Transcarent members requiring their services.

Under the Transcarent business model, there are no hidden fees, price gouging, or overtreatment. Moreover, Transcarent puts their proverbial "money where their mouth is" by taking full financial risk for the costs of their members' care. Transcarent's pricing model only charges their self-insured clients when it delivers tangible value through better health outcomes and lower costs (see Figure 9.8).

To make this happen, Transcarent's app really does cover the map.

Brand Promise in Action

Embedded within Transcarent's brand promise is the ability for its members to get the care they require, even expensive inpatient care, easily and

Figure 9.8   Screenshot of Transcarent app.

Source: Transcarent.

without question. To make this happen, Transcarent announced on September 26, 2023, the launch of its National Independent Provider Ecosystem with "10 of the most innovative and highest-quality health systems across America."[9]

In exchange for incremental volume and upfront payment, these health systems have agreed to preferred access for Transcarent members for specific care episodes at pre-contracted bundled prices. As of April 2024, their network includes Advocate, Intermountain, the Hospital for Special Surgery, and Mass General Brigham, among many others.

This agreement enables Transcarent to extend its virtual care platform into locally delivered, high-quality affordable care whenever and wherever necessary. Tullman's comments describing the ecosystem's launch read like a primer for exchange-based business models tailored to healthcare's unique operating environment:

> *Our close collaboration with these 10 leading health systems will allow us to better design care pathways, provide higher-quality care and faster access. By aligning with health systems who can guarantee both quality of care and competitive pricing, we can reduce administrative burden and, just as important, demonstrate true measurable value for the people who pay for care — employers and their employees.*
>
> *We'll also more closely integrate the digital experience with the hands-on care that we know only health professionals can provide. It's not an either/or, it's both!*

Beyond hospital care, Transcarent is attacking high drug prices. In November 2022, the company selected Prescryptive to be the backbone of Transcarent Pharmacy Care (TPC). TPC offers members a transparent, flexible, and integrated pharmacy benefit that enables searches for lowest-cost drug prices and prescription transfers when necessary. The press release describes how this benefit works to drive better pharmacy purchasing:

> *Prescryptive's prescription intelligence platform will power a new kind of pharmacy experience for Transcarent's millions of members with transparent pricing, 100% pass-through of manufacturer rebates, no spread pricing and access to Prescryptive's national network of more than 60,000 retail, home delivery and specialty pharmacies.*

Through the partnership, Transcarent Pharmacy Care Members will be able to shop for their own prescriptions for the first time with a digital prescription. Consumers can simply tap to view real-time price data, select a pharmacy to fill their medication or a home delivery option, know the price they will pay and make more informed decisions.[10]

TPC reduces real-time prescription costs by as much as 30% by incorporating low-cost drug suppliers into its value chain. These include GoodRx, Walmart, and Mark Cuban's Cost-Plus Drug Company. Glen Tullman and Mark Cuban are intellectual soulmates in using their capital, expertise, and passion to deliver CB^2E^2 healthcare to American health consumers.

Tullman and Cuban were on stage together on January 11, 2024, for the closing session of the Consumer Electronics Show. Energetic and optimistic, both believe that the key to fixing U.S. healthcare is making it less complex, more consumer-friendly, and by directly focused on measurable outcomes.

Healthcare is complex everywhere in the world. The U.S. is exceptional in making healthcare even more complex than it needs to be.

Aggregators like Transcarent hold the key to unshackling American consumers from the strangling grip of Healthcare Inc. They are applying digital technologies in novel ways to eliminate healthcare's sclerotic operating practices and improve its anemic productivity as well as to delight customers by solving their health and healthcare jobs-to-be-done.

BAYLOR SCOTT & WHITE'S PLATFORM PLAY

Exchange companies like Transcarent are placing enormous pressure on incumbent healthcare companies to embrace consumerism. By developing its own seamless consumer interface, Baylor Scott & White Health (BSW) is positioning to become a convenient, high-volume, high-quality, appropriate-cost healthcare system. BSW's strategy is to simultaneously increase its consumer connectivity while expanding its market reach.

BSW's bold pivot into consumerism reflects healthcare's changing supply–demand dynamics. As Transcarent and other exchange companies become more established in the marketplace, they will control enough consumer activity to encourage more suppliers/providers to join their networks.

In this process, consumers gain value at the expense of suppliers. Successful suppliers recover lost per-unit revenues by delivering more units of service. Overall revenues increase even as per-unit service prices decline. This is how value-based care delivery generates high investment returns.

Operating businesses, like BSW, adapt to this new form of competition by joining exchanges, building their own platforms, cooperating, and/or consolidating with competitors, enhancing their value-propositions, and/or developing loyalty programs that attract customers with perks, special offers, and amenities. These strategies are expensive to deploy. Being an early adopter is often essential to long-term success.

The hospitality industry provides context for the strategic challenge confronting health systems. Understanding how big "platform" players like Marriott and Hilton have responded to the competitive threat posed by exchange companies (e.g., Hotels.com, Airbnb) illuminates the wisdom of BSW's strategy.

Hotel management companies like Marriott and Hilton focus their efforts on building brand loyalty by creating great customer experiences. Through brand consolidation, they have expanded their range of hotel offerings (price points, amenities, decor). They also build robust loyalty programs and bundle services with affiliated partners (e.g., airlines, rental car companies, retailers). In essence, hotel platform companies are doing everything they can to retain existing customers even as they accept incremental demand from hospitality exchange companies.

Recognizing the need to establish its own independent and powerful marketplace offering, BSW is following the playbook charted by successful consumer platform companies like Marriott, Target, American Airlines, and Amazon.

Moving Beyond Epic

As discussed earlier in this chapter, most U.S. health systems rely on pure or hybrid versions of Epic's MyChart to serve as their digital front door. This is the equivalent of Marriott relying on Sabre to operate its vital consumer portal.

In the digital era, nothing is more important than connecting with customers and making their consumer experience easy, productive, and rewarding. Like Sabre, the Epic EHR is a transactional record system, not an effective consumer interface. Co-author Dave's experience trying to reschedule a dermatology appointment through MyChart illustrates the dangers of this approach.

As discussed in the chapter on Force#5, Epic has a stranglehold on the marketplace for electronic health records in the U.S. Two-thirds of all patient records flow through their "walled garden" network. We believe this gives Epic monopoly pricing control within the vitally important EHR marketplace.

Health systems using Epic's EHR essentially become members of an "Epic Society" that provides guidance on the development and application of the MyChart app. At Epic's annual meeting each summer in Verona, Wisconsin, health system members of the "Epic Society" vote on which MyChart features they would like to adjust and improve. Majority rules. Epic implements those changes.

Can anyone imagine Amazon agreeing to cede management of its customer engagement platform to a third party? That simply would never, ever happen.

McCanna's Moment

When Pete McCanna joined Baylor Scott & White as the organization's president in September 2017, he saw value in BSW's relatively new consumer-facing app. McCanna wanted to expand the app's capabilities and reach.

Historically, health systems have maintained tight control of patient access to hospital and clinic services through strong physician relationships. Great health system leaders were those who cultivated physicians to practice at their institutions. "No" was not a word in their vocabulary when it came to engaging high-volume admitting doctors.

McCanna understands that a paternalistic view of health systems' commercial relationships with patients is anachronistic. He believes consumerism in healthcare is "an unstoppable force," so health systems like BSW must cultivate direct relationships with their patient customers to sustain market relevance.

As discussed previously, effective consumer connectivity in a digital marketplace requires "one app that covers the map." Accordingly, McCanna has increased BSW's technology and talent investments to make this vision a reality.

Not long after McCanna's arrival, the rebranded MyBSWHealth app came to life. Unlike almost every other health system and like almost all travel companies, BSW created a bespoke digital app on top of its Epic EHR. McCanna wasn't going to accept design advice exclusively from the Epic Society or other third parties for "improving" BSW's vital customer engagement platform.

When McCanna became BSW CEO in January 2022, he authored a new vision statement for the organization with this powerful mantra, "Empowering You to Live Well." Accompanying the new vision statement was a hard strategic pivot to embrace consumerism.

Essentially, BSW's strategy is to transfer agency to its patients/customers for managing their health. This requires giving consumers better tools for managing their health and healthcare. As Clay Christensen might observe, granting consumers agency is now BSW's "job-to-be-done."

MyBSWHealth app is leading this charge. McCanna wants the app to become the industry's "finest customer engagement platform" as BSW becomes an "indisputable leader" in healthcare consumerism. Achieving this goal has led BSW to engage human design engineers, journey mappers, and other non-traditional health system professionals to imagine, improve, and enliven their customers' digital experiences.

Putting it all together, BSW's digital strategy for consumers has the following three core components:

1. It relies on developing direct relationships with customers through their digital devices. BSW wants to become the primary partner for consumers on their individual health and healthcare journeys. That means out-hustling others seeking that role (retailers, big tech, Epic, upstart digital tech companies) by pairing a cohesive digital experience with a robust care delivery network.

2. It requires an ecosystem that incorporates health and wellbeing in addition to healthcare services. Health systems, in McCanna's opinion, essentially operate hospitals and clinics. While essential, delivering superior clinical care is not enough to create an all-encompassing customer relationship. Accordingly, BSW has expanded its offerings in partnership with an array of specialized health and wellbeing service providers.

3. Finally, and perhaps most importantly, BSW has to offer "frictionless" delivery 24/7 in whatever venue customers prefer. This is much easier said than done. BSW has overhauled and reengineered its workflows to make sure the company delivers when customers hit the "easy button" to trigger specific actions.

The results are impressive. As of early 2024, there are 3.1 million active MyBSWHealth accounts with more than 1,000 new accounts joining daily. In 2023, 1.65 million members scheduled appointments through the app.

The majority of (88%) of total BSW patients with three or more annual visits (i.e., "frequent fliers") maintain active MyBSWHealth accounts. The app now handles 31% of all patient balance payments.

Since 2020, more than 325,000 individuals with no previous BSW connection have created accounts. The team is continuously refining metrics to better understand the dynamics of customer loyalty as well as ways to increase engagement, attract new customers, and earn more "wallet share."

Almost all healthcare companies assert they're advancing customer engagement and tout the strength of their consumer platforms. Very few, however, are making the concerted investments in capital, talent, and network expansion to make that vision a reality.

Standing out from the crowd, BSW is designing and implementing its digital future on its own terms. Pete McCanna is a football fan. He believes BSW has a little lead on the industry now but that it's still early in the game. Like all great coaches, McCanna wants to "extend that lead by halftime."

CONCLUSION: CONSUMERISM NOW

Consumerism is propelling a paradigm shift in health and healthcare service provision. Consumer engagement is THE essential ingredient reshaping a complex healthcare ecosystem. Solving real consumer problems is THE strategy required for market success.

While health systems like Northwestern wait for Epic to deliver them to the digital promised land, they are losing the battle for consumers' hearts and minds at the very time that consumers' healthcare service choices are expanding. Engaging consumers requires "one app that covers the map" – single-site, omni-channel platforms that delight customers with comprehensive offerings, great service, and ease of use.

Powerful new market entrants, like One Medical and Transcarent, have integrated omni-channel platforming into their business models. Some healthcare incumbents, like Baylor Scott & White Health, have custom-built apps that deliver equivalent high-level consumer engagement. While a distinct minority, BSW and others like them are positioning for increased market relevance within a consolidating and digitizing healthcare economy.

Promise and peril are the two sides of expanding healthcare consumerism. Engaging consumers is not rocket science but it is rare in healthcare. Healthcare organizations that rise to the challenge can prosper. Those that don't may perish.

KEY INSIGHTS ON AGGREGATORS' ADVANTAGE

- Consumer-driven health requires "one app that covers the map" to realize its full potential. Decentralized whole-person health requires seamless digital platforms that empower users to manage their health and healthcare needs.
- As an industry, healthcare has been slow to engage consumers. Most incumbent providers and payers remain too committed to transactional, volume-driven business models where consumer experience is an afterthought.
- Great software eats intermediaries. Healthcare is a target-rich environment for digital technology companies that can improve services provision and lower costs by eliminating the armies of healthcare intermediaries that create administrative friction and diminish consumer and caregiver experience.
- Many traditional healthcare companies appreciate the need to become more consumer-centric but seem incapable of making the transition. They "declare victory" at engagement level 1.0 (Administrative), missing the opportunity to connect with "Automated" and "Empowered" users.
- Newer market entrants, including One Medical and Transcarent, along with some enlightened incumbents like Baylor Scott & White Health, are developing engaging omni-channel platforms that provide trusted information, guidance, and access to vital services.

10 | Empowered Caregivers

When co-author Paul was the CEO of Amedisys, he spent one week each month in the field engaging with caregivers and their patients. Supporting caregivers so they in turn could serve patients was the secret sauce that propelled Amedysis' stratospheric growth. Here's an example of the kind of service no money can buy that occurred while Paul was on a field visit to northern Maine.

A series of winter storms dumped over a foot of snow on the streets of Bangor, Maine. As the town struggled to clean the roads, many residents were snowed-in and unable to leave their homes. Amanda DeWitt, an Amedisys hospice aide, trucked over to see a patient who lived at the end of a now-impassable driveway.

Amanda put on snowshoes and hiked up the mile-long driveway to visit the patient and his wife. Before Amanda left, she brought firewood in to heat the home. On subsequent visits, Amanda snowmobiled up the driveway with an attached dogsled to deliver groceries and medications.

Snowshoeing and snowmobile driving weren't part of Amanda's job description. That didn't matter. She did what she needed to do. *It's at bedsides and kitchen tables throughout America where the magic of great caregiving occurs – one patient and one caregiver at a time.*

Amedysis lore contains innumerable stories like Amanda's. Collectively, these triumphant stories fuel caregivers' passion for serving patients. Together they have created a culture of superior caregiving where professionals thrive knowing they can do whatever is necessary to serve their patients.

In the last chapter, we described how some healthcare companies fully engage with consumers to help them solve their health and healthcare "jobs to be done." This is impossible to accomplish without engaged employees, like Amanda, who go the extra mile for customers.

Brand love is the power that moves consumers to embrace a company's products and services. Empowering caregivers is the best strategy for engaging consumers and earning their brand love. Despite its compelling mission, healthcare isn't igniting employee passions like it should. Often, it's just the opposite.

THE WAY HEALTHCARE'S WORKING ISN'T WORKING

"Drowning" in Silverlake, Washington

On October 11, 2022, the emergency room at St. Michael Medical Center (SMMC) reached the breaking point. Only five nurses were on duty to care for over 45 patients. Panic ensued.

Unable to think of any other solution, Kelsay Irby, R.N., called 911 and begged for help: "We're drowning . . . We're drowning . . . We're in dire straits . . . Can someone come up here and help us?" The call center dispatched two firefighters to the hospital's ER. For 90 minutes, they took vital signs, moved patients, cleaned rooms, and changed bedsheets. After operations stabilized, the hospital manager thanked and dismissed the firefighters.[1]

St. Michael is part of Virginia Mason Franciscan Health (VMFH), headquartered in Tacoma, Washington. At a community meeting later that fall, SMMC's CEO Chad Melton described the hospital's severe understaffing. SMMC already employed 180 contract workers and was searching desperately for 300 more. Despite their focused effort, no candidates had interviewed for vacancies in the ER department.

The situation remained fraught. The UFCW 3000 union representing SMMC workers called for CEO Melton and Chief Nursing Officer Jeanell Rasmussen to resign. In response, VMFH emphasized that it was "redoubling" its recruitment and professional development efforts. SMMC offers among the highest pay rates for nursing staff in Washington state.

For her part, Irby is exhausted, angry, and disheartened. She made the following comments at the meeting:

> *I know that I speak for myself and several coworkers that when we leave at the end of the day, going, "I honestly don't even know if it's worth it," it's not just about the money. It is about going into healthcare to be able to take care of patients. When we can't do that, when we go home at the end of our shift and feel like we failed you because we are not heard by our management, there are no words.*

A New York City Exodus

On January 9, 2023, over 7,000 nurses walked off the job at Mount Sinai Hospital and Montefiore Medical Center in New York City after four months of failed negotiations between the hospitals and their union, the New York State Nurses Association (NYSNA). Although higher pay was among their demands, the nurses' primary concern was improving nursing–patient staffing ratios.

Interviewed for a *New York Times* article, nurses described double and triple workloads on extended shifts, particularly in ERs, ICUs, and critical care units. The stress and added burden have clearly taken a toll even on the most dedicated nurses. Here's how they describe their plight:

> *We are leaving the profession in droves because we go home with moral injury. We go home crying because we are not able to meet the needs of our patients.*
> —Benny Mathew, a Montefiore emergency nurse
> *We're literally just giving medication and moving to the next patient. We're not providing quality of care. We're not able to listen to the patient.*
> —Karen Paltoo, a Mount Sinai stroke nurse

After two chaotic days, the hospitals settled the strike with higher wages and the establishment of concrete, enforceable staffing ratios. The hospitals will bear the added costs of higher pay for more nurses without a commensurate increase in revenues.

The way healthcare works isn't working. Despite high pay, nurses (healthcare's workhorses) are leaving the profession in droves. The passion that drove them to become caregivers has withered. SMMC's, Mount Sinai's and Montefiore's current staffing challenges are extreme but not unique. Even as their profitability evaporates, American hospitals everywhere are struggling to find enough doctors, nurses, technicians, and hourly workers to provide adequate care.

Throwing money at the problem hasn't worked. An October 2022 report by Definitive Health cited research that found 47% of healthcare workers plan to leave their positions by 2025.[2] More of the same approach of paying higher salaries for intolerable working conditions will yield more of the same dismal results.

Despite the increasing service demands, healthcare productivity is decreasing, due in large measure to accelerated turnover, excessive administrative burdens, and more chaotic work environments. Productivity goes down when workforce stress increases. As illustrated by the Washington and New York City case studies, workplace stress inside healthcare organizations is at an all-time high.

Demographic trends within the U.S. population compound both healthcare's labor supply (a shrinking pool of potential workers) and demand (more patients with chronic diseases) workforce challenges. Real improvement can only occur by reigniting healthcare workers' passion for caregiving.

CHANGING MINDSETS

Noted author Simon Sinek has observed that "working hard for something we don't care about is stress; working hard for something we love is passion." The irony of healthcare's workforce dilemmas is that few professions can match its potential for providing intrinsic meaning to its frontline workers.

Healthcare needs a managerial mindset change. Igniting clinicians' passion for caregiving can only happen as part of a broader strategic initiative to optimize clinicians' human potential as part of cohesive teams, supported by user-friendly technologies and systems, within purpose-driven organizations.

It sounds hard, and maybe it is, but the rewards and financial returns of connecting employees with organizational purpose are exponential. Before they will commit heart and soul to their jobs, however, caregivers must receive more support and guidance from their employers. It's time for healthcare organizations to give their employees what they need, want, and increasingly expect.

Asking What Companies Can Do for Their Employees

The concept that well-treated employees deliver great customer service and higher operating profitability is not new. In the 1980s, renowned consultant and bestselling author Frederick Reichheld began studying the economics of loyalty.

Reichheld believed businesses that retain good customers, productive employees, and supportive investors achieve superior performance levels over time. By contrast, businesses that ignore loyalty confront a future filled with uneven profitability, low growth, and loss of market relevance.

During the 1990s, Reichheld founded Bain and Company's global Loyalty Practice. He and the practice are still going strong. Under Reichheld's leadership, Bain quantified loyalty economics, created the Net Promoter Score, and has advised scores of Fortune 100 companies. Even in digital work environments filled with dazzling technologies, loyalty-based businesses thrive and outperform their competitors.

In his 2011 book *The Ultimate Question 2.0*, Reichheld stressed the importance of having inspired employees in creating loyal customers:

> *[Many executives] forget that it's impossible to create loyal customers without first inspiring a team of employees so they become promoters themselves. Who would go out of their way for a customer unless he or she is proud and inspired to be part of the team?*
>
> *And while there are many ingredients of employee engagement – the right training and development, rewards, opportunity for growth, the feeling of being valued and so forth – the real foundation is this: Employees must be able to treat customers and colleagues in a manner that makes them proud.*
>
> *When leaders and their teams consistently treat people right, when they can be relied upon to do the right thing, then an organization can truly be worthy of loyalty.*

Golden Rule Management

Co-author Paul has always believed in Reichheld's approach to people management. When he took the helm of the home care and hospice company Amedisys in 2014, Paul had the chance to put Reichheld's loyalty theories into practice. Drawing on his theology background, Paul dubbed his approach "Golden Rule" management.

At the time, Amedisys was struggling. The company had just fired its founder and long-time CEO, paid a large government fine, and overinvested in an underperforming technology platform. Its stock was trading in the mid-teens.

After spending a short time at the corporate headquarters to get the lay of the land, Paul packed a suitcase and spent the next two months interviewing Amedisys home care and hospice workers in the field. Aside from clinicians, the employees were often underappreciated, low-skilled, and low-income women. They were doing the hard work of providing hands-on care to very sick and dying people.

Paul asked these frontline workers what he and the company could do to make their work lives better. Their answers filled a dozen notebooks and became the basis for his "Golden Rule" turnaround strategy. Paul bet Amedisys' future on the proposition that treating its employees with care, support, and respect would turbocharge the company's operating performance, fuel growth, and attract investment.

It worked. Employee retention increased. Quality scores improved. Profits soared. Under Paul's leadership, Amedisys redefined the home-care sector and became its leading company. The company's stock price moved consistently upward and peaked at over $300 a share in January 2021.

Paul retired as the company's CEO in April 2022. He celebrated by taking a long and meandering road trip. In 30 days, he visited over 100 Amedisys care centers throughout the South, saying thank you to the very caregivers who made the company's transformation possible. "Golden Rule" management clearly worked for Paul and Amedisys. There's no reason it won't work equally well for other healthcare organizations.

Unlocking underutilized human potential triggered Amedisys' success. Post-COVID, optimizing human potential is still the key imperative for healthcare leaders. They desperately need to regain their employees' loyalty to transform archaic business practices and deliver value-based care. These leaders need to figure out how to win back discouraged employees.

The real question, of course, is how to ignite the spark. During COVID, remote work, video connectivity, and new technologies changed the character of work in fundamental ways. Living through COVID also led many workers to reexamine why and how they work. Under this scrutiny, record numbers changed professions, moved to new locations, and/or developed new relationships with their managers and coworkers.

There's no going back to the pre-pandemic world of work. Companies must move forward by creating new world-of-work paradigms. Doing this requires embracing employee loyalty as a foundational goal, asking what they require to succeed, listening to their answers and then responding with proactive policies, programs, and procedures. This is how Satya Nadella engineered Microsoft's turnaround.

Since Nadella became CEO in 2014, Microsoft's market value has more than quintupled. Nadella believes that Microsoft's success has come through energizing its employees to find value for themselves, the company, and the world. This belief came through loud and clear during a 2018 interview with psychologist Michael Gervais when he asked Nadella to define mastery:

> For me, it [mastery] comes down to being in touch, deeply in touch, with what gives you purpose. One of the things that I say a lot is, "What if you took what you do at Microsoft and flipped it? Hey, I don't work at Microsoft, Microsoft works for me."
>
> And that is because you are a someone who has a particular passion, a particular personal philosophy, and you are able to, in fact, turn what is considered work into an instrument of you realizing the deeper meaning in pursuing your personal philosophy, or passion.
>
> To me, mastery is that—that ability to lead a more purposeful life, and then take all of life and turn it into that platform. Because I think that's all we have, so we may as well make use of it.[3]

What Nadella observed in 2018 is even more applicable in today's post-COVID work environments. It takes self-actualizing platforms for individuals to integrate their work and life activities efficiently and effectively. When optimized, work–life integration gives joy and purpose to employees while they create value for their companies, customers, coworkers, and the world.

The good news is that the right loyalty mindset aligns perfectly with an evolving work–life paradigm that elevates the individual, sustains the company, and improves the world.

The Wheel of Corporate Good Fortune

The concept of work–life balance no longer works. Life infuses work 24/7 and vice versa. The challenge and opportunity for companies today is to create enriching work environments that welcome and engage employees as whole persons with individualized needs and preferences.

When work and life integrate seamlessly, liberated employees expand their reach and capabilities. They create value for themselves, customers, their companies, and everyone around them.

Value creation of this magnitude requires companies to address immediate challenges for employees in concert with tailored development plans. Great companies do not let the urgent overshadow foundational worker support systems. They accommodate both employees' short- and long-term needs.

Cultivating human empowerment requires a managerial mindset that explores what companies can do to help employees become their best selves, professionally and personally. *Motivated employees go the extra mile for customers when they know the company goes the extra mile for them.*

This is the loyalty effect that Fred Reichheld describes. It's the harmonic synergies that co-author Paul unleashed at Amedisys by engaging frontline caregivers. It's how Satya Nadella enables Microsoft employees to achieve mastery at home as well as on the job.

Figure 10.1 depicts how companies can create a continuous process for engaging employees. The process has seven components that intermingle with one another to anticipate opportunities, develop capabilities, accommodate personal circumstances, provide accountability, and bring joy to the workplace. Importantly, this engagement platform simultaneously aligns and satisfies both employee and company needs.

CHANGING MECHANICS

When companies work for employees, they create an environment that fosters honesty, trust, respect, accountability, adaptability, and recognition. Teams thrive when members understand their roles and can count on one another. Everybody wins.

Technologies can help optimize the components of high-functioning corporate cultures. They can reduce friction. They can nudge behaviors. They can speed learning. They can anticipate problems. They can identify opportunities.

What technologies cannot do is create the human-centered mindset that sustains individual and group engagement with noble purpose.

When Companies Work for Employees

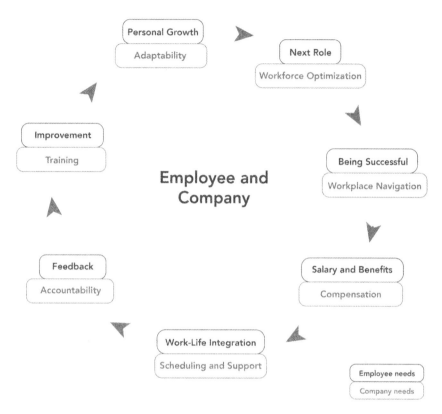

Figure 10.1 Aligning employee and company needs.

That requires leadership. Current and projected shortages of healthcare workers is an industry-wide challenge.

Most solutions for addressing staffing shortages add incremental costs without addressing the causes of employee burnout and turnover. For example, nursing is a hospital's largest expense, typically representing a quarter of the operating budget. Mandated staffing levels, however, is a twentieth-century solution for a twenty-first-century problem.

By contrast, human-centered technologies are the cost-effective twenty-first-century solutions for easing burden and related staffing shortages. Proven technologies and strategies exist that can increase productivity, reduce stress, and grant greater autonomy to frontline caregivers.

Successful companies create cultures and environments that make employees proud and inspire them to be their best selves at work. In this sense, companies work for their employees, not the reverse. The most effective way to address healthcare's staffing shortages is by reigniting the passion existing employees already have for patient care.

Inspired healthcare professionals don't burn out and leave the industry. They're engaged in their work. They're more productive as respected members of cohesive care teams that solve their work–life challenges and give them the tools they require to excel. Applied technologies can make all the difference.

Technological advances are enabling human–machine collaboration in novel and powerful ways. They are transforming healthcare delivery the old-fashioned way – by optimizing human potential. No other business strategy generates a higher return on investment.

Tech-enabled applications that can turbocharge performance already exist. They have proven their ability to reduce drudgery and increase effectiveness, as well as reduce stress, burden, and burnout in healthcare settings. Changing healthcare's workplace mechanics is long overdue. The workforce systems and processes that most healthcare companies employ originated decades ago and haven't evolved.

The simple but elusive goal is to use these human-centered technologies to create work environments that are calm, reassuring, respectful, and productive. All employees, but particularly caregivers, require autonomy, tools, and support to fully engage in their work. Here's the magic. Fully engaged employees turbocharge organizational energy, productivity, and profitability. They go above and beyond to serve customers' needs, and they love doing it.

Eighty percent of the current healthcare workforce is deskless. The best workforce solutions must move beyond the desktop. They must integrate within employee workflows on portable devices that support real-time decision-making.

Solutions that automate or streamline low-value activity create more time for employees to pursue higher-value activities, manage their self-care, and engage whole-heartedly with customers/patients. Imagine the positive impact that rewired managerial mindsets and human-centered mechanics could have on the almost dystopian working conditions that have exasperated nurses in New York City and throughout the country.

Machine Intelligence and the Healthcare Worker

The alignment of employer and employee needs occurs within a continuous activity flow that addresses real challenges and exploits real opportunities in real time. In Figure 10.2, we've augmented the "wheel" graphic with applicable workforce enablement strategies and tools to illustrate how the mechanics of effective workforce management benefit both companies and their employees.

Beginning with the "Next Role/Workforce Optimization" nexus point, we highlight the specific tools and approaches companies can employ to optimize employee wellbeing and organizational performance. Both occur within high-performing organizations that foster human–machine collaboration through digital solutions.

- **Next Role/Workforce Optimization**

    Employees want to understand their career progress and what it will take to advance to their next role. Companies need to align their

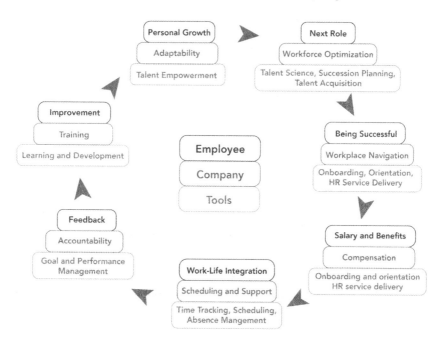

When Companies Work for Employees

Figure 10.2   Tools that improve employee–company alignment.

workforces to deliver their products and services. Talent science uses cognitive assessment tools to give employees and their managers insights into employees' orientation and behavioral attributes.

Armed with this information, managers and employees can explore options for career advancement that match personal preferences and organizational needs. Everybody wins. Employees find positions that fit their lifestyles and personalities. Organizations retain employees by giving them more internal mobility based on their own behaviors, strengths, and preferences.

- ## Being Successful/Talent Empowerment

    Employees want to be successful. Organizations need to orchestrate the movement of their workforces to optimize performance. Talent empowerment offers personalized career-planning guidance that helps employees improve in their current roles and/or prepare them for advancement within the organization.

    For employee fulfillment, talent empowerment must generate advice and opportunities tailored to their professional goals and individual preferences. A key component of talent empowerment is acknowledging employee successes appropriately through organizational and peer-to-peer recognition practices. For example, some employees crave public praise while others prefer quieter, more one-on-one feedback.

- ## Salary and Benefits/Compensation

    Employees want to know how they'll benefit financially as they fulfill their responsibilities to the organization and its customers. Companies need to compensate their employees fairly and transparently to encourage engagement and enhance performance.

    Paying employees accurately and on time is essential. It is also essential that employees understand the components of their compensation and benefits structure. For example, nurses should understand when they can earn premium compensation for working nights and weekends.

- ## Work–Life Integration/Scheduling and Support

    Work–life balance is a myth. Work–life integration is a necessity. Employees need the flexibility to adjust their working schedules to the demands of their personal life. Companies need to develop strategies for supporting their employees in a way that sustains their engagement. Giving employees scheduling control and flexibility can achieve both objectives.

For example, self-scheduling, shift trading and swapping, and shift billboards that use digital tools enable nurses to proactively allocate their time easily. Companies can become more expansive in orchestrating their work environments by encompassing hybrid/virtual options, shorter shifts, weekend-only shifts with full-time pay, etc. Digital scheduling tools also give employees the ability to share their work schedules easily with others (e.g., with family members) and for nursing leaders to see current and upcoming staffing.

- **Assessment/Accountability**

  Employees want to know how they're doing in their roles. Companies want to maintain a consistently high-performing workforce. Providing regular and meaningful performance assessments is essential.

  Done properly, performance assessments become a vehicle for providing and receiving feedback, setting goals, acknowledging successes, and finding opportunities for improvement. Often, incorporating 360-degree assessment tools enrich the ongoing dialogue between managers and employees.

- **Improvement/Training and Development**

  Employees want to improve their knowledge base and skill sets. Companies need to train and develop their workforces to maintain competitiveness. Digital tools incorporated into workflows can accelerate learning, minimize errors, and measure engagement.

  For example, placing digital QR codes at convenient locations (e.g., nurses' stations) can launch short videos, information bulletins, or courses for employees. A quick tour of unit layout helps orient temporary nurses. QR codes on new equipment can provide operating instructions and/or short how-to videos. Companies can also create social connections attached to personalized development programs that build peer-to-peer bonds and deepen learning experiences.

- **Personal Growth/Adaptability**

  Employees want to grow as individuals and develop new capabilities. Companies need to adapt to ever-changing environments. Companies and their employees must embrace lifelong learning

Figure 10.3

within and outside employment for employees to maintain upward mobility and for companies to meet new market demands.

As the pace of change accelerates, employing digital tools to enhance performance and advance skill development will be an area where human–machine collaboration creates differentiation. Keeping aging employees engaged at the level each wants will keep seasoned employees for patients who can guide new generations of employees. For example, mentoring and preceptor programs provide opportunities for seasoned nurses nearing retirement to continue working and sharing expertise.

WOMEN AND HEALTHCARE

Unmet demand for workers has been and will continue to be a significant challenge for the healthcare industry. This shortfall creates a natural opportunity for women to fill the void and lead a revitalized healthcare workforce.

Women dominate healthcare as consumers and caregivers. *Optimizing their role as caregivers, consumers, and leaders is essential to industry transformation.* Bill Clinton's 1992 presidential campaign focused "like a laser beam" on revitalizing the U.S. economy with the famous mantra, "It's the economy, stupid!" In healthcare today, the defining mantra should be "It's women, stupid!"

A 2019 Oliver Wyman report found that women make 80% of health-care decisions and constitute 65% of the healthcare workforce but only fill 30% of healthcare C-suite positions.[4] Only 13% of the healthcare industry's CEOs are women. Simple math suggests that healthcare needs more women leaders.

If the Oliver Wyman 80% figure is accurate, healthcare decisions shaped by women account for $3.76 trillion of the projected $4.7 trillion in 2024 U.S. healthcare expenditure. By extension, healthcare decision-making by women constitutes 15% of the entire U.S. economy. That represents enormous purchasing power.

Women are the primary caregivers in the U.S. today. No one disputes this. Women encounter the health system when they have children, as primary caregivers for their children (80% of decisions regarding a child's health), and as primary caregivers for their parents (59% of healthcare decisions regarding parents are made by women, generally daughters or relatives).

Consequently, women have more direct and frequent experience with healthcare than men. They generally also have a wider range of healthcare experiences than men who often avoid interaction with the system until middle or old age.

The stress or burden placed on women for caregiving is disproportionate and exceedingly unfair. Caregiving.com has found that the average caregiver is a 49-year-old woman taking care of an aging parent. Women provide 62% of unpaid care. Women over 50 disproportionately leave employment to care for aging parents. A 2016 AARP report estimates that this costs these women $324,000 in aggregate wages and Social Security benefits over their lifetimes.[5]

The actual cost is probably much higher today. Women caregivers are 2.5 times more likely to experience poverty later in life than those who are not caregivers. Michigan State University researched the health effects of the caregiving burden and found women caregivers reported twice as much chronic stress as non-caregivers.

Unpaid care has increased to epidemic proportions. A 2021 AARP report pegged the annual cost of unpaid care at $600 billion.[6] More people, particularly women, are providing unpaid care as the U.S. population ages and there are fewer clinical and non-clinical caregivers. According to the Family Caregiver Alliance, the number of unpaid caregivers grew 21% between 2015 and 2020. They expect that trend will continue.

The challenges and complexity of unpaid caregiving are also increasing. Ninety-six percent of the caregivers attend to their patients' ADLs (Activities of Daily Living) for an average of 19 days per month. Surprisingly, 46% of unpaid caregivers report that they perform medical and nursing tasks usually done by clinical professionals. Due to a lack of insurance coverage and/or financial resources, 57% of unpaid caregivers say they *must* undertake these clinical tasks.

According to a 2019 report by the Boston Consulting Group, women fill 75% of entry-level positions with healthcare payers and providers.[7] Those women promoted to more senior roles "cluster" disproportionately into administrative and non-operational roles. The report concludes that "recruitment [of women] isn't a problem, it's retention and advancement."

This lack of equitable promotions occurs even though women receive most advanced healthcare degrees. Despite their disproportionately higher levels of academic training, women held only 18 of the 150 leadership positions at the 50 largest healthcare companies.

The BCG report concludes that "gender diversity is worse in healthcare . . . than in other industries. These [large healthcare] companies have a wealth of talent to develop into senior positions, yet the industry still relies primarily on male leaders." Scott Barry Kaufman in an opinion piece in *Scientific American* suggested that "people don't get hyped up about gender equality in female-dominated fields (like healthcare)." It's time they should.

A 2020 McKinsey study found correlation between greater diversity in C-suites and boards of directors (gender, age, ethnicity, and economic status) and higher organizational profitability. When a company's board and management resemble their customers demographically, EBITDA (i.e., organizational cash-flow) doubles.[8] This is a remarkable statistic!

Since women are making 80% of the healthcare decisions and represent 75% of the healthcare workforce, it's almost unfathomable that women are so underrepresented in healthcare's leadership ranks. Healthcare companies with this upside-down leadership structure are clearly missing the mark and are prone to making strategic mistakes.

There's nothing more important to a company's future than knowing and understanding its customers. Diversity in healthcare leadership creates significant corporate value. It makes sense. If the people driving the company look like the people buying the company's products or services, they will pinpoint more accurately what their customers want, need, and desire.

Co-author Paul witnessed this first-hand as Amedisys' chair and CEO. The company's profitability increased as its leadership diversified. Collectively, the company made better and more informed strategic decisions.

Simply put, it's time for women to take a greater leadership role in U.S. healthcare. This is particularly true as the industry seeks to transform by solving consumers' health and healthcare "jobs to be done." Progress is occurring. Two of the top five health insurance companies are run by women (Karen Lynch at CVS and Gail Boudreaux at Elevance). Kim A. Keck now runs the national Blue Cross Blue Shield Association. Two large and influential Blue plans have also recently appointed women CEOs.

The U.S. needs more gifted women to lead the charge for revolutionary industry transformation. The BCG report referenced above affirms this logic in compelling language:

> *This isn't an issue of fairness; gender diversity offers substantial benefits to organizations. According to BCG research, How Diverse Leadership Teams Boost Innovation, they are more innovative and generate higher financial returns.*
>
> *In the current healthcare environment, companies must innovate faster than ever to contend with disruptive forces such as new payment models, digital and e-health, and the increasing involvement of patients in decisions about their care. Given these pressures, companies need to tap all available insights, ideas, and perspectives.*[9]

There is an enormous opportunity to drive better performance by diversifying the leadership of healthcare organizations to reflect the customers they serve. Indeed, empowering women leaders may be among the most effective strategies for engaging the healthcare workforce and reigniting their passion for caregiving and health promotion. Women healthcare leaders are more likely to change managerial "mindsets" and organizational "mechanics" to empower healthcare workforces to go the extra mile for customers.

THE DOCTOR DILEMMA

This chapter's organizing principle is that enlightened companies with engaging caregivers who solve consumers' health and healthcare "jobs to be

done" will gain competitive advantage as the healthcare ecosystem trans-
forms. In the process, a "new" value-based medicine will emerge to replace
the "old" value-depleting medicine that currently dominates the U.S.
healthcare.

This transition from Old Medicine to New Medicine will be exceptionally difficult for physicians. Their selection, training, enculturation,
compensation, and protection is a root cause of healthcare's dysfunction.
The medical profession's outsized prestige, privilege, and political power has
distorted its ability to deliver high-quality healthcare services consistently,
cost-effectively, and equitably. Medical protectionism exacts high financial
and human toll from American society.

In his 1984 Pulitzer prize–winning book, *The Social Transformation of
Medicine*, author Paul Starr chronicles American medicine's history. Prior to
the 1900s, doctors had low social status. There were too many quacks. Most
care took place in the home. Pay was low. The profession lacked professional standards. Most doctors lived hand to mouth.

As the century turned, several cultural, economic, scientific, and legal
developments converged to elevate the profession's status in American society. Stricter licensing reduced the supply of physicians and closed most existing medical schools. Legislation and legal rulings restricted corporate
ownership of medical practices and enshrined physicians' operating autonomy. Scientific breakthroughs have given medicine more healing power and
prestige. Medicine's gains have largely come at the expense of public health
programming and funding.

Through the decades that have followed, the American Medical Association and state medical societies have frustrated external attempts to control medical delivery and institute national health insurance. The medical
establishment's insistence on fee-for-service payment and the absolute right
of patients to choose their doctors has curtailed responsible payment
reform, limited accountability, and diminished U.S. health status.

Physician incomes and prestige rose from the 1920s onward as the
medical profession limited practitioner supply, established payment guidelines, encouraged specialization, controlled service delivery, and socialized
capital investment. Within the medical profession, specialists have gained
public stature and higher compensation relative to primary care physicians.
These factors explain the dramatic increase in specialty physicians as a percentage of U.S. doctors.

The business of U.S. healthcare today has not evolved. Physicians still exhibit the professional behaviors that emerged during the early 1900s. Gleaming new medical centers testify to the profession's success in socializing capital investment and maintaining autonomy over healthcare operations. Protectionism is alive and well-practiced in U.S. medicine.

Consequently, U.S. healthcare is a well-documented negative outlier among high-income countries. It costs far more to deliver care and delivers inferior health outcomes. Multiple institutional restraints prevent American medicine from reorganizing to deliver a higher societal return. They include the following:

- **Overdeveloped Specialty Care**

  As many as 80% of U.S. physicians now practice as specialists. The remaining 20% practice primary care. With increasing frequency, health systems and health insurers now employ these remaining primary care physicians to either amplify or restrict referrals into high-cost specialty care services.

  As witnessed in other national health systems (e.g., Portugal) and with enhanced U.S. primary care companies (e.g., One Medical), independent and integrated primary care practices are much more effective at diagnosing, preventing, and managing chronic diseases. By contrast, the U.S. system by and large only treats the symptoms of chronic disease, not its root causes. This treatment-centric approach has disastrous consequences.

  The U.S. healthcare system's maldistribution of facilities and practitioners relative to consumer needs reflects an inherent cultural bias within medicine and financial incentives that reward specialty care service provision, particularly for commercially insured patients. Acute care hospitals and ambulatory facilities are expensive playgrounds for America's overabundant specialty care physicians.

- **Underused Facilities**

  No capital-intensive industry uses its high-cost facilities less than healthcare. Most hospitals and ambulatory centers run one shift per day, four-and-a-half days per week. They are ghost towns after 4 p.m. Monday to Thursday, noon on Friday and over the weekends.

  Medicine's bias toward specialty care and accommodation of doctors' preferred and inefficient practice patterns has led to a massive overbuilding of acute care capacity in the U.S. Imagine the

productivity pickup if hospitals eliminated unnecessary and preventable admissions while running two full shifts every day.

- **Restricted Physician Supply and Service Provision**

U.S. medicine restricts the number and distribution of practicing
doctors by limiting admissions to medical schools and demanding
excessive training. For example, it requires 15 years (four years of college, four years of medical school, three years of residency, and four
years of fellowship) to become a cardiac surgeon even for high-
volume, easy-to-perform routine procedures like angioplasty.

U.S. medicine further restricts physician supply and amplifies demand for their services in the following four ways:

1. By promulgating state-based regulations that prevent other
   medical professionals (e.g., nurse practitioners, physician as-
   sistants, pharmacists) to practice at the top of their license.
2. By promulgating regulations that limit or prevent medical
   professionals to cross state lines to practice.
3. By using regulatory and/or practice rules to require redun-
   dant and/or inefficient practices that limit consumer access
   to service provision (e.g., mandated physician office visits to
   refill prescriptions).
4. By establishing payment rules that reward physician-led
   activities and limit CB^2E^2 service provision (e.g., requiring a
   dermatologist instead of aides or even machines to conduct
   routine screenings for signs of skin cancer).

Restricting supply and service provision supports higher compensation levels for practicing physicians, particularly specialists. The
mechanisms that enable this artificial manipulation of physician demand and service supply include the following:

1. Undue influence by medical societies on the promulgation
   of state-based medical regulations.
2. Determination of Medicare compensation levels by the
   American Medical Association.
3. The setting of accreditation standards by specialty medical
   associations.

Homeostasis is a biological term that describes the self-regulating processes by which living organisms maintain equilibrium. Homeostasis requires

multiple interdependent systems to adjust their function to maintain balance and stability. Disease manifests when systems become chaotic and imbalanced. Cancer cells proliferate and destroy vital organs. The body then withers and ultimately dies. Entropy wins.

U.S. medicine's dysfunction has disrupted the balance required to maintain health and treat disease within a high-functioning society. U.S. medicine cannot return to homeostasis without a radical rewiring of physician selection, training, acculturation, and compensation.

No group will experience the impact of value-based reform more than doctors. From Old Medicine's ashes will emerge a revolutionary, people-centered New Medicine that will make America healthy again.

Old Medicine vs. New Medicine

In 2007, Donald Berwick and his colleagues at the Institute for Healthcare Improvement introduced the concept of healthcare's "Triple Aim." In Berwick's words, "Improving the U.S. healthcare system requires simultaneous pursuit of three aims: Improving the experience of care, improving the health of populations, and reducing per-capita costs of healthcare."

Since then, many have argued that "improving the work life of healthcare providers, including clinicians and staff" should become the fourth aim. More recently, some have argued that "health equity" should become the fifth aim.

Together, these five aims establish the foundations of a New Medicine that overcomes antiquated but well-established and counterproductive practices embedded within Old Medicine. Achieving this "Quintuple Aim" requires clinical practice models that emphasize interdisciplinary as well as interprofessional team-based care, human–machine collaboration, and lifelong learning.

Retooling America's clinical workforce to practice New Medicine is an enormous undertaking. No initiative of this scope occurs in a vacuum. Across all industry sectors, companies are adapting to remarkable advances in digital technologies and analytics. Healthcare is no exception. Harnessing digital technology's potential is a team-based enterprise. Clinical training and leadership development must evolve to create healthcare's workforce for tomorrow.

Old Medicine applies a heroic model of physician leadership that discourages team-oriented behaviors. Reflective of a time when most physicians worked independently, such an approach grants enormous autonomy to physicians but impedes standardization, compromises patient safety, and diminishes care outcomes.

New Medicine relies on continuous performance improvement supported by massive data sets and incisive analytics. Integrated technologies improve medical decision-making at the point of care. Optimizing performance requires ongoing clinical education that is relevant, seamless, and connected to operational workflows. It must facilitate learning without adding more administrative burden to already overworked clinicians.

The chart illustrated in Figure 10.3 contrasts Old Medicine's learned behaviors with those required to excel within New Medicine's evolving ecosystem.

In New Medicine, collaborative, team-based leaders engender trust and share information freely. They replace command-and-control leaders who practice hierarchical decision-making and cherish individual autonomy. Outcomes improve as dynamic teams prioritize patients' needs, collaborate, and hold one another accountable.

Human capital is New Medicine's most precious resource. Leadership development tools and data support self-assessment, self-awareness, and personal and professional growth. Coaching, training, and guidance can equip physicians and other clinicians to control their emotions, become more empathetic, and encourage patients to become active participants in their care regimens.

Inculcating New Medicine's aligned educational programming into daily work routines is a powerful tool for unifying organizational culture, enhancing capabilities, optimizing performance, and realizing workforce potential. In this organic and systematic way, educational programming creates the principal channel for developing the essential learned leadership behaviors required for "new medicine" to thrive.

New Medicine's Transformative Market Dynamics

The healthcare marketplace is reorganizing to serve digitally enabled boomer and millennial consumers. It's shifting away from fragmented, high-cost and centralized Old Medicine (think physicians in hospitals) to lower-cost,

Old Medicine		New Medicine
Individualistic	Mindset	Team-Based
Hierarchical	Worldview	Outcomes-Driven
Autonomous	Orientation	Collaborative
Specialized	Focus	Broad
My Way	Attitude	Our Way
Trust Myself	Decision Bias	Trust Others
Do It Myself	Action Bias	Delegate
Assumed	Trust	Earned
Command	Communication Style	Persuade
Personal	Recognition/Accountability	Group

Figure 10.4 It's time for a change: "Old Medicine" vs. "New Medicine" leadership models.

more convenient and customer-friendly New Medicine delivered through omni-channel platforms. Engaging consumers in managing their health and healthcare needs is a prerequisite for New Medicine providers.

Consequently, a new practitioner paradigm is also emerging. That paradigm is shifting surgeries and other routine procedures to high-volume focused factories that deliver high-quality outcomes at low costs through standardization.

The new paradigm also emphasizes active patient engagement with equally empowered caregivers to achieve better routine and complex care outcomes. Next-generation business models (see Figure 10.5) move beyond the referral-treadmill underlying fee-for-service (FFS) and administrative-services-only (ASO) medicine. They accommodate risk-based payment

New Medicine's Practitioner Paradigm

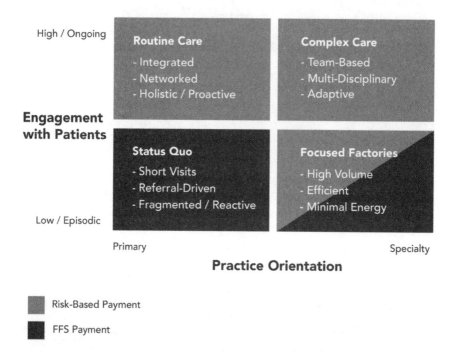

Figure 10.5   New Medicine's practitioner paradigm.

models, full-risk bundles for episodic care, and capitation for population health.

New Medicine emphasizes teamwork, shares information, grants greater autonomy to frontline personnel, and applies advanced data technologies to improve real-time decision-making. Given the geometric increases in medical knowledge and delivery complexity, doctors practicing new medicine must rely on teams of high-performing medical professionals to achieve high-quality outcomes consistently.

Harnessing technology to serve clinicians and consumers is also essential to continuous performance improvement that doesn't overly burden caregivers. Integrated healthcare companies must embrace consumerism, holistic service delivery, and full-risk business models to deliver value-based care and manage the health and healthcare needs of large populations.

Practicing New Medicine requires a highly skilled, diverse, interdisciplinary, interprofessional, and interdependent workforce to meet consumer and market demands for better, higher-value service delivery. Status-quo approaches will fail. Success requires organizational cultures that promote respect, resourcefulness, cooperation, and resilience.

Incumbents and new market entrants that delight consumers while meeting their health and healthcare needs will differentiate their service delivery and gain market share. Those that don't will lose market relevance. The difference between New Medicine's winners and losers will be their relative abilities to train tomorrow's healthcare workforce.

CONCLUSION: BELIEVE IN PEOPLE AND HUMAN-CENTERED TECHNOLOGIES

Helen Keller observed, "The only thing worse than being blind is having sight but no vision." Old Medicine, addicted to FFS and ASO contracting, is lumbering into an uncertain future with a voracious appetite for resources but no vision for transforming itself.

A new world order is emerging that is shaking Old Medicine's foundations to the core. Revolutionary New Medicine centers on meeting consumers' needs, creating value, emphasizing wellbeing, and using technology to improve outcomes and convenience.

Orthodoxies rarely concede without a fight, but individual healthcare incumbents can choose to accommodate New Medicine and retain market relevance. They can participate in New Medicine's reformation, but it will require massive cultural and organizational change.

The future belongs to team-based, consumer-oriented health companies that deliver high-value services consistently and with a smile. Not known for their agility, incumbent healthcare companies must exhibit the flexibility and adaptability required to sustain market relevance within the disrupting healthcare marketplace.

The January 2023 nursing strike in New York City illustrates the deep frustration that many, perhaps most, healthcare workers feel for their institutional work environments. While recruiting new employees will help ease the staffing burden, it is a costly solution that fails to address the underlying sources of anger, frustration, and disconnection between caregivers and their patients.

In an interview with *National Public Radio* regarding the strike, President of the American Nurses Association Jennifer Mensik Kennedy highlighted the need to improve healthcare work environments, so nurses feel valued:

> *We definitely need more nurses. But what we've found [over] decades of research and programs is that when we have really good work environments for nurses — where nurses are valued, nurses are listened to and nurses can provide quality, safe care — those hospitals, those organizations, don't experience the shortages that other hospitals do.*[10]
>
> *There are solutions that organizations can put in place to attract nurses and retain nurses. And nurses will go to those organizations where they feel valued and they feel like at the end of the day, at the end of this shift, that they were able to provide good quality care to people.*

We have reached a point in societal evolution where employees cannot fulfill their responsibilities without the aid of human-centered technologies. The speed and complexity of modern life are beyond the capabilities of human beings to adapt without proactive intervention by their employers.

The pressure to adapt organizational cultures and practices is greater in healthcare than in other industries because healthcare incumbents have clung to outdated, hierarchical managerial approaches and tools. The good news is that healthcare companies do not have to accept status-quo practices and continue their downward spiral. They can engage with their employees to create more holistic and humane work environments by incorporating human-centered technologies into daily workflows. Properly implemented, digital tools liberate employees, rekindle passion, reduce burden, and turbocharge performance.

To change managerial mindsets and organizational mechanics, healthcare companies must embrace employee loyalty as the organization's defining cultural value. This requires engaging employees in determining how to improve operations and in designing optimal workflows.

Concurrently, organizations must employ the right digital tools in the right way so employees can deliver the highest value care. Ironically perhaps, optimizing human connection and potential in the digital age requires expansive human–machine collaboration and empowered participation by all involved.

A core problem of struggling organizations is that they rely on transactional mechanisms to drive retention and recruitment. Transactional exchange has limited application and often creates collateral damage. Great companies do more than compensate their employees well. They also feed their souls. They give meaning and purpose to life at work.

Healthcare's transactional mindset and the dysfunction it creates are corrosive. They constitute the fundamental reasons why so many healthcare organizations are failing financially, losing productive employees, and routinely disappointing consumers.

Since the way healthcare works today isn't working, it's time to change course and elevate the character and quality of employees' work lives. Cultivating loyal employees is the key to organizational transformation. Finding novel ways to serve and delight customers is the path to long-term sustainability. Empowered employees are healthcare's future. Bring them in, treat them well, and let them show the way.

KEY INSIGHTS ON EMPOWERED CAREGIVERS

- Healthcare is a people-centered business. Successful healthcare companies empower their caregivers to go the extra mile for customers.
- Caregivers are at a breaking point. They are leaving well-paying positions in enormous numbers. Throwing money and bodies at the problem doesn't fix it.
- Healthcare companies must change mindsets by asking what they can do for their employees. A "Golden Rule" managerial approach empowers employees by engaging them in meaningful work and giving them a role in resource allocation decisions and in designing company workflows.
- Empowered employees have higher work satisfaction, higher retention rates, and generate higher customer satisfaction scores.
- Women make most healthcare decisions for themselves and their families but are underrepresented in healthcare leadership. This must change.
- Healthcare companies must also change workplace mechanics by employing digital tools and workflows that relieve administrative burden, giving employees more autonomy in managing their work–life integration and by providing personalized career development activities/opportunities.
- Unleashing untapped human potential has the highest return of all workplace investments.

Conclusion:
Guns *and* Butter

Death is very likely the single best invention of life. It's life's change agent. It clears out the old to make way for the new.

—Steve Jobs in a 2005 commencement address
at Stanford University

Figure 1
Source: Associated Press

War is expensive.

In the largest attack on European soil since World War II, the Russian army invaded Ukraine on February 24, 2022. Entering the third year of that conflict and with no end in sight, Russia's Ukrainian war efforts now consume over 40% of its total economy. Spending on troops, military equipment, and munitions has reduced or eliminated investments in almost all other economic sectors. A singular focus on guns means there is much less to spend on butter.

President Lyndon B. Johnson initially believed the U.S. could have both guns and butter. Johnson declared this belief in stirring language during his State of the Union address on January 12, 1966:

> *Our Nation tonight is engaged in a brutal and bitter conflict in Vietnam. . . But we will not permit those who fire upon us in Vietnam to win a victory over the desires and the intentions of all the American people.*
>
> *This Nation is mighty enough, its society is healthy enough, its people are strong enough, to pursue our goals in the rest of the world while still building a Great Society here at home.*[1]

Just 18 months later, budgetary realities forced Johnson to conclude the opposite. On August 3, 1967, he sent a special message to Congress with the ominous title "The Hard and Inescapable Facts." In it, Johnson described an increasing budget deficit and the steps his administration was taking to address it. This included a sizable tax increase. Six months later, President Johnson announced his decision not to seek re-election. His inability to deliver both guns and butter became his downfall.[2]

U.S. healthcare has a version of the "guns or butter" dilemma. In his influential 1994 book *Medicine's Dilemmas: Infinite Needs and Finite Resources*, Dr. William Kissick observes that healthcare differs from other economic activities because the demand for healthcare services is insatiable. Consequently, no country has sufficient resources to provide all the healthcare services that its population is capable of consuming.

By deduction, Kissick concludes that there are no ideal policies for reforming U.S. healthcare. All attempts to control the system's cost growth will organically cause a decline in care access and/or care quality. In other words, like LBJ discovered when trying to fund the Great Society programs and the Vietnam War, it's impossible for U.S. healthcare to have more care access, higher-quality care delivery, *and* lower costs.

Upon initial inspection, Dr. Kissick appears right. His logic explains the pattern of increasing costs that has riddled U.S. healthcare for decades. Moreover, inadequate care access in low-income communities combined with an aging population and expensive breakthrough therapies suggest that healthcare's cost will continue to rise as a share of U.S. gross domestic product (GDP).

Like gravity, increasing demand for healthcare services at ever-higher costs appears to be an economic reality that policymakers must accept and accommodate. That's why the Centers for Medicare and Medicaid Services (CMS) projects that healthcare expenditures will consume almost 20% of the U.S. economy by 2031 (up from 17.3% of GDP in 2022).

Upon closer inspection, however, Kissick's logic collapses. Relative to health systems in other high-income countries, the U.S. system is a major negative outlier. It's not only twice as expensive per capita, but it also generates inferior health status metrics, and contains massive inequities. Consequently, America is well on its way to becoming the land of the sick and the home of the frail. This is a future no one wants for the United States.

Underlying this disastrous situation is a gargantuan industrial complex (Healthcare Inc.) that emphasizes volume-based care delivery, engages in profiteering, tolerates unacceptable levels of medical error, exploits perverse economic incentives, underinvests in preventive care, and stubbornly resists change. This system must die before a better one can take its place. This is the hard and inescapable fact that drives Part I of this book.

The five macro forces pressing down on Healthcare Inc. are demographic determinants, funding fatigue, chronic pandemics, technological imperatives, and pro-consumer/market reforms. Individually, each is a powerful force demanding system-wide transformation. Collectively, these macro forces are irresistible.

The good news is that U.S. healthcare can have guns *and* butter. As described in Part II of this book, disruption of Healthcare Inc. is already well underway. The five bottom-up market forces challenging Healthcare Inc.'s entrenched and outdated business practices are whole health, care redesign, care migration, aggregators' advantage, and empowered caregivers.

Innovative and disruptive companies are exploiting the opportunities created by the macro forces to create health and healthcare businesses that are **Cheaper**, **Better**, more **Balanced**, **Easier** to use, and **Empowering** for caregivers and consumers. These **CB²E²** companies are gaining market traction by offering products and services that solve consumers'"jobs to be done." As Steve Jobs might say, they are the marketplace's change agents. They are clearing away old healthcare as they give birth to a new American healthcare that creates greater care access, delivers higher-quality outcomes, *and* lowers costs.

While Healthcare Inc. can and will forestall the forces of transformation, it cannot reverse their momentum. This is why the healthcare ecosystem will change more in the next 10 years than it has in the last 100 years. This constructive evolution is long overdue. U.S. healthcare of, for, and by the American people is at our doorstep. It is a bracing and liberating time for those with the vision to see the future and the courage to embrace it.

HEALTHCARE INC. WILL "END IN A WHIMPER"

Astute readers will notice an abundance of literary references throughout our book. We'll end with one final example from the pen of T.S. Eliot. "The Waste Land," published in 1922, is among the most influential works of modernist poetry.

Another Lost-Generation artist like Ernest Hemingway, Eliot composed "The Waste Land" over several years amid the devastation, dislocation, and disillusionment that followed World War I. It is a long, 434-line poem with these five sections: The Burial of the Dead; A Game of Chess; The Fire Sermon; Death by Water; and What the Thunder Said.

Eliot explores isolation, fragmentation, and dissociation within the poem's stanzas. These are a literary manifestation of the social, economic, political, and cultural trends that Robert Putnam examined in *The Upswing* and we discussed in Chapter 6.

In his review of multiple data sources over 120 years (1895–2015), Putnam concludes that the U.S. society has moved from a deeply individualistic society in the Gilded Age to a collectivist one at mid-century and then back to one today with a highly toxic level of individualism. Putnam describes this evolution of societal norms as an expansive "I-We-I" pattern.

U.S. healthcare today resembles Gilded Age norms in its political divisiveness, economic disparities, and callousness. Despite the obvious benefits of healthier populations, American society has lost the ability to advance our collective health.

The fragmentation, inefficiency, and ineffectiveness of the U.S. healthcare system are bankrupting the country and contributing to the decline in Americans' health status. In the first section of "The Waste Land," Eliot has a godlike figure proclaim, "I will show you fear in a handful of dust." American adults today fear payment of medical bills more than contracting disease. This "dust" must and will blow away.

"The Waste Land" passes from one scene to another within an isolated industrialized world. In the poem's final section, the Fisher King despondently sits by a polluted river, void of life, and contemplates his kingdom's decline:

> *I sat upon the shore,*
> *Fishing, with the arid plain behind me.*
> *Shall I at least set my lands in order?*

Like U.S. auto executives in the 1980s, Eliot's Fisher King is experiencing a reckoning. The Big Three automakers responded by making "Quality Job 1." Getting back to basics and serving customers was the key to their redemption and salvation.

Healthcare executives today are experiencing a similar reckoning. Like what happened to U.S. automakers in the 1970s, disruptive change is coming to Healthcare Inc. from the outside-in. It's adapt-or-die time for healthcare's incumbent payers, providers, and suppliers. Delivering value-based care is the key to their redemption and salvation.

The Fisher King's last line is, "These fragments I have shored against my ruins." In essence, the Fisher King is trying to "set his lands in order" by protecting the remaining few good pieces of his kingdom against decay. Like a phoenix rising from the ashes, "these fragments" will become the foundation for a better, future kingdom.

The precious "fragments" with which the future of U.S. healthcare is being rebuilt are the democratized and decentralized delivery of whole-person health (3D–WPH). In the same organic, bottom–up, and relentless way that Black Americans migrated north in search of better lives, enlightened healthcare companies are making strategic bets that the industry's future lies in helping all Americans to get healthier together.

They are collectively weaving an ever-strengthening collage of care that will deliver better health outcomes tailored to individual needs and preferences at lower costs. New technologies that foster human–machine collaboration will enable pre-emptive diagnostics, 24/7 service provision, health promotion, and productive redeployment of wasteful healthcare spending. As this value-based, health-driven movement achieves scale and critical mass, the bloated remnants of Healthcare Inc. will fade into the dustbins of history.

Like war, U.S. healthcare is expensive. Funding Healthcare Inc.'s profligacy and poor results limits investments to address vital societal needs. The way U.S. healthcare's working isn't working. It's time, as the Fisher King notes, to "set our lands in order." . . . In the process, quoting from Eliot's famous 1925 poem *The Hollow Men,* Healthcare Inc. will end "not with a bang, but a whimper."

Notes

Introduction: Healthcare's Roaring 2020s

1. Sean P. Keehan, Jacqueline A. Fiore, John A. Poisal, Gigi A. Cuckler, Andrea M. Sisko, Sheila Smith, Andrew J. Madison, and Kathryn E. Rennie. "National Health Expenditure Projections, 2022–31: Growth to Stabilize Once the COVID-19 Public Health Emergency Ends." Health Affairs 42, no. 7 (July 1, 2023): 886–98. https://doi.org/10.1377/hlthaff.2023.00403.
2. "The Role of Administrative Waste in Excess US Health Spending," Health affairs.org, October 2022. https://www.healthaffairs.org/do/10.1377/hpb20220909.830296/#:~:text=Top%20Findings%20From%20The%20Literature,care%20administration%20than%20comparable%20countries.
3. Jeffrey Pfeffer et al., "The magnitude and effects of 'sludge' in benefits administration: How health insurance hassles burden workers and cost employers," *Academy of Management Discoveries*, July 31, 2020, https://doi.org/10.5465/amd.2020.0063.
4. "NHE Fact Sheet | CMS," n.d., https://www.cms.gov/data-research/statistics-trends-and-reports/national-health-expenditure-data/nhe-fact-sheet#:~:text=Projected%20NHE%2C%202022%2D2031%3A,to%2019.6%20percent%20in%202031.
5. "It's Time to Operate," *Fortune 81* (January 1970), 79.
6. "Products – Health E Stats – Prevalence of Overweight, Obesity, and Extreme Obesity Among Adults Aged 20 and Over: United States, 1960–1962 Through 2017–2018," n.d., https://www.cdc.gov/nchs/data/hestat/obesity-adult-17-18/obesity-adult.htm#1.

7. USAFacts, "US Obesity Rates Have Tripled Over the Last 60 Years," USAFacts, March 21, 2023, https://usafacts.org/articles/obesity-rate-nearly-triples-united-states-over-last-50-years/.

8. "Adult Obesity," Obesity Prevention Source, April 14, 2016, https://www.hsph.harvard.edu/obesity-prevention-source/obesity-trends-original/obesity-rates-worldwide/#:~:text=(9)%20A%20closer%20look%20at,(9).

Chapter 1: Demographic Determinants

1. Jonathan Vespa, Lauren Medina, and David M. Armstrong, "Demographic Turning Points for the United States: Population Projections for 2020 to 2060," report, *Population Estimates and Projections*, March 2018, https://www.census.gov/content/dam/Census/library/publications/2020/demo/p25-1144.pdf.

2. Craig Muder, "Satchel Paige Pitches for A's at Age 59," Baseball Hall of Fame, n.d., https://baseballhall.org/discover/inside-pitch/satchel-paige-pitches-at-age-59.

3. Cynthia M. LeRouge et al., "Challenges and Opportunities with Empowering Baby Boomers for Personal Health Information Management Using Consumer Health Information Technologies: An Ecological Perspective," AIMS Public Health, September 2, 2014, https://www.ncbi.nlm.nih.gov/pmc/articles/PMC5689789/#:~:text=However%2C%20about%2060%20percent%20of,%2C%20osteoporosis%2C%20hypertension%20and%20depression.

4. Larry Husten, "Lancet Review: Will Most Babies Born Now Live to 100?" October 1, 2009, http://www.cardiobrief.org/2009/10/01/lancet-review-will-most-babies-born-now-live-to-100/.

5. "FastStats," Body Measurements, n.d., https://www.cdc.gov/nchs/fastats/body-measurements.htm.

6. Zachary J. Ward et al., "Projected U.S. State-Level Prevalence of Adult Obesity and Severe Obesity," *New England Journal of Medicine/the New England Journal of Medicine* 381, no. 25 (December 19, 2019): 2440–50, https://doi.org/10.1056/nejmsa1909301.

7. Sean P. Keehan et al., "National Health Expenditure Projections, 2022–31: Growth to Stabilize Once the COVID-19 Public Health Emergency Ends," *Health Affairs* 42, no. 7 (July 1, 2023): 886–98, https://doi.org/10.1377/hlthaff.2023.00403.

8. "World Bank Open Data," World Bank Open Data, n.d., https://data
.worldbank.org/indicator/NY.GDP.MKTP.CD?locations=1W&most_
recent_value_desc=true.

9. Clay Routledge and Will Johnson, "The Real Story Behind America's
Population Bomb: Adults Want Their Independence," *USA TODAY*,
October 12, 2022, https://www.usatoday.com/story/opinion/
2022/10/12/why-americans-not-having-babies-low-birth-
rate/8233324001/.

10. Anthony DeBarros, "A Visual Breakdown of America's Stagnating
Number of Births," *The Wall Street Journal,* June 23, 1AD, https://www
.wsj.com/articles/a-visual-breakdown-of-americas-stagnating-
number-of-births-9a2e6e2d.

11. Mike Schneider, "Immigration Fuels Uptick in US Population Growth,"
AP News, December 20, 2023, https://apnews.com/article/population-
estimates-census-south-carolina-florida-a21094d38c216097c1ddd
06164a133eb.

12. "Quick Facts on Social Security," n.d., https://www.uvm.edu/~dguber/
POLS21/articles/quick_facts_on_social_security.htm.

13. Robert Thomas Malthus (18 January 2010). *An Essay on the Principle of
Population*. Oxfordshire, England: Oxford World's Classics. p. 13. ISBN
978-1450535540.

14. "The Great Horse Manure Crisis of 1894," Historic UK, November 21,
2023, https://www.historic-uk.com/HistoryUK/HistoryofBritain/
Great-Horse-Manure-Crisis-of-1894/.

Chapter 2: Funding Fatigue

1. David W. Johnson, "How Big Is the Revenue Cycle Management
(RCM) Business? You Tell Us," 4sight Health, July 11, 2023, https://
www.4sighthealth.com/how-big-is-the-revenue-cycle-management-
rcm-business-you-tell-us/.

2. "The Sveriges Riksbank Prize in Economic Sciences in Memory of
Alfred Nobel 1972," NobelPrize.org, n.d., https://www.nobelprize.
org/prizes/economic-sciences/1972/hicks/facts/.

3. Nancy Ochieng et al., "Funding for Health Care Providers During the
Pandemic: An Update," KFF, January 27, 2022, https://www.kff.org/
coronavirus-covid-19/issue-brief/funding-for-health-care-providers-
during-the-pandemic-an-update/.

4. "CMS Office of the Actuary Releases 2021–2030 Projections of National Health Expenditures," CMS, March 28, 2022, https://www.cms.gov/newsroom/press-releases/cms-office-actuary-releases-2021-2030-projections-national-health-expenditures.

5. "National Health Spending Grew Slightly in 2021," CMS, December 14, 2022, https://www.cms.gov/newsroom/press-releases/national-health-spending-grew-slightly-2021.

6. "Fiscal Data Explains the National Debt," n.d., https://fiscaldata.treasury.gov/americas-finance-guide/national-debt/.

7. J.P. Morgan Chase, "2023 Economic Outlook: Insights for What's Ahead," December 8, 2022, https://www.jpmorgan.com/insights/outlook/economic-outlook/economic-trends#:~:text=GDP%20growth%20is%20decelerating%3B%20while,of%20Labor%20Statistics%2C%20J.P.%20Morgan.

8. "Fiscal Data Explains the National Debt," n.d., https://fiscaldata.treasury.gov/americas-finance-guide/national-debt/.

9. "Interest Costs on the National Debt Are on Track to Reach a Record," pgpf.org, n.d., https://www.pgpf.org/blog/2023/02/interest-costs-on-the-national-debt-are-on-track-to-reach-a-record-high#:~:text=Net%20interest%20payments%20on%20the,highest%20level%20in%2021%20years.

10. Kaufman, Hall & Associates, LLC, "National Hospital Flash Report," 2023, https://www.kaufmanhall.com/sites/default/files/2023-01/KH_NHFR_2023-01.pdf.

11. "CMS Issues Hospital IPPS Final Rule for FY 2024," American Hospital Association | AHA News, August 1, 2023, https://www.aha.org/news/headline/2023-08-01-cms-issues-hospital-ipps-final-rule-fy-2024.

12. Sandro Galea and Nason Maani, "The Cost of Preventable Disease in the USA," *The Lancet*, October 2020, https://www.thelancet.com/journals/lanpub/article/PIIS2468-2667(20)30204-8/fulltext.

13. William H. Shrank, Teresa L. Rogstad, and Natasha Parekh, "Waste in the US Health Care System," *JAMA* 322, no. 15 (October 15, 2019): 1501, https://doi.org/10.1001/jama.2019.13978.

14. Sam Roberts, "Infamous 'Drop Dead' Was Never Said by Ford," *The New York Times*, December 28, 2006, https://www.nytimes.com/2006/12/28/nyregion/28veto.html.

15. Margot Sanger-Katz, Alicia Parlapiano, and Josh Katz, "A Huge Threat to the U.S. Budget Has Receded: And No One Is Sure Why," *The New York Times*, September 8, 2023, https://www.nytimes.com/interactive/2023/09/05/upshot/medicare-budget-threat-receded.html.

16. Ibid.

17. Ezekiel J. Emanuel, Aaron Glickman, and David Johnson, "Measuring the Burden of Health Care Costs on US Families," *JAMA* 318, no. 19 (November 21, 2017): 1863, https://doi.org/10.1001/jama.2017.15686.

18. Robert Gibson, "National Health Expenditures, 1978," ncbi.nlm.nih.gov, 1979, https://www.ncbi.nlm.nih.gov/pmc/articles/PMC4191067/.

19. John A. Poisal et al., "National Health Expenditure Projections, 2021–30: Growth to Moderate as COVID-19 Impacts Wane," *Health Affairs* 41, no. 4 (April 1, 2022): 474–86, https://doi.org/10.1377/hlthaff.2022.00113.

20. "Nonfarm Business Sector: Labor Productivity (Output per Hour) for All Workers," March 7, 2024, https://fred.stlouisfed.org/series/PRS85006092.

21. "Crede & Family, Organized by Dawn McCrobie," gofundme.com, n.d., https://www.gofundme.com/f/crede-amp-family.

22. "Bloomberg – Are You a Robot?" December 14, 2020, https://www.bloomberg.com/news/articles/2020-12-14/white-house-official-recovers-from-severe-covid-19-friend-says?leadSource=uverify%20wall#xj4y7vzkg.

23. David U. Himmelstein et al., "Medical Bankruptcy: Still Common Despite the Affordable Care Act," *American Journal of Public Health* 109, no. 3 (March 1, 2019): 431–33, https://doi.org/10.2105/ajph.2018.304901.

24. Christopher M. Whaley et al., "Nationwide Evaluation of Health Care Prices Paid by Private Health Plans: Findings from Round 3 of an Employer-Led Transparency Initiative," RAND, September 18, 2020, https://www.rand.org/pubs/research_reports/RR4394.html.

25. UnitedHealth Group, "Price Variation of Health Care Services in the U.S.," 2019, https://www.unitedhealthgroup.com/content/dam/UHG/PDF/2019/affordability-Diagnostic-Tests-Price-Variation.pdf.

26. Kevin Kennedy, William Johnson, Sally Rodriguez, and Niall Brennan, "Past the Price Index: Exploring Actual Prices Paid for Specific Services by Metro Area," HCCI, February 12, 2020, https://healthcostinstitute.org/in-the-news/hmi-2019-service-prices.

27. Jonathan Hiskes, "Crowdfunding for Medical Bills a Band-Aid, Not a Cure-all, UW Bothell Study Finds," UW News, March 13, 2017, https://www.washington.edu/news/2017/03/13/crowdfunding-for-medical-bills-a-band-aid-not-a-cure-all-uw-study-finds/.

28. Rachel Bluth, "GoFundMe CEO: 'Gigantic Gaps' in Health System Showing up in Crowdfunding," KFF Health News, April 2, 2019, https://khn.org/news/gofundme-ceo-gigantic-gaps-in-health-system-showing-up-in-crowdfunding/.

Chapter 3: Chronic Pandemics

1. "Statistics About Diabetes," ADA, n.d., https://diabetes.org/about-us/statistics/about-diabetes.

2. "Chronic Disease Publications, Graphics, and Media," CDC, n.d., https://www.cdc.gov/chronicdisease/center/news-media/index.htm.

3. "United States Cancer Statistics," CDC, n.d., https://www.cdc.gov/cancer/uscs/index.htm.

4. "CDC – NCHS – National Center for Health Statistics," n.d., https://www.cdc.gov/nchs/index.htm.

5. World Health Organization (WHO), "Cancer," February 3, 2022, https://www.who.int/news-room/fact-sheets/detail/cancer#:~:text=Reducing%20the%20burden,of%20patients%20who%20develop%20cancer.

6. "More Than 4 in 10 Cancers and Cancer Deaths Linked to Modifiable Risk Factors," *American Cancer Society*, November 21, 2017, https://www.cancer.org/research/acs-research-news/more-than-4-in-10-cancers-and-cancer-deaths-linked-to-modifiable-risk-factors.html.

7. "Health and Economic Benefits of Diabetes Interventions – Power of Prevention," n.d., https://www.cdc.gov/chronicdisease/programs-impact/pop/diabetes.htm#:~:text=total%20annual%20cost%20of%20diabetes5&text=%241%20out%20of%20every%20%244,caring%20for%20people%20with%20diabetes.&text=%24237%20billion%E2%80%A1(a)%20is,(a)%20on%20reduced%20productivity.

8. "Health and Economic Benefits of Diabetes Interventions – Power of Prevention," n.d., https://www.cdc.gov/chronicdisease/programs-impact/pop/diabetes.htm.

9. "New American Diabetes Association Report Finds Annual Costs of Diabetes to be $412.9 Billion," ADA, n.d., https://diabetes.org/

newsroom/press-releases/new-american-diabetes-association-report-finds-annual-costs-diabetes-be.

10. Zara Abrams, "USC Launches Large-Scale Study in Dementia and Diabetes in Adults with Hispanic Ancestry," October 26, 2022, https://keck.usc.edu/news/usc-launches-large-scale-study-of-dementia-and-diabetes-in-adults-with-hispanic-ancestry/.

11. "What Is Alzheimer's Disease?" | CDC, n.d., https://www.cdc.gov/aging/aginginfo/alzheimers.htm.

12. United States Joint Economic Committee, "The Economic Costs of Alzheimer's Disease," United States Joint Economic Committee, July 6, 2022, https://www.jec.senate.gov/public/index.cfm/democrats/issue-briefs?ID=02F4CADC-954F-4E3B-8409-A4213E3C0759.

13. "Alzheimer's Disease Facts and Figures," Alzheimer's Disease and Dementia, n.d., https://www.alz.org/alzheimers-dementia/facts-figures.

14. "Balaji Ravichandran: Sugar Is the New Tobacco," The BMJ, March 15, 2013, https://blogs.bmj.com/bmj/2013/03/15/balaji-ravichandran-sugar-is-the-new-tobacco/#:~:text=Sugar%20as%20a%20toxin&text=The%20econometric%20analysis%2C%20he%20said,toxin%20in%20its%20own%20right.

15. "Adult Physical Inactivity," CDC, November 20, 2023, https://www.cdc.gov/physicalactivity/data/inactivity-prevalence-maps/index.html#overall.

16. "Excessive Alcohol Use," CDC, July 11, 2022, https://www.cdc.gov/chronicdisease/resources/publications/factsheets/alcohol.htm.

17. World Health Organization (WHO), "No Level of Alcohol Consumption Is Safe for Our Health," *Who.Int*, January 4, 2023, https://www.who.int/europe/news/item/04-01-2023-no-level-of-alcohol-consumption-is-safe-for-our-health.

18. John P. Ansah and Chih-Yu Chiu, "Projecting the Chronic Disease Burden Among the Adult Population in the United States Using a Multi-state Population Model," *Frontiers in Public Health* 10 (January 13, 2023), https://doi.org/10.3389/fpubh.2022.1082183.

Chapter 4: Technological Imperatives

1. *Fortune Magazine,* January 1970 issue, page 2.
2. "10 Administrators for Every 1 Doctor. We Deserve a Better Healthcare System – PNHP," PNHP, April 7, 2022, https://pnhp.org/

news/10-administrators-for-every-1-doctor-we-deserve-a-better-healthcare-system/.

3. Ibid.

4. Nikhil R Sahni, Brandon Carrus, and David M. Cutler, "Administrative Simplification and the Potential for Saving a Quarter-Trillion Dollars in Health Care," *JAMA* 326, no. 17 (November 2, 2021): 1677, https://doi.org/10.1001/jama.2021.17315.

5. Thomas L. Friedman, *Thank You for Being Late: An Optimist's Guide to Thriving in the Age of Accelerations*, Farrar, Straus & Girous, 2016.

6. Deborah Debono et al., "Nurses' workarounds in acute healthcare settings: a scoping review," ncbi.nlm.nih.gov, May 11, 2013, https://www.ncbi.nlm.nih.gov/pmc/articles/PMC3663687/.

7. Albert Boonstra et al., "Persisting Workarounds in Electronic Health Record System Use: Types, Risks and Benefits," *BMC Medical Informatics and Decision Making* 21, no. 1 (June 8, 2021), https://doi.org/10.1186/s12911-021-01548-0.

8. H. James Wilson, "How Humans and AI Are Working Together in 1,500 Companies," *Harvard Business Review*, November 19, 2019, https://hbr.org/2018/07/collaborative-intelligence-humans-and-ai-are-joining-forces.

9. Kalley Huang, "Alarmed by A.I. Chatbots, Universities Start Revamping How They Teach," Nyt.Com, January 16, 2023.

10. Berber Jin and Miles Kruppa, "ChatGPT Creator Is Talking to Investors About Selling Shares at $29 Billion Valuation," Wsj.Com, January 5, 2023.

11. David Burda, "Podcast: Did ChatGPT Write This Podcast on AI and Healthcare? 1/26/23," 4sight Health, January 26, 2023, https://www.4sighthealth.com/podcast-did-chat-gpt-write-this-podcast-on-ai-and-healthcare-1-26-23/?utm_source=4sight+Health+Readers&utm_campaign=8ef38af7b0-CMS+Misdirection_COPY_01&utm_medium=email&utm_term=0_96b6d85309-8ef38af7b0-147462757.

12. "U.S. Revenue Cycle Management Market Size, Share & Trends Analysis Report by End-user, by Product Type, by Component, by Delivery Mode, by Physician Specialty, by Sourcing, by Function, and Segment Forecasts, 2023–2030," April 14, 2022, https://www.grandviewresearch.com/industry-analysis/us-revenue-cycle-management-rcm-market.

13. Jan Hatzius et al., "The Potentially Large Effects of Artificial Intelligence on Economic Growth," by Goldman Sachs Co. LLC, March 26,

2023, https://www.key4biz.it/wp-content/uploads/2023/03/Global-Economics-Analyst_-The-Potentially-Large-Effects-of-Artificial-Intelligence-on-Economic-Growth-Briggs_Kodnani.pdf.

14. "The Productivity Imperative for Healthcare Delivery in the United States," McKinsey & Company, February 27, 2019, https://www.mck insey.com/industries/healthcare/our-insights/the-productivity-imperative-for-healthcare-delivery-in-the-united-states.

15. Martin Jinek et al., "A Programmable Dual-RNA–Guided DNA Endonuclease in Adaptive Bacterial Immunity," *Science,* 337, no. 6096 (August 17, 2012): 816–21, https://doi.org/10.1126/science.1225829.

16. Rob Stein, "In a 1st, Doctors in U.S. Use CRISPR Tool to Treat Patient With Genetic Disorder," *NPR*, July 29, 2019, https://www.npr.org/sections/health-shots/2019/07/29/744826505/sickle-cell-patient-reveals-why-she-is-volunteering-for-landmark-gene-editing-st .

17. Office of the Commissioner, "FDA Approves First Gene Therapies to Treat Patients with Sickle Cell Disease," U.S. Food And Drug Administration, December 8, 2023, https://www.fda.gov/news-events/press-announcements/fda-approves-first-gene-therapies-treat-patients-sickle-cell-disease#:~:text=Casgevy%2C%20a%20cell%2Dbased%20gene,type%20of%20genome%20editing%20technology .

18. Walter Isaacson, *The Code Breaker,* Simon & Schuster, (2021), pp. 250–251.

19. Bill Gates, "The Road Ahead Reaches a Turning Point in 2024," *Gatesnotes .Com*, December 19, 2023, https://www.gatesnotes.com/The-Year-Ahead-2024 .

20. "RBC Capital Markets | Navigating the Changing Face of Healthcare Episode," n.d., https://www.rbccm.com/en/gib/healthcare/episode/the_healthcare_data_explosion.

Chapter 5: Pro-Consumer/Market Reforms

1. Julia Shaver, "The State of Telehealth Before and After the COVID-19 Pandemic," *Ncbi.Nlm.Nhi.Gov*, December 2022.

2. Euny C. Lee et al., "Updated National Survey Trends in Telehealth Utilization and Modality (2021–2022)," 2023, https://aspe.hhs.gov/sites/default/files/documents/7d6b4989431f4c70144f209622975116/household-pulse-survey-telehealth-covid-ib.pdf.

3. "FTC Challenges Private Equity Firm's Scheme to Suppress Competition in Anesthesiology Practices Across Texas," Federal Trade Commission, September 21, 2023, https://www.ftc.gov/news-events/news/press-releases/2023/09/ftc-challenges-private-equity-firms-scheme-suppress-competition-anesthesiology-practices-across.

4. Christina Farr, "Epic's CEO Is Urging Hospital Customers to Oppose Rules That Would Make It Easier to Share Medical Info," *CNBC*, January 23, 2020, https://www.cnbc.com/2020/01/22/epic-ceo-sends-letter-urging-hospitals-to-oppose-hhs-data-sharing-rule.html.

5. Gabriel Perna, "How Epic took over the hospital EHR market," modernhealthcare.com, September 18, 2023.

6. Atul Gawande, "Why Doctors Hate Their Computers," *The New Yorker*, n.d., https://www.newyorker.com/magazine/2018/11/12/why-doctors-hate-their-computers.

7. "Health IT and EHR Information," n.d., https://ehrintelligence.com/news/study-shows-physician-burnout-directly-related-to-ehrs.

8. Admin, "21st Century Cures Act – A Summary," HIMSS, October 29, 2020, https://www.himss.org/resources/21st-century-cures-act-summary#:~:text=The%2021st%20Century%20Cures%20Act%2C%20signed%20December%2013%2C%202016%2C,improve%20mental%20health%20service%20delivery.

9. "Health Business Insights | Oracle," n.d., https://www.cerner.com/perspectives/21st-century-cures-act-an-open-letter.

10. "2020 ONC Annual Meeting | HealthIT.gov," n.d., https://www.healthit.gov/news/events/2020-onc-annual-meeting.

11. Jessica Kim Cohen, "Azar: 'Scare Tactics' Won't Stall Interoperability Rules," Modern healthcare.com, January 27, 2020.

12. Christopher M. Whaley et al., "Nationwide Evaluation of Health Care Prices Paid by Private Health Plans: Findings from Round 3 of an Employer-Led Transparency Initiative," RAND, September 18, 2020, https://www.rand.org/pubs/research_reports/RR4394.html.

13. "2020-12-31 08:51 | Archive of HHS.gov," November 15, 2019, https://www.hhs.gov/about/news/2019/11/15/trump-administration-announces-historic-price-transparency-and-lower-healthcare-costs-for-all-americans.html.

14. Meena Seshamani, "Fifth Semi-Annual Hospital Price Transparency Compliance Report," 2023, https://static1.squarespace.com/static/60065b8fc8cd610112ab89a7/t/64beb5900a0c5603529e96a8/

1690219961931/July+20+2023+PRA+Hospital+Price+Transparency+
Compliance+Report+2.pdf.

15. David W. Johnson, "Healthcare's Jobs to Be Done (2-Part Series)," 4sight Health, February 3, 2023, https://www.4sighthealth.com/series-healthcares-jobs-to-be-done/.

16. Ibid.

17. "How Does U.S. Life Expectancy Compare to Other Countries? – Peterson-KFF Health System Tracker," Peterson-KFF Health System Tracker, January 30, 2024, https://www.healthsystemtracker.org/chart-collection/u-s-life-expectancy-compare-countries/#Life%20expectancy%20and%20per%20capita%20healthcare%20spending%20(PPP%20adjusted),%202021.

18. David W. Johnson, "It's the Payment Models, Stupid! (Part 1): Maryland Leads the Way," 4sight Health, October 17, 2023, https://www.4sighthealth.com/its-the-payment-models-stupid-maryland-leads-the-way-part-1/.

19. "CMMI Director Finds Mixed Results for Bundled Payments, Gives High Marks to Global Budgets," Fierce Healthcare, September 22, 2020, https://www.fiercehealthcare.com/payer/cmmi-director-finds-mixed-results-for-bundled-payment-models-high-marks-for-total-cost-care.

20. Elizabeth H. Bradley, Heather Sipsma, and Lauren A. Taylor, "American Health Care Paradox – High Spending on Health Care and Poor Health," *QJM*, October 24, 2016, hcw187, https://doi.org/10.1093/qjmed/hcw187.

21. Maria T. Peña et al., "How Do Dual-Eligible Individuals Get Their Medicare Coverage?" KFF, March 25, 2024, https://www.kff.org/medicare/issue-brief/how-do-dual-eligible-individuals-get-their-medicare-coverage/#:~:text=(described%20below).-,Dual%2Deligible%20plans,benefits%20across%20the%20two%20programs.

22. "CMS Announces Transformative Model to Give States Incentives and Flexibilities to Redesign Health Care Delivery, Improve Equitable Access to Care," September 5, 2023, https://www.cms.gov/newsroom/press-releases/cms-announces-transformative-model-give-states-incentives-and-flexibilities-redesign-health-care.

23. "Innovation in Behavioral Health (IBH) Model." n.d., https://www.cms.gov/priorities/innovation/innovation-models/innovation-behavioral-health-ibh-model.

Chapter 6: Whole Health

1. Lisa Schencker, "Northwestern Lake Forest Hospital Lays Out Plan for $389 Million Expansion, Modernization Project," *Chicago Tribune*, December 20, 2022, https://www.chicagotribune.com/2022/12/20/northwestern-lake-forest-hospital-lays-out-plan-for-389-million-expansion-modernization-project/.

2. Dan Diamond, "America Has a Life Expectancy Crisis. But It's Not a Political Priority," *Washington Post*, January 9, 2024, https://www.washingtonpost.com/health/2023/12/28/life-expectancy-no-political-response/.

3. Vivek H. Murthy, "Our Epidemic of Loneliness and Isolation: The U.S. Surgeon General's Advisory on the Healing Effects of Social Connection and Community," 2023, https://www.hhs.gov/sites/default/files/surgeon-general-social-connection-advisory.pdf.

4. Robert D. Putnam, *The Upswing,* Simon & Schuster, (2021), pp. 10–11.

5. Ibid., page 11–12.

6. Jennifer Tolbert, Patrick Drake, and Anthony Damico, "Key Facts About the Uninsured Population, KFF," KFF, December 18, 2023, https://www.kff.org/uninsured/issue-brief/key-facts-about-the-uninsured-population/#:~:text=The%20uninsured%20rate%20dropped%20in,to%202022%20(Figure%201).

7. Joel Achenbach, Dan Keating, Laurie McGinley, Akilah Johnson, and Jahi Chikwendiu, "An Epidemic of Chronic Illness Is Killing Us Too Soon," *Washington Post*, October 3, 2023, https://www.washingtonpost.com/health/interactive/2023/american-life-expectancy-dropping/.

8. Washington Post Staff, "The Post Spent the Past Year Examining U.S. Life Expectancy. Here's What We Found," *The Washington Post*, December 18, 2023, https://www.washingtonpost.com/health/2023/10/02/takeaways-us-life-expectancy-crisis/.

9. Frances Stead Sellers and Catarina Fernandes Martins, "U.S., Portugal Show Contrasting Paths to Public Health, Life Expectancy," *The Washington Post*, October 17, 2023, https://www.washingtonpost.com/health/interactive/2023/portugal-us-health-systems-life-expectancy/.

10. "World Bank Open Data," World Bank Open Data, n.d., https://data.worldbank.org/indicator/NY.GDP.PCAP.CD?most_recent_value_desc=true&view=chart.

11. Maudlyne Ihejirika, "4 South Side Hospitals Plan to Merge, Building One Hospital – *Chicago Sun-Times*," *Chicago Sun-Times*, January 24, 2020, https://chicago.suntimes.com/business/2020/1/23/21077674/hospital-merger-south-side-advocate-trinity-south-shore-mercy-hospital-st-bernard.

12. Thomas Fisher, The Emergency: A Year of Healing and Heartbreak in a Chicago ER, One World, (2023).

13. Lisa Schencker, "Chicago's Lifespan Gap: Streeterville Residents Live to 90. Englewood Residents Die at 60. Study Finds It's the Largest Divide in the U.S.," *Chicago Tribune*, June 6, 2019, https://www.chicagotribune.com/business/ct-biz-chicago-has-largest-life-expectancy-gap-between-neighborhoods-20190605-story.html.

14. "Press-release," n.d., https://www.illinois.gov/news/press-release.21790.html.

15. William Bornhoft, "Minnesota Saw Life Expectancy Decline in 2020 with COVID-19 Deaths," *Minneapolis, MN Patch*, August 23, 2022, https://patch.com/minnesota/minneapolis/minnesota-saw-life-expectancy-decline-2020-covid-19-deaths.

16. "How Does the U.S. Healthcare System Compare to Other Countries?" pgpf.org, n.d., https://www.pgpf.org/blog/2022/07/how-does-the-us-healthcare-system-compare-to-other-countries.

Chapter 7: Care Redesign

1. "FORTUNE 500: 1956 Archive Full List 1–100," n.d., https://money.cnn.com/magazines/fortunc/fortune500_archive/full/1956/index.html.

2. Mark Dowie, "Pinto Madness," Mother Jones, n.d., https://www.motherjones.com/politics/1977/09/pinto-madness/.

3. "Mirror, Mirror 2021: Reflecting Poorly," *Commonwealth Fund*, August 4, 2021, https://doi.org/10.26099/01dv-h208.

4. Annette Lavezza et al., "Activities of Daily Living Assessment Early in Hospitalization Is Associated with Key Outcomes," *The American Journal of Occupational Therapy* 77, no. 5 (September 1, 2023), https://doi.org/10.5014/ajot.2023.050167.

5. Ibid.

6. Samantha Artiga and Elizabeth Hinton, "Beyond Health Care: The Role of Social Determinants in Promoting Health and Health Equity," KFF,

July 9, 2019, https://www.kff.org/racial-equity-and-health-policy/issue-brief/beyond-health-care-the-role-of-social-determinants-in-promoting-health-and-health-equity/.

7. "What Works for Health (WWFH)"; "Improving Wisconsin's Health"; "Making Wisconsin the Healthiest State"; "Mobilizing Action Toward Community Health (MATCH); "UW Population Health Institute (UWPHI)," n.d., http://improvingwihealth.org/wwfh/index.php.

8. "INFOGRAPHIC: What Makes Us Healthy vs. What We Spend on Being Healthy | Bipartisan Policy Center," June 5. 2012, https://bipartisanpolicy.org/report/what-makes-us-healthy-vs-what-we-spend-on-being-healthy/.

9. "Explore Health Topics," County Health Rankings & Roadmaps, n.d., https://www.countyhealthrankings.org/what-impacts-health/county-health-rankings-model.

10. "Humana to Exit Employer Group Commercial Medical Products Business," February 23, 2023, https://press.humana.com/news/news-details/2023/Humana-to-Exit-Employer-Group-Commercial-Medical-Products-Business/default.aspx#gsc.tab=0.

11. "Amazon, Berkshire Hathaway and JPMorgan Chase & Co. To Partner on U.S. Employee Healthcare," n.d., https://www.jpmorganchase.com/news-stories/january-announcement.

12. "Employers Should Expect More from the U.S. Health Care System," n.d., https://www.jpmorganchase.com/content/dam/jpmc/jpmorgan-chase-and-co/documents/JPMC_Morgan-Health-Report_ADA.pdf.

13. "Yahoo Is Part of the Yahoo Family of Brands," n.d., https://finance.yahoo.com/blogs/the-exchange/castlight-health--most-overpriced-ipo-of-the-century-134049448.html?guccounter=1&guce_referrer=aHR0cHM6Ly93d3cuZ29vZ2xlLmNvbS8&guce_referrer_sig=AQAAABJls-UwWezdBUTbkMkJyD2rdPjrCcOsJuhU5ZwocEilzriqKfJXuKlpOwzf22xC_3r1I52OstoQUZE8Z7nqPdFvY5cF749BUpDeAveH8L40I1GCD_6bbo6dKnMvImz-aKZGfuJdPbZOnwj9wM2i8rd9ev2ayjWleJAQ3zwrLwVW.

14. "When Nissan Had a Better Idea," January 19, 2001, https://archive.nytimes.com/www.nytimes.com/books/98/03/15/home/halberstam-reckoning.html?_r=2&oref=slogin.

15. "The Reckoning," Goodreads, n.d., https://www.goodreads.com/en/book/show/75416.

16. Chicago Tribune, "THE RECKONING," *Chicago Tribune*, August 9, 2021, https://www.chicagotribune.com/1986/10/05/the-reckoning-9/?clearUserState=true.

Chapter 8: Care Migration

1. "Ambulatory Surgery Center Growth Accelerates: Is Medtech Ready?" Bain, June 26, 2020, https://www.bain.com/insights/ambulatory-surgery-center-growth-accelerates-is-medtech-ready/.
2. "Site-Neutral Payment," American Hospital Association, n.d., https://www.aha.org/site-neutral/outpatient-pps/site-neutral-payment.
3. David W. Johnson, "David Johnson: Right-sizing Physician Training? The Case for Surgical Mechanics," HFMA, November 6, 2023, https://www.hfma.org/finance-and-business-strategy/innovation-and-disruption/right-sizing-physician-training-the-case-for-surgical-mechanics/.
4. Michelle R. Davis, "77 Percent of Older Adults Want to Remain in Their Homes as They Age," AARP, November 1, 2022, https://www.aarp.org/home-family/your-home/info-2021/home-and-community-preferences-survey.html.
5. "Aging in Place," National Institute on Aging, n.d., https://www.nia.nih.gov/health/aging-place#:~:text=Many%20people%20want%20to%20stay,safely%20as%20possible%20at%20home.
6. Ashish K. Jha MD MPH, "End-of-Life Care, Not End-of-Life Spending," *JAMA Network*, July 13, 2018, https://doi.org/10.1001/jamahealthforum.2018.0028.
7. Riz Hatton, "Equipment, Property Cost $1.4M per Operating Room at ASCs," n.d., https://www.beckersasc.com/benchmarking/equipment-property-cost-1-4m-per-operating-room-at-ascs.html.
8. Doximity, "Physician Compensation Report," 2021, https://c8y.doxcdn.com/image/upload/v1/Press%20Blog/Research%20Reports/Doximity-Compensation-Report-2021.pdf.
9. "One in Two Americans Have a Musculoskeletal Condition," Science-Daily, March 16, 2016, https://www.sciencedaily.com/releases/2016/03/160301114116.htm#:~:text=Summary%3A,according%20to%20a%20new%20report.
10. "Ezra Receives 510(K) FDA Clearance for AI That Enhances MRI, Enabling Fast, Low-Cost Scans," June 1, 2023, https://ezra.com/

press-releases/ezra-receives-510-k-fda-clearance-for-ai-that-enhances-mri-enabling-fast-low-cost-scans.

11. "What Do We Know About Spending Related to Public Health in the U.S. and Comparable Countries? – Peterson-KFF Health System Tracker," Peterson-KFF Health System Tracker, September 30, 2020, https://www.healthsystemtracker.org/chart-collection/what-do-we-know-about-spending-related-to-public-health-in-the-u-s-and-comparable-countries/#Preventive%20care%20spending%20by%20government/compulsory%20schemes%20as%20a%20share%20of%20total%20national%20health%20expenditures,%202018.

12. Ibid.

13. PyCoach, "Is Data the New Oil of the 21st Century or Just an Over-rated Asset?" *Medium*, February 5, 2024, https://towardsdatascience.com/is-data-the-new-oil-of-the-21st-century-or-just-an-overrated-asset-1dbb05b8ccdf.

Chapter 9: Aggregators' Advantage

1. Voice of The Market, "2021 Year-end Digital Health Funding: Seismic Shifts Beneath the Surface," Rock Health, We're Powering the Future of Healthcare. Rock Health Is a Seed and Early-stage Venture Fund That Supports Startups Building the Next Generation of Technologies Transforming Healthcare., January 10, 2022, https://rockhealth.com/insights/2021-year-end-digital-health-funding-seismic-shifts-beneath-the-surface/.

2. Hall Kaufman Jr. and Kaufman, Hall & Associates, LLC, "State of Consumerism in Healthcare 2021: Regaining Momentum" (Kaufman, Hall & Associates, LLC, September 2021), https://www.kaufmanhall.com/sites/default/files/2021-09/kh-2021-state-of-consumerism-survey-report_final-9.15.pdf.

3. "Explore Health Topics," County Health Rankings & Roadmaps, n.d., https://www.countyhealthrankings.org/explore-health-rankings/measures-data-sources/county-health-rankings-model.

4. Wan He et al., "90+ in the United States: 2006–2008," report, *American Community Survey Reports* (U.S. Government Printing Office, November 2011), https://0.tqn.com/z/g/usgovinfo/library/nosearch/90_plus_in_us.pdf.

5. "Individuals' Access and Use of Patient Portals and Smartphone Health Apps, 2020," HealthIT.gov, n.d., https://www.healthit.gov/data/data-briefs/individuals-access-and-use-patient-portals-and-smartphone-health-apps-2020.

6. "Teladoc Finalizes Blockbuster Deal with Livongo in Less than 3 Months," Fierce Healthcare, October 30, 2020, https://www.fiercehealthcare.com/finance/teladoc-finalizes-blockbuster-deal-livongo-less-than-three-months.

7. Transcarent, "Employees Want Three Things out of Their Health Benefits Journey – and another 'health navigator' isn't one of them. ...," March 26, 2021, https://www.linkedin.com/posts/transcarent_employees-want-three-things-out-of-their-activity-6781180498627694592-IwOW/.

8. Micah Caswell, "A CFO's Guide to Health Plan Fiduciary Leadership," PBGH, May 22, 2023, https://www.pbgh.org/a-cfos-guide-to-health-plan-fiduciary-leadership/.

9. "Transcarent Launches National Independent Provider Ecosystem," Transcarent, n.d., https://transcarent.com/press-releases/transcarent-launches-national-independent-provider-ecosystem.

10. "Transcarent Selects Prescryptive Health to Power a New, Different and Better Integrated Pharmacy Experience," Transcarent, n.d., https://transcarent.com/press-releases/transcarent-selects-prescryptive-health-to-power-a-new-different-and-better-integrated-pharmacy-experience.

Chapter 10: Empowered Caregivers

1. Nathan Pilling, "Faced with an Overwhelmed ER, a St. Michael Medical Center Nurse called 911 for Help," *Kitsap Sun*, October 12, 2022, https://www.kitsapsun.com/story/news/2022/10/12/overwhelmed-st-michael-medical-center-nurse-called-911-help/10472123002/.

2. Ethan Popowitz et al., "Addressing the Healthcare Staffing Shortage," 2022, https://www.definitivehc.com/sites/default/files/resources/pdfs/Addressing-the-healthcare-staffing-shortage.pdf.

3. https://qz.com/work/1279814/ask-what-your-company-can-do-for-you-says-microsoft-ceo-satya-nadella.

4. Oliver Wyman and Terry Stone, "New Report: Women Make 80% of Buying Decisions but Represent Only 13% of CEOs," n.d., https://

www.oliverwyman.com/our-expertise/perspectives/health/2019/jan/
women-in-healthcare-make-80--of-purchasing-decisions--yet-13--of
.html#:~:text=Healthcare%20is%20an%20industry%20where,65%20
percent%20of%20the%20workforce.

5. "Journal Articles Post," Web Starter Kit, n.d., https://www.aarpinternational
.org/the-journal/current-edition/journal-articles-blog/2016/01/
challenges-facing-older-women.

6. Susan C. Reinhard et al., "Valuing the Invaluable: 2023 Update," March
8, 2023, https://doi.org/10.26419/ppi.00082.006.

7. Michelle Stohlmeyer Russell et al., "Women Dominate Health Care –
Just Not in the Executive Suite," BCG Global, August 23, 2022, https://
www.bcg.com/publications/2019/women-dominate-health-care-not-
in-executive-suite.

8. Vivian Hunt et al., "Diversity Wins: How Inclusion Matters," May 2020,
https://www.mckinsey.com/~/media/mckinsey/featured%20insights/
diversity%20and%20inclusion/diversity%20wins%20
how%20inclusion%20matters/diversity-wins-how-inclusion-matters-
vf.pdf?shouldIndex=false.

9. Rocío Lorenzo et al., "How Diverse Leadership Teams Boost Innovation,"
BCG Global, January 22, 2023, https://www.bcg.com/publications/2018/
how-diverse-leadership-teams-boost-innovation.

10. Rachel Treisman, "NYC Nurses Are on Strike, but the Problems They
Face Are Seen Nationwide," NPR, January 11, 2023, https://www.npr
.org/2023/01/11/1148333140/new-york-city-nurse-strike-staffing-
shortages.

Conclusion: Guns *and* Butter

1. "Annual Message to the Congress on the State of the Union," the
American Presidency Project, n.d., https://www.presidency.ucsb.edu/
documents/annual-message-the-congress-the-state-the-union-27.

2. "Special Message to the Congress: The State of the Budget and the
Economy," the American Presidency Project, n.d., https://www.presi
dency.ucsb.edu/documents/special-message-the-congress-the-state-
the-budget-and-the-economy.

Glossary of Acronyms

AALL:	American Association for Labor Legislation
ACA:	Affordable Care Act or Obamacare
ACF:	Acute care facilities
ACS:	American Cancer Society
ADL:	Activities of daily living
AHA:	American Hospital Association
AHEAD:	Advancing All-Payer Health Equity Approaches and Development
AIDS:	Acquired Immune Deficiency Syndrome
AI:	Artificial intelligence
ALF:	Assisted living facility
AMA:	American Medical Association
APC:	Advanced primary care
ARP:	American Rescue Plan
ASC:	Ambulatory surgical center
ASO:	Administrative services only
B2B:	Business to business
BHI:	Behavioral health integration
BLS:	U.S. Bureau of Labor Statistics
CB^2E^2:	Cheaper, Better, Balanced, Easier, Empowered

CCM:	Chronic care management
CCRC:	Continuing care retirement community
CDC:	Centers for Disease Control and Prevention
CHIP:	Children's Health Insurance Program
CMMI:	Center for Medicare and Medicaid Innovation
CMS:	Centers for Medicare and Medicaid Services
COPD:	Chronic obstructive pulmonary disease
COPC:	Central Ohio Primary Care
CPT:	Current procedural terminology
CRISPR:	Clustered Regularly Interspaced Short Palindromic Repeats
EBITDA:	Earnings before interest, taxes, depreciation and amortization
ED:	Emergency department
EHR:	Electronic health records
ER:	Emergency room
FDA:	Food and Drug Administration
FFS:	Fee-for-service
FTC:	Federal Trade Commission
GDP:	Gross domestic product
GenAI:	Generative artificial intelligence
GPO:	Group purchasing organization
HCCI:	Health Care Cost Institute
HCDD:	Heart disease, cancer, diabetes, dementia
HEDIS:	Healthcare Effectiveness Data and Information Set
HHS:	U.S. Department of Health and Human Services
HITECH:	Health Information Technology for Economic and Clinical Health
HMO:	Health maintenance organization
IBH:	Innovation in Behavioral Health
ICD:	International classification of disease
ICU:	Intensive care unit
IHI:	Institute for Healthcare Improvement

IOP:	Inpatient-only procedure
IRF:	Inpatient rehabilitation facility
JAMA:	Journal of the American Medical Association
JPMC:	JP Morgan Chase & Co.
KFF:	Kaiser Family Foundation
KO:	Knocked out
LLM:	Large language model
MA:	Medicare Advantage
MedPAC:	Medical Payment Advisory Commission
MHI:	Median household income
ML:	Machine learning
MRI:	Magnetic resonance imaging
MSK:	Musculoskeletal system
MVTSA:	Motor Vehicle and Traffic Safety Act
NCCDPHP:	National Center for Chronic Disease Prevention and Health Promotion
NCHS:	National Center for Health Statistics
NEBR:	National Bureau of Economic Research
NHTSA:	National Highway Traffic Safety Administration
NIA:	National Institute on Aging
NIH:	National Institutes of Health
NLP:	Natural language processing
NPS:	Net Promoter Score
NYSNA:	New York State Nurses Association
ONC:	Office of the National Coordinator for Health Information Technology
OR:	Operating room
PBM:	Pharmacy benefit manager
PCH:	Personal care home
PCM:	Principal care management
PERS:	Personal emergency response systems

PPE: Personal protective equipment

RA: Rheumatoid arthritis
RCM: Revenue cycle management
ROI: Return on investment
RPM: Remote patient monitoring
RTM: Remote therapeutic monitoring
RVU: Relative value units

SAD: Standard American Diet
SADLE: Standard American Diet, Lifestyle and Environment
SDoH: Social Determinants of Health
SMMC: St. Michael Medical Center
SNF: Skilled nursing facility

TB: Tuberculosis
TCM: Transitional care management
TPA: Third party administrator
TPC: Transcarent Pharmacy Care

UHC: UnitedHealthcare
UHG: UnitedHealth Group
UP4C: Universal primary, pre-natal, post-natal and palliative care
USCS: U.S. Cancer Statistics
UTI: Urinary tract infection
UX: User experience

VA: Veterans Affairs
VBC: Value-based care
VMFH: Virginia Mason Franciscan Health

WHO: World Health Organization

Acknowledgments

It takes a village to write a balanced book about healthcare policy. The industry is so large, complex, and counterintuitive that an informed understanding can only emerge after in-depth engagement with knowledgeable peers across the expansive healthcare ecosystem.

Even with our formidable networks and decades of experience, co-authors Dave and Paul debated and continue to debate the finer points of the megatrends reshaping the massive U.S. healthcare industry. Not for the faint of heart, incisive healthcare policy analysis is a full-contact enterprise. Necessary improvements will come at the expense of well-positioned incumbents, most of whom are loathe to relinquish their privileges.

While we have the scars and bruises that emerge when questioning the validity and logic of the powers that be, we also receive ongoing support and encouragement from a growing army of healthcare revolutionaries and reformers. Like us, there are growing numbers who believe all Americans deserve access to appropriate and affordable healthcare services. The U.S. healthcare system can and must do better, much better.

Healthcare revolutionaries also believe the U.S. system needs to invest more expansively in pro-health services and programs, so that Americans can live longer and healthier lives with less need for expensive treatment interventions. Promoting this transformative vision for U.S. healthcare is worth the slings and arrows that come with it.

First and foremost, we wish to acknowledge and thank the legions of healthcare revolutionaries doing the hard, bottom-up work required for industry transformation. If nothing else, we hope our book encourages their essential and often difficult work. More than ever, our country needs you. Dare to be different and dare to be great.

This includes the millions of clinicians and caregivers who do the hard daily work of caring for patients. At their core is a desire to help people get better and to coax them back to health when they are most vulnerable.

Despite all the current system's dysfunction and blockages, it is truly inspiring to witness selfless caregiving in action. In recognition of their efforts, the U.S. system must transform to ease caregivers' burdens and free them to do what they do best – to care and heal.

In our previous books, co-authors Dave and Paul have recognized hundreds of individuals who have advanced our thinking and contributed to its articulation. We cannot thank them enough. For this book, we've narrowed our focus to acknowledging those who contributed specifically to its writing.

Foremost among this group are the members of our core working group from 4sight Health and our publisher, John Wiley & Sons. Michelle Lange, 4sight's Managing Editor, oversaw the manuscript's production. Michelle was ably assisted by Lara Dufresne, who conducted the first round of copy-editing, created and elevated the book's graphics, and compiled its glossary. Kelly Stone has supercharged the book's marketing and distribution.

The Wiley team has been beyond what we could have hoped for, a true advocate and partner. An efficient, hands-on and effective collaborator in bringing our book into final form. Cheryl Segura is the Wiley team leader. Working with a new publisher can be anxiety inducing. Not in this instance. Cheryl has assembled a small army of professionals, notably Amanda Pyne, Sangeetha Suresh, Sharmila Srinivasan, Sundhar Karuthudian, Arun Arumugan, and Karen Weller, to assist in title refinement, book cover art, editing, copy-editing, pre-marketing and permissions. Collectively, they've kept the pages turning as we've moved toward publication.

Our book also incorporates several 4sight case studies written in partnership with thought leaders and change-makers. These include commentaries on consumerism with Jeff Jones and Dugan Winke and commentaries on platforming, transformative change and workforce dynamics with Infor's Matthew Bragstad, Marcus Mossberger, Matt Wilson and Briana Zink.

We'd also like to recognize the contributions of Kerry Weems, former CMS administrator and regular 4sight contributor who died after a short illness in August 2023. We miss Kerry enormously for his quick wit and penetrating analysis. The healthcare industry lost a titan in Kerry Weems. We'll all have to up our games to compensate for his absence.

Brenda Battle of UChicago Medicine and Meghan Woltman of Advocate Health Care provided timely information and insights regarding health system transformation on Chicago's South Side. Though not always agreeing, James Hereford and Brad Benson from MHealth Fairview provided informed perspectives on the MPact Health Care initiative to revitalize the University of Minnesota's healthcare enterprise.

We'd like to acknowledge and celebrate 4sight's long-standing and expansive thought leadership partnership with Cain Brothers. Cain Brothers is the nation's leading healthcare-only investment bank. First under the leadership of Rob Fraiman and now under the leadership of Wyatt Richie, 4sight partners with senior bankers at Cain Brothers to explore sector-specific market dynamics.

The next person we'd like to acknowledge is Zeke Emanuel, the noted physician, researcher, author and health policy maven. Few individuals have the stature and orientation to advance system reform for the healthcare industry in its entirety. Zeke is among these honored few. He works tirelessly to make affordable healthcare services universally available. We're enormously grateful to Zeke for his pioneering work and willingness to write this book's foreword.

Beyond the foreword, Zeke and co-author Dave collaborated on the creation of the Healthcare Affordability Index (with Aaron Glickman) and a two-part series in "Health Affairs" on state-based reform efforts (with Merrill Goozner and Matthew Guido).

Next, we'd like to acknowledge and thank the individuals and organizations that facilitated the in-depth case studies that we present to illustrate market forces in action. The JPMorgan/Morgan Health/Apree case study illustrates how the healthcare marketplace is organizing itself to deliver democratized and distributed whole-person health (3D-WPH) in Columbus, Ohio. It's a remarkable story.

Many contributed to the case study. We'd like to single out Dan Mendelson, the CEO of Morgan Health, and Don Trigg, the CEO of Apree Health. Both Dan and Don shared their time and perspectives generously. They also made key members of their teams available for interviews and follow-up questions.

Likewise, we'd like to recognize Glenn Tullman, the CEO of Transcarent, and Pete McCanna, the CEO of Baylor Scott & White Health. Each spear-headed case studies for our "Aggregators' Advantage" chapter. Healthcare's Holy Grail is the quest to give consumers the information, guidance and access they require to conduct their individual healthcare journeys seamlessly. Transcarent and BSW Health are working to make that quest a reality.

Co-author Dave serves on the boards of the Healthcare Financial Management Association (HFMA) and The Community Builders (TCB). Each deserve mention because of the pioneering work they're doing to promote health and community wellbeing.

At HFMA, Dave is chairing the "Health Futures" task force which is seeking to address the "reverse" tragedy of the commons discussed in the "Pro-Consumer/Market Reforms" chapter. HFMA CEO Ann Jordan and 2023/24 Board Chair (and Mayo Clinic's CFO) Dennis Dahlen have guided this initiative into a formidable undertaking that is positioned to advance industry-wide payment reform and metrics. Co-author Paul is a member of the task force. Its work has influenced our thinking on payment reform enormously.

TCB is the nation's largest non-profit developer of affordable housing. Not content with simply building and managing properties, TCB dedicates enormous effort through its Community Life division to enrich residents' lives through pro-active engagement. Every day, TCB communities show how it's not only possible but essential to improve health and wellbeing as part of an all-encompassing effort to build strong and sustainable communities where people thrive.

Like "Healthy Futures," TCB's "Community Life" has provided invaluable source material that informs our perspectives on healthcare system reform. Both organizations are key players in helping all Americans to get healthier together. We cannot thrive as a nation until we improve the overall health of the U.S. population.

Co-author Paul was CEO of Amedisys for 8 years, and is still the Chairman. Seeing care effectively delivered in the home and outside of institutions drove our thinking about an overreliance on hospital and institutional care. Paul is also the Executive Chairman of Unified Women's Health and Careforth. Unified's mission is to proactively advance women's health and Careforth's is devoted training and support for non-clinical caregivers.

The authors have learned about the importance of "food as medicine" from Paul's experience on the board of Purfoods, which ships healthy meals to those who can't find healthy food or can't afford it. Through Paul's co-founding and launching of Healthpilot with Dr. Jonathan Kolstad, we better understand how technology can help consumers make better healthcare choices. Through Paul's service on the Nashville Health Care Council board, we have witnessed the building of a large, complex, interconnected and effective healthcare ecosystem. There's a reason that Nashville has earned the nickname "Healthcare City."

Paul would like to thank the following healthcare leaders, in particular, for sharing their insights and travails. Healthcare requires a collective revolution with expansive cross-pollinized sharing of ideas, experiences and investment risks.

Paul's list of incisive cross-pollinators includes company leaders: Richard Ashworth, Nick Muscato, Kendall Hagood, Robert LaGalia, Harriet Booker, Markus Hockson, Matt Marek, Tom Boleson, Chris Choi, Seth Teich, Jake Calvin, Cindy Baier, Apryl Childs-Potter, David Dill, Bobby Frist, Haley Hovious, Russ Thomas, Sam Hazen, Mary Langowski, Sarah Iselin, Rob Jay, Catherine Tabaka and Jim Rechtin. It also includes thought leaders: Jamie Shapiro, Gunjan Khanna, Dave Tamburri, Leonora Zilkha Williamson, Jon Kaplan, Fred Reichheld, Trevor Fetter, Senator Bill Frist, Nancy-Ann DeParle and Jonathan Kolstad. Finally it includes pioneering investors: Kevin Ryan, Kevin Cox, Akshay Kumar, Scott Werry, Megan Preiner, Vishal Agrawal, John Keenan, Jim Moore, Paul Hondros, Tom Sipp, Robb Vorhoff, Chris Comenos, Carmine Petrone, Ben Edmonds, Andy Cavanna, David Schuppan, Adam Boehler, Navid Farzad, Bryan Bui, Ian Sacks, Nader Niani, Peter Ehrich, Bryan Cressey, Vineeta Agrawal and Julie Yoo.

The United States' healthcare dilemma for innovators resembles the life of a hermit crab. Individual companies have to adapt, live and thrive within an evolving eco-system not designed to reward value creation. With collective effort and constructive decision-making, however, progressive companies are advancing transformation and minimizing the typical dislocation that comes from disruptive innovation. This organic, bottom-up reorganization of the U.S.'s largest industry has been occurring, using Hemingway's description of bankruptcy, "gradually and then suddenly." It cannot come soon enough!

About the Authors

Co-authors Dave and Paul first met one another in the wake of the 2008–2009 financial crisis at the boutique healthcare investment bank, B.C. Ziegler and Co. in Chicago. Neither stayed very long at Ziegler. Both of them were working on projects ahead of their time. Failing fast is a key to success.

After the abject failure of the big banks to serve nonprofit health systems during the financial crisis, Dave was pioneering a leaner, more analytic and customer-centric model at Ziegler. At the same time, Paul was seeking to launch a new type of venture fund through Ziegler to invest in promising companies with tech-enabled, value-based business models. Neither venture worked particularly well, but each provided valuable insights into how the healthcare marketplace was evolving.

More importantly, Dave and Paul's serendipitous meeting at Ziegler triggered a deep friendship grounded in a shared passion for fixing America's broken healthcare system. The two friends and authors have similar academic training in literature, philosophy, and theology. As such, Dave and Paul are generalists operating within a siloed healthcare ecosystem. Their diverse range of knowledge, experiences, and collaborative instincts lead them to participate a large array of healthcare businesses.

As informed and driven generalists with deep expertise in healthcare operations, Dave and Paul strive to connect the dots between business theory and its application. They understand healthcare's unique and suboptimal operating characteristics. They also understand how the industry's siloed business practices are succumbing to the powerful macro and market forces described within this book's covers.

Like the Cleveland Clinic's former CEO, Toby Cosgrove, Dave and Paul increasingly believe "the state of our nation depends on the state of our health."

David W. Johnson

After a long and dynamic investment banking career, David Johnson launched 4sight Health in 2014 as a boutique healthcare media and advisory company. 4sight operates at the intersection of healthcare economics, policy, strategy, and capital formation. The company's mantra is *outcomes matter, customers count, and value rules.*

Dave is a voluminous reader, speaker, podcaster, lecturer and writer, with expertise in health policy, economics, statistics, behavioral finance, innovation, organizational change, and complexity theory. He is the author of *Market vs. Medicine: America's Epic Fight for Better, Affordable Healthcare* (2016) and *The Customer Revolution in Healthcare: Delivering Kinder, Smarter, Affordable Care of All* (2019). The 2023 documentary *American Hospitals: Healing a Broken System* features Dave prominently. He also won the *2024 National Silver and 2023 Regional Bronze Azbee Awards* for excellence in business journalism.

Dave earned an AB in English Literature from Colgate University and a master's in public policy from Harvard Kennedy School. He was a Language Arts Peace Corps Volunteer in Liberia, West Africa, where he taught very large (100+ students) classes, coached a championship soccer team and survived a coup.

Dave currently serves on the boards of the Healthcare Financial Management Association (HFMA) and The Community Builders (TCB). He formerly was an Overseer at Harvard Medical School; a Visiting Committee Member at UChicago Harris School of Public Policy and a Board; and Executive Committee and Finance Committee member of the Chicago Council on Global Affairs.

Paul Kusserow

Paul Kusserow is the Chairman and former President and CEO of Amedisys (Nasdaq: AMED), the country's leading home care company. He is also Executive Chairman of Unified Woman's Healthcare, a leading woman's healthcare company; and Careforth, a care enablement company for caregivers in the home. He is a co-founder and Chairman of Healthpilot, a

Medicare choice optimization technology company, and an Operating Partner at Ares Management.

Paul started his career as a management consultant at McKinsey & Company. He started his healthcare career at Tenet Healthcare (NYSE: THC), a leading hospital and ambulatory surgery company, as Senior Vice President of Strategy and Ventures. After Tenet, Paul was the Senior Vice President of Strategy, Business Development and Innovation at Humana (NYSE: HUM), a Fortune 75 healthcare company. Prior to joining Amedisys, Paul was the President and Vice Chairman of Alignment Healthcare (Nasdaq: ALHC), a technology-enabled Medicare Advantage plan in Southern California.

He is a Fellow at the Center for Healthcare Marketplace Innovation at the Haas School at University of California, Berkeley, and recently was a lecturer at Vanderbilt University.

He is the author of *The Anatomy of a Turnaround: Transforming an Organization by Prioritizing People, Performance and Purpose* (McGraw Hill, 2023).

Paul serves on the Boards of Scion Health, Purfoods and Matrix Medical Management. He previously served on the Boards of Oak Street Health (NYSE: OSH), New Century Health, Picwell, and Availity, where he served as Chairman.

He graduated with a BA in Religious Studies from Wesleyan University where he was a member of Phi Beta Kappa, an Olin Fellow, a Brown Scholar, and Student Fellow at the Center for the Humanities. He received an MA in English Language and Literature from Oxford University where was a Rhodes Scholar.

Index